Mind to Mind MARKETING

Communicating with 21st-century customers

Harry Alder

KOGAN
PAGE

First published in 2001

Apart from any fair dealing for the purposes of research or private study, or criticism or review, as permitted under the Copyright, Designs and Patents Act 1988, this publication may only be reproduced, stored or transmitted, in any form or by any means, with the prior permission in writing of the publishers, or in the case of reprographic reproduction in accordance with the terms and licences issued by the CLA. Enquiries concerning reproduction outside these terms should be sent to the publishers at the undermentioned addresses:

Kogan Page Limited
120 Pentonville Road
London N1 9JN
UK

Kogan Page Limited
163 Central Avenue, Suite 2
Dover NH 03820
USA

© Harry Alder, 2001

British Library Cataloguing in Publication Data

A CIP record for this book is available from the British Library.

ISBN 0 7494 3366 3

Typeset by Saxon Graphics Ltd, Derby
Printed and bound by Creative Print and Design (Wales) Ebbw Vale

Contents

Introduction

Several important trends point to major changes in the way we do business, and especially in the way companies communicate with their customers. One is the trend towards individual customer relationships, termed relationship or 'one to one' marketing, as opposed to mass marketing. Another is towards 'mass customization', in which mass-produced goods are 'customized' to an individual customer's requirements. Flexible, 'intelligent' production systems have made this possible. The revolution in information technology has also made a particularly strong impact on all our lives. The idea of a trend from 'atoms' (material products) to bits (invisible, weightless 'products' – information) is also a product of the 'information age'. Similarly, the trend from goods to services, and miniaturization – big to little, tiny to invisible.

These trends are set to impact conventional marketing at a deep level, and in some remarkable ways. Not only will 'high tech' business advance in pace and scale, but also the nature of the seller–buyer relationship will change forever. The big change will concern the mind: the *mind* of the customer; the *mind* of the seller; and how they mutually communicate *mind to mind*. The 1990s were called the decade of the brain. The emerging science and technology of the mind is already transforming our understanding of thinking, feeling, consciousness, intention, and interpersonal communication. It stimulates the 'big questions'. At the same time it is set to make its mark on the down to earth world of business and marketing.

21ST-CENTURY CORNER SHOP

At first sight, contemporary business trends seem to favour customers. They enjoy the fruits of whatever the latest technology can provide and share the benefits of free enterprise and competition. They enjoy the benefits of deregulation and the growth of the Internet. But, from the perspective of the individual customer, not all the change is positive. Personalized letters, loyalty schemes and extensive customer care programmes, for example, don't seem to overcome the poor, impersonal service of which customers all too often complain. The 'corner shop' proprietor, who knew every customer and anticipated his or her needs and preferences, seems to have no place in super-efficient retail marketing. Yet, paradoxically, some of the marketing trends to which I refer herald a 21st-century equivalent of just such a relationship: a global 'corner shop'.

MASS MARKETING MALAISE

The central place of the customer in trade and commerce is a relatively recent, far from universal phenomenon. Moreover, 'the customer is always right', and its modern-day derivatives, have little supporting substance. These sentiments are largely marketing rhetoric. Indeed, with all the current emphasis on customer service, most businesses continue to sell to customers *en masse*. The target – by its nature – is not a customer, but a 'market segment'. Sometimes it comprises millions of customers, or 'consumers', segmented on a geographical, socio-economic or whatever basis.

The nearest the mass marketer gets to an individual customer is the stereotypical, or 'modal', customer. This is the Special Person that focus groups and questionnaires seek to identify. The person for which an annual avalanche of new products is designed, and to which powerful, ubiquitous, round-the-clock advertising is targeted. This customer caricature is, nonetheless, the best representation of the 'person' who may or may not buy. However, a stereotypical, mass-market customer is no more real than a modal family with 2.4 children and 1.25 cars. It doesn't exist. Put another way, a 'real' customer does not figure in the mass marketing model.

MAGICAL TECHNOLOGY

Customers have to admit that they have gained much through the economies of scale of mass marketing and runaway technological advances. Staggering choice and magical (to over-40s) technology at throwaway prices are so ubiquitous we get to accept them. However, beyond the relatively tiny vestige of authentic corner shops, customers have, it seems, forfeited any special, personal relationship with suppliers of goods and services.

The influence of mass marketing over half a century or so can hardly be overstated. It was spawned by the revolution in production methods pioneered by such trailblazing industrialists as the car maker Henry Ford. It has enabled a bewildering variety of products to be delivered to an ever-demanding, increasingly informed customer populace. It has created wants that never existed, and demand for products that were once not even dreamt of. However, mass marketing addresses a nameless, faceless abstraction of who or what the customer is. To the 21st-century customer, and the modern-day marketer who watches and listens, the mass marketing model is an anachronism, and deficient in the extreme.

BARGAIN BASEMENT COMPUTING POWER

Yet marketing technology advances unabated. We now have automated telecommunications, queuing systems, synthetic computer telephonists, answering machines, electromechanical tellers, interactive advertising, personalized mail and electronic commerce. The customer, it would seem, has never had it so automated.

But the higher the high tech becomes, the more it seems that any true relationship between buyer and seller has been lost for ever. However sophisticated the marketing, the individual customer doesn't seem to count. He or she is powerless in the path of global mega-corporations and universal automation courtesy of bargain basement computing power.

Technology has been a mixed blessing for customers. Rather than being directed at remembering and understanding customers better, it was directed at making more products at lower unit prices and attracting enough customers to turn over the stocks. Business owners, product makers, managers and financiers seem to get more of the growing cake. Super databases seem to contribute more to junk mail than personal customer service. But that has been courtesy of short-sighted marketers rather than product developers, technologists and information buffs. The fruits of technology are there for the taking, as smaller, nimble competitors know only too well. Customers got variety and throw away prices, of course. The question is, whether, into the bargain, they had to lose all vestige of hope of a corner shop rela-tionship – or even just respect as a person.

A NEW WAY OF MARKETING

Proponents of individual customer, 'one to one', or relationship marketing (RM) maintain that the days of mass marketing are numbered. But the dominance of mass marketing in marketing theory and practice should not be understated. When it is replaced, its replacement will have to be something special. Such a development requires no less than a paradigm shift in the business function we call marketing – a new way of marketing equal to the 21st-century customer.

Other aspects of business have already experienced their own paradigm shifts. In recent years, massive change has been the rule rather than the exception, and the youthful majority (who use calcu-lators and can set the video) have come to accept it routinely. Change features new communication techniques, undreamt-of levels of consistent quality and 'throwaway' products, to name token examples only. Yesterday's space age and sci-fi technologies have become familiar and expected. Yet human customers and the humans who purport to serve them have changed little in the nature and effec-tiveness of their communication.

Such a degree of change has not yet reached mainstream marketing. Businesses have not delivered. Customer service has not kept pace with product quality, reliability and value for money. For marketing in general, and customer relationships in particular, the big change is still to come. As I write, marketing remains just another business function that has had its mass market heyday. Twenty-first century marketing will need to embrace what and who the customer is.

High on the agenda will be what customers *feel* and what affects how they feel, their thinking as well as behavioural characteristics. What's on their mind. What makes them tick. And such will be the first serious venture of marketing into the mysterious 'black box' of the human mind. For the first time in commercial history, new forms of two-way, buyer–seller communication technology are set to make this level of personal understanding possible. The paradigm shift will be of a scale and sophistication that no corner shop proprietor dreamt of.

MASS PRODUCTION ALIVE AND WELL

Mass marketing is at the 'chaotic boundary', as it has been termed, of such fundamental change. Mass *production,* however, of a kind that even Henry Ford could not foresee, is alive and well. It has been a party to the trends I identified at the outset and seems to be on target to meet the needs of new-century customers. It now boasts intelligent robotics, sophisticated quality control, nanotechnology and more. Mass production seems capable of satisfying seemingly limitless consumer demand. Customers take the benefits of product and production technology for granted. In cars and electronic goods, for instance, reliability, quality and value for money are now more remarkable by their absence. Henry Ford's 'any colour provided it's black' philosophy has long been replaced by a staggering choice of products and product features.

Known as mass customization, one of the positive paradoxes of mass production is a reversion to 'customized' products. Made to measure Levi jeans and individually specified car options roll endlessly off mass production lines. Flexible production runs of many thousands can now cater for the bespoke demands of individual customers.

DIRECT MARKETING

With all these undenied benefits, today's customers are none too happy to be talked at by machines, and targeted by impersonal, faceless mega-corporations and hyper retailers. The simplest customer expectations – respect, personal service, courtesy, care, and individual attention – are valued and desired all the more for their absence.

Personal service as the customer would define it seems beyond the wit of the cream of high technology.

However, all is not bad news on the customer relationship front. Some forms of marketing seem to be headed in the right direction, even if the corner shop relationship has been lost. All kinds of direct marketing, for instance, have experienced growth, such as mail order, tele-marketing and e-commerce. However 'mass' a market they serve, they reflect the new 'status' of the individual customer. That's a limited status, however, for so-called direct marketers, but better than a mass-market segment.

The customer remains no more than an anonymous representation of a modal entity – a name with an address and telephone number and some socio-demographic data thrown in. But, however impersonal it all seems from the customer's perspective, it's a rifle rather than shotgun approach. Direct marketing is headed in the direction of the individual customer.

Direct marketing, such as by post or telephone, does not imply a customer relationship. Any 'relationship' in direct marketing is typically with a mail-merged name and an appropriate salutation. Postal address, bank sort code and club card PIN stand in for the real customer. The individual customer remains far less a 'one off' than the customized car, designer jeans or 'tailored' financial services he or she can readily buy. Such customers exhibit 'buying characteristics', but don't have thoughts, feelings and aspirations. Other than through 'representative' focus groups and nation-wide statistics, the customer's voice, let alone what goes on in his or her mind, doesn't get heard.

Consequently, the marketing 'message', directed *at* the individual customer, is largely one-way traffic. The feedback and mutual communication vital to even the most basic relationship remain conspicuously absent. Marketing data usually extends no further than whether, what and when a customer buys or doesn't buy, and an analysis of occasional 'tell us what you think' cards. Insofar as any face to face or even telephone relationship is established, it will more likely be in the event of complaints. In most cases, direct customer contact happens by default rather than as a planned marketing strategy.

Positive relationship building is no part of such a marketing strategy. The customer relationship lies secondary to short-term, measurable, transaction-by-transaction profitability. Yet most marketers acknowledge that customer relationships are crucial to eventual success. It's just that they are not sufficiently committed to the notion, or don't have the know-how to create relationships. Radical change in marketing theory and practice is patently overdue.

THE FUTURE IS ONE TO ONE

Relationship marketing, at the centre of this revival of customer focus, was popularized by the book *The One-to-One Future*, by Don Peppers and Martha Rogers. It involves 'getting to know' each customer with a view to a long-term, mutually beneficial relationship. In this information age, one to one marketing is based on information. The better the quantity and quality of customer information, the better the seller will be able to communicate with customers and win their loyalty. The aim is for the 'corner shop' relationship, but on a bigger scale, and without the need to store the information in one person's head. Customer intelligence is gathered and used as part of a long-term relationship strategy rather than as a by-product of the occasional contact.

Although growing globally, one to one marketing is sufficiently novel not to have entrenched rules and systems. There are no standard questionnaires. There is no dominant corporate model. No one has decided what customer information is needed, how it can be obtained and how it might best be analysed and interpreted.

In such a commercial wilderness, companies that can transform their customer relationships will gain a competitive edge. A genuine, ongoing 'feel' for the customer is a unique business feature that is hard to emulate, however large a competitor's investment and however advanced their technology. It takes creativity, ingenuity and know-how, rather than capital and technology, to understand and communicate with the customer. A few customer-centred ideas can bring dividends, without the heavy costs of shotgun, hit and (usually) miss advertising. A handful of satisfied, loyal, ambassadorial customers, in turn, can outperform a high-fee professional advertising agency.

CUSTOMER RELATIONSHIP STRATEGY

However, a few important principles should underlie a successful customer relationship strategy. For example:

- Two-way communication needs to be established. The channels should make communication easy and enjoyable.
- You need to know what your customer thinks, and quickly. Responses, comments and personal information have to be elicited

from the customer on a positive, ongoing basis. You will not be praised for doing well and you will get complaints all too soon when you make mistakes. Relationships don't just happen, any more than revolutionary products do.

- You need to know how your customer behaves. A detailed record of every transaction has to be maintained.
- You need to listen, carefully. Individual feedback provides the important information on which your relationship strategy will be managed.
- You need to keep at it. It's a long-term strategy.
- You have to 'walk the talk' and deliver on promises. That means consistent, tangible performance. These are entry-level require-ments for relationship marketing – it is grown-up business.
- You don't have to hang on to customers you don't want. The customer may be 'always right', but not right for your business.
- You have to reward your best customers.
- You have to make profit. Gaining 'lifetime share of customer' is a serious, highly profitable business enterprise.

That's a tall strategic order, but the winnings are big. Moreover, as with the 'quality movement', a decade or two ago, competition may force marketers to excel in this crucial area, not as an optional extra, but for survival.

CUSTOMER PROFITABILITY

When measured for management accounting purposes, profit is usually attributed on a product category, or market segment basis. It is rarely attributed to the customers who provide it. The best, most loyal customers are therefore not only not thanked and rewarded, they are not even identified. Relationship marketing, on the other hand, focuses on customer profitability – that is, *individual* customer profitability. Pareto's 80–20 rule usually means that the least profitable customers get the lion's share of attention and costs. So marketing inputs, without the vital individual profitability, are at best irrational, and are more likely to be counterproductive.

When the individual customer comes first, measurement focuses on long-term *share of customer*, or lifetime customer value (LCV) and other such loyalty factors, rather than market share and financial transactions in a given accounting period. It's a new kind of customer relationship. New, at least, to a mass marketing generation. It's a better way of measuring a customer's worth.

Unlike mass marketing, relationship marketing is consistent with some of the important trends I identified earlier. As far as the customer is concerned, it takes marketing in the right direction. Importantly, for present purposes, relationship marketing forms an important foundation for a 'mind to mind' customer strategy.

PSYCHOGRAPHIC SWINGERS

Segmenting customers according to mental criteria is not new. Customers are sometimes classified, for instance, into psychographic, personality-type characteristics. Terms such as 'swinger', 'techno-boomer' or 'hedonist' are used to describe different customer personality types. These, however, typically relate to mass-market segments, and simply supplement existing socio-demographic categories, which still rule the market research roost. Other than slotting him or her into the appropriate psychographic pigeonhole, they do not reflect the actual customer. The target customer remains a modal ideal, albeit with a clever-sounding psychographic label. The 'swinger' or 'techno-boomer' descriptor becomes simply part of the stereotypical customer specification. It no more reflects a true understanding of your customer than socio-economic status and postal code.

Although personality or 'mind' based, these psychographic classifications are nonetheless 'folk' labels, and never better than caricatures. Nor are they standardized and validated. So they have little use as a universal marketing tool, even when applied just for positioning to mass-market segments. Even with the latest psychographic classifications, no attempt is made to understand how a real, flesh and blood customer thinks and feels.

In the case of direct selling, for instance, whilst *transactions* are with individuals, for marketing purposes customers are grouped into segments, whether according to socio-economic and demographic rating or some form of personality type. The same label means the same marketing *message*. The customer is differentiated statistically, such as by value of purchases, earnings and postal code, but not as a person.

Having said this, the popularity of psychographic segmentation acknowledges the importance of customer characteristics beyond raw demographics. When used for market segmentation, it allows another dimension of customer understanding. When used on a one to one basis, psychographic profiling recognizes the importance of how the individual customer thinks.

MIND MODELS AND META PROGRAMS

Some developments in cognitive science, and 'mind modelling', drawn mainly from neuro-linguistic programming (NLP), can now be successfully applied to relationship marketing. In particular, we can classify *individual* customers according to their particular thinking style, temperament, disposition and a whole range of personality traits.

These broad mind-categories are sometimes termed 'Meta Programs'. Once identified, together they form a unique psychographic profile of the individual customer and, importantly, a predictor of their buying behaviour. By building up a profile of this information, a seller gets to understand how customers think. This includes the way they perceive things, their predispositions, how they 'interpret' promotional messages, and, in consequence, how they habitually behave. The type and content of marketing messages can then be tailored to reflect these personal characteristics. With this level of understanding, real two-way communication can be established. The seller now understands and speaks the customer's language. What I describe as a 'mind to mind' relationship is formed.

MIND TO MIND RELATIONSHIP

A mind to mind relationship involves a special kind of one to one relationship. In such a relationship, the customer is the sum of his or her thoughts, feelings, attitudes and aspirations, rather than just the sum of his or her historical buying behaviour. The company that takes account of these personal qualities will establish rapport with their customers, in the same way that close friends and colleagues can empathize and have worthwhile relationships. Customers in such a relationship buy *because they like you*, whatever the rationale of a particular purchase. They get pleasure and avoid pain – the universal human motivators – in the relationship and the buying experience as well as in anticipation of product benefits. And they keep buying as long as mutual loyalty is maintained.

The relationship goes deeper than even individual behaviour. Just as in a close family, the nature of the relationship will outlive the occasional lapse in behaviour. Put another way, as a seller, provided you establish the relationship, you are allowed one or two mistakes.

SEGMENTS OF ONE

In a marketing sense, the customer becomes a 'segment of one'. A mind to mind relationship develops over a period, based on the exchange of information and mutual trust, just as with personal friends and colleagues we come to know well. For this to happen, a fundamental change in the nature of marketing is required. Instead of personalizing a 'segment', and treating a mass market *like* a customer, mind to mind marketing focuses on real customers, whether they number 10 or 10 million.

In fact, to treat the customer as a segment is to miss the point of a one to one relationship. Segments, such as geographical, socio-economic or even psychographic, are fine for secondary statistical and planning purposes, and perhaps for relatively small, niche groups. But the essence of marketing is the individual customer.

Marketing in the dimension of the customer's mind is not a discretionary tool. It involves the sort of relationship that customers will increasingly demand, and which competitor companies will increasingly adopt. Behaviour, including buying behaviour, starts in the mind anyway. According to the timeless adage, 'As a man thinketh, so is he', customers 'act out' what they think about most. Your customer's mind is the key to your marketing success. Communicating on that level is essential if you want to compete for their loyalty. We have now identified important thinking characteristics and have the technology both to marshal and interpret such information.

A successful mind to mind relationship will involve two important factors that relationship marketing lacks: 1) standard, psychographic characteristics that can be applied to individual customers; 2) methods and instruments to obtain and manage the information.

Psychographic characteristics might include, for example:

- brain dominance (left–right, rational–intuitive, heart–mind);
- sensory preference (visual, auditory, kinaesthetic);

- a preference for knowing, having or getting, doing, being, or relating to other people.

You will meet these in the coming chapters. They are based on common, individual neurophysiological and psychological character- istics. At one level, they form the psychographic market segments for market positioning, just as with 'swinger'-type folk categories. At another level they are the channels that form the basis of ongoing customer communication. Chapter 3 summarizes some of these 'Meta Programs', which are then covered in detail in Chapters 5 to 8.

CORPORATE PERSONALITY

These thinking classifications reflect the *customer* side of the two-way, mind to mind relationship. As an inanimate corporation (usually), the seller, at the other side, does not have a mind, of course, any more than does a stereotypical, modal customer. Having said that, even an imper- sonal multinational company – an IBM, Federal Express, or Marks & Spencer, for instance – may be *perceived* as having a personality. Not just an image, but the culture, attitudes and actual behaviour behind the public image – a quasi-personality. How the customer perceives the seller personality will determine the nature of the relationship as much as the way the seller perceives the customer.

Customers personify a company, whether as the sum of its human representatives, a human-like image or a living metaphor. That corporate 'personality' is the seller's 'mind' in a mind to mind rela- tionship. The customer acts *as though* the seller company has a mind (and heart) of its own. It is hard to love or hate an inanimate legal entity. It is easy to relate to someone who thinks and feels as you do – someone who understands, or can at least appreciate, the way you think and feel.

Customers, for better or worse, get to know and relate to that 'personality'. They often attribute to a company, or even to products, personal qualities. For example, they refer to a company in terms like 'caring', 'arrogant', 'conservative', 'fuddy-duddy', 'brash' and 'stuck- up' – terms that we usually apply to people. In such a relationship emotions can become engaged and passions aroused. And such is the stuff of customer loyalty. A passionate product or company fan is an ambassador worth his or her weight in advertising gold. Conversely, an angry customer or ex-customer can do damage to a company's image out of all proportion to the amount of business they contributed.

There is another, more obvious aspect of corporate personality. Even a big organization has human faces – salespeople, customer service staff, receptionists, telephonists, service engineers and the like. The company is also personified in the face of the spokesperson, chairperson or chief executive who appears in the press and on television. These are real people. They have their own, very different, personalities, however conditioned they are to a company's ethos, or faithful to customer service 'scripts'. Together, they create a collective 'personality'. As seller representatives – anyone who might influence the customer's perception of the seller company – they may reflect or not reflect the corporate personality. Either way, just by association with the seller, they will affect the customer relationship. The marketing magic (and it's some trick) is, first to portray a single personality rather than several, and second to portray the personality you would like rather than let it happen by default, which it will.

WALKING THE MARKETING TALK

A mind to mind strategy therefore requires consistency between the behaviour and attitudes of staff at the coalface of customer contact, or in the media, and the collective corporate personality, which the seller seeks to communicate and establish. A well-established corporate personality will ride the storm of the occasional inconsistencies of individual staff. Genuine long-term loyalty makes allowances and excuses, just like a mother does for her child. The relationship *itself*, based on a mutual investment of information, is of value.

A company's personality is based, not just on an image, but on words and deeds. More specifically, on its customers' perception, or interpretation, of its words and deeds. What the customer:

- thinks you said;
- thinks you meant;
- thinks you did or didn't do;

and why he or she thinks you did or didn't do it.

If, in the mind of the customer, you stay true to the image you communicate, you will establish a rewarding, loyal relationship. A company has to think and act like a person – with values, needs and feelings – if it is to 'come across' in the human way that loyalty demands. Even more importantly, a company has to communicate with each customer in a way that reflects his or her own meta programs, or thinking characteristics. Those characteristics differ from customer to customer. So in a quite literal sense, the relationship is based on a meeting of minds.

My book *Corporate Charisma* (Piatkus) addresses the seller side of the mind to mind marketing relationship, and describes how you can create and manage your company's corporate personality. This is summarized, and related to the two-way, mind to mind relationship, in Chapter 9 of this book.

A 21ST-CENTURY MARKETING PARADIGM

I have referred to a new kind of customer relationship as a 'paradigm shift' in marketing. This is not to suggest that the customer has not occupied an important position in the past. Successful or 'excellent' companies are often cited for 'best practice', and their secret usually boils down to positive customer relationships, however achieved. A recurring feature, however, is the short-term or cyclical nature of a company's rise to customer acclaim. In some cases success is the result of a technological innovation, well timed and efficiently distributed. Today's high-flier companies can soon become the sad objects of business case studies. So, while there are always exceptions to the rule, 'successful companies' don't often change history. Precious few survive long enough. In any event, whatever the examples set, the impersonal 'market' survives from a mass marketing age that has less and less significance to customers today. Marketing as we know it has not yet cracked the vital loyalty, relationship factor.

For all the growth of one to one relationship marketing, examples of mind to mind marketing are difficult to find. However, some businesses – perhaps those we least expected – are beginning to recognize and prepare for the radical changes needed. Thankfully, the worldwide movement towards relationship marketing puts the individual customer in the number one position. It has already given us some examples of best practice and the extraordinary results of a one to one relationship. Bottom-line benefits of a one to one customer relationship have been documented in companies of widely differing type and size.

ONE CUSTOMER AT A TIME

Restructuring, right sizing, quality movements, re-engineering and other panaceas have bombarded business. Many of these, by their all-or-nothing nature, demand an upheaval that few organizations can cope with along with carrying on their day to day business. Popular strategic initiatives such as re-engineering and total quality management (TQM) typically require major corporate surgery, without the certainty of a cure. After many years of incremental evolution, the massive people and systems changes required are risky, if not unrealistic. However, you can start to understand and relate to your customers at the level of the mind economically and incrementally, with immediate results. Rather than 'all or nothing', relationship marketing can be implemented on an incremental 'try it and see' basis. It addresses customers one to one, and you can make changes one customer at a time. We have the necessary database technology, and the mind models developed by NLP, which I describe in Chapter 3, are also now to hand. From that foundation, forming a mind to mind relationship between sellers and buyers is primarily intuitive, and its major requirement is common sense.

ABOUT THIS BOOK

Each of the topics I have introduced is covered to some degree of detail throughout the book. So have patience. And I suggest you read according to the ingenious method of starting at the beginning and proceeding to the end. That way, there is more chance of it all making sense and you will ask yourself fewer annoying questions. Some material I thought might seem heavy, or just useful to refer back to, I have confined to the back as appendices. There are no books on the subject *per se*, nor indeed any literature except at the periphery, such as one to one marketing, mass customization and similar current marketing topics, so you will find no bibliography. However, an Internet search on the various NLP Meta Programs I use will prove fruitful, and any of my own NLP books will give further background in those areas.

Chapter 1 questions the ideal that marketing has traditionally espoused during its relatively young life: the Customer is King. I weigh the impact of technology and the trends I have already referred to and consider the need for something better. If you like, a new marketing paradigm for the 21st century. Part of this process meant exorcising a few marketing myths, and, in particular, critically appraising the relevance of the 'marketing mix' model. Although I have no loyalties to marketing as a function, I have tried to do this respectfully and have taken account of marketing principles and practice both pre and post 'the customer is king' turning point some 40 years ago. Not to be too apocalyptic, I refer to marketing as 'at the crossroads'.

In Chapter 2, we focus, as marketing does, on the customers. In particular, their thoughts, feelings, values, needs and aspirations, rather than their demographic status, then how this whole mind dimension can be incorporated into better marketing. This includes how the buyer perceives a 'product', the nature of which is changing due to the Internet and rampant technology. How the seller sees things, from a 'quasi-mental' rather than corporate or economic perspective is also addressed. I then present the idea of mind to mind marketing and the benefits for companies ready to go further along the already popular one to one route. To ensure this is relevant to mainstream marketing, I have included a section on positioning and segmentation, which I relate to the mind to mind concept.

Chapter 3 introduces some NLP principles and methods that apply to marketing generally and in particular to one to one customer relationships. In this chapter you will also meet 'Meta Programs', which are one of the bases of the mind to mind marketing paradigm I describe.

Chapter 4 addresses customer relationships as a vital part of any business and, specifically, the importance of customer loyalty in relationship to CRM and database technology – both of which are growing apace.

Chapter 5 introduces the first group of Meta Programs relating to 'brain dominance' and the universal dilemma of communicating to 'heart and mind'. Left-brain and right-brain communication strategies are suggested, and I include a questionnaire for measuring your own left–right brain preference.

Chapter 6 covers sensory (visual, auditory, kinaesthetic) preference as an important aspect of customer perception and a basis for segmentation. This includes, for instance, the impact of colour on customers' behaviour.

Chapter 7, 'How customers decide', looks at another important segmentation Meta Program in the form of the Life Content model and its application to relationship and mind to mind marketing. 'Convincer strategy' is included as an example of another useful Meta Program, in this case revealing buying and decision-making behaviour, and offering a remarkable new form of customer intelligence.

Chapter 8 covers the rest of the few Meta Programs I have used to illustrate the power of a mind to mind approach to data gathering and customer loyalty. I also outline some proprietary psychographic profiles and well-known personality instruments, used increasingly in a commercial context but confined to date to large segments rather than individual customer profiling.

The final chapter, Chapter 9, addresses the other 'mind' in the mind to mind relationship – the mind or personality of the seller. A case is made for a corporate personality and I show how this is a vital part of any mind to mind strategy.

This book is not a handbook or a comprehensive implementation programme for the mind to mind paradigm it presents. Implementation of some of the concepts you will meet is perhaps a decade away. Even the leading ambassadors of one to one marketing and CRM software gurus have hardly begun to incorporate the psychographic dimension into individual customer relationships, settling often for transaction and profitability analysis.

Having said that, there is plenty of room for optimism even in the immediate future. First, many of the methods you will meet lend themselves to implementation in small chunks at low risk and cost. That means you can 'suck it and see'. As with 'common or garden' one to one marketing, still hardly embryonic in global terms, you will soon see the difference in bottom-line results. Moreover, firms that are well down the one to one road will find mental segmentation an obvious progression from their mainly demographic and historical sales-related data gathering, without the upheaval associated with re-engineering-type innovation. Even on such an incremental basis I hope to show that benefits are there for the taking for those who are ready to think outside the box.

By adopting a flexible approach to database 'mind' content and information-gathering methods I have kept it all at a DIY-feasible level, especially for the thousands of smaller enterprises who I guess will trailblaze in marketing innovation anyway.

Finally, the seller 'mind' has already been covered more definitively in my book *Corporate Charisma* (Piatkus), in which is included a full implementation programme. The mind to mind project puts it all together, and that is today's big challenge, even for 'excellent' companies.

The principles, especially those surrounding the 'marketing concept', will be familiar if not old hat. That is to be expected, as the corner shop one to one relationship of yesteryear epitomizes just where many businesspeople want to get back to. Any novelty will be in doing this on a mega, fairly automated scale, rather than within a local neighbourhood and resident in one proprietor's head. If the ideas seem simplistic, that's also fine. Things do seem blindingly obvious when you understand them properly. Better still if a so-called mind to mind paradigm for the 21st century seems like common sense: that has been my aim all along. Even the magic apple tricks of gravity, a mind-defying spherical earth, and central locking qualify as common sense in the end. It usually helps to read with an open mind anyway.

1

Marketing at the crossroads

Theodore Levitt is credited with the historic constitutional marketing pronouncement 'the customer is king'. That was in 1960 in his seminal *Harvard Business Review* article 'Marketing Myopia'. Over the years his groundbreaking ideas have gradually percolated into marketing theory so that today there is hardly a company that would dare to draft its mission without some ever more ingenious deification of the customer. Customer care. Customer service. Customer first. The customer surely is king.

But is this the case? Do customers agree? What's missing in modern marketing, and what sort of change is needed? How does all this relate to the wider business and social trends we have identified? In particular, how might marketing theory and practice in the coming years incorporate customers at the level of the mind?

'Customer first' catch-phrases now have a familiar ring. Even with hindsight, Levitt's idea was hardly novel. Along with other inspirational thoughts and discoveries throughout history, like the wheel and sliced bread, it turns out to be common sense. 'The customer is king' has a useful sound bite rating – invaluable for any concept that is to occupy consultants, academics and gurus. And great for chairperson's speeches and mission statements. But after a generation of politically correct customer adulation, the real customer occupies no such privileged position in the world of modern business.

A MOST DETESTABLE SPECIES

In our present preoccupation with the customer, we can easily under-estimate the impact of what at the time bordered on heresy: some marketing academic notion that the moaning, whimpering, interfering buying public should be allowed to upset the efficient professionalism of the store or factory doing an honest job of fulfilling orders. Put another way, that customers should get in the way of commerce and industry. And yet more heresy: some ivory tower delusion that mass production technologists, scientific managers and hard-pressed shop-keepers would ever pander to an ungrateful, miserly, mostly detestable species termed euphemistically the customer. Ask hotel or supermarket checkout workers about customers, and carefully watch their facial expressions and body language (never mind what they say, unless they are off the premises, out of earshot of managers and customers). For that matter, ask a politician about voters, a vicar about parishioners, or a nurse about patients, at a less than positive juncture in their respective workdays.

The minds of sellers have not changed, just the words they use. So, however succinct or catchy the slogans, however comprehensive and comforting the customer's charter, the reality of customer supremacy remains firmly in theory rather than practice. The customer is not, and never has been, king. At least in customers' minds, where it matters. The so-called customer revolution was only a revolution in theory – an ideal, a good idea. It became the profitable stock-in-trade of consultants, business writers and even marketing professionals. But what is happening today, in a new century, after a generation of business school rhetoric? After a thousand AGM president's speeches quoting lofty customer-centred mission statements? Whatever it is, it's far from Levitt's ideal of customer-centred marketing.

REACTIONARY MARKETING

Businesses often react to competition and declining profit after much of the damage has already been done. And the reaction can be both desperate and radical. Re-engineering, restructuring, employee empowerment and cultural change programmes, for example, typically involve major, company-wide disruption. These responses usually suffer from three major defects, however, which do little for long-term customer relationships. They are outlined below.

STAFF ATTITUDES

First, changes do not take proper account of the attitudes of staff, and the culture of the organization – the 'mind' of the seller organization. For example, mass customer service training 'scripts' (a popular 1980s panacea), and the behavioural training supporting them, have rarely succeeded in changing entrenched staff attitudes. Such training budgets are wasted. Staff, as well as customers, are more cynical about 'having a nice day' than they were in the old days. Companies face the indictments of arrogance, condescension and resentment. Nowadays, customers add hypocrisy, and worse. This calls for something more substantial. Something deeper has to happen in the customer's mind. But that presupposes a change in the seller's mind. The customer, as a real person, must be *perceived* differently. Suppliers' attitudes and beliefs have to align with their outward behaviour. A corporate mission has to be 'congruent' with its people, and especially those it lets loose on customers. Smiles and 'surface' changes will not suffice. Most of all, marketers need to act creatively rather than react. And all this happens in the mind.

STAFF EMPOWERMENT

Second, staff need to be 'empowered' to fulfil new roles and establish customer relationships. But they will not be keen to be 'empowered' to do two or three times their previous job function in a delayered structure, bereft of managers. Staff will usually respond to greater discretion and responsibility without money rewards, but they don't want to be left out on a limb, especially in an era of job insecurity. So empowerment needs to go beyond words. Top management has to 'walk the talk' and support staff to the hilt in any customer interface. Again, the nature and scale of change are not amenable to top-down communication or traditional sheep-dip methods. Empowerment also affects the company culture and the attitudes of managers and staff – the 'quasi-mind' that has to communicate with the mind of the customer in a mind to mind relationship.

THE INTERNAL VERSUS EXTERNAL DILEMMA

The third defect is that such changes as we commonly witness, however painful, are internal to the organization, rather than externally directed to markets and customers. They focus, for example, on *internal* order processing and production, *internal* empowerment (staff), and intrinsic product features and quality changes. In other words, on *our* rather than *your*. Such changes are supplier- rather than customer-centred. The need, however, is for greater *perceived* benefits on the part of customers. That requires an external rather than internal perspective.

Few customers care what goes on 'inside' the seller's company provided they get what they want at the right price and are treated with respect. That doesn't mean you will get away without a quality product. It means, rather, that 'quality' will always be as perceived by the customer. So one of your customer-first tasks is to create and manage that perception. Product quality is not the only factor that determines whether a customer buys or is loyal. If 'quality' includes a look in the eye of the checkout assistant or some unspoken arrogance, so be it. The customer's perception is whatever goes on in the customer's mind.

Customers, for whatever reason, are rarely absent from managers' thinking. But positive customer consideration is rarely *central* (as is, say, hitting budget or getting that hoped-for promotion) other than in rhetoric. So with all the product quality advances of recent years and the vast expenditure on customer service initiatives, the average customer feels no better treated, and no more satisfied. Marketing reacts but doesn't seem to make things better. It has failed to understand and tap the customer's perception – to get to his or her mind.

THE IMPACT OF CHANGE

We seem to have exhausted metaphors to describe the pace and scale of change in society generally and production and information technology in particular. As consumers, we are all affected. Neither is any marketer or businessperson spared the upheaval. Universal 'delayering', or 'downsizing', is as much a result of technological and social change as economic recession. It has altered the way we do business and, indeed, the way we live our lives as a society. In particular, businesses can no longer win, keep, and relate to customers in the way that they perhaps have done in the past. So the marketing function, whilst ostensibly supporting vital sales, and crucial to any business, has not been spared radical change, including layoffs. Nor has the customer, who, for the most part, has benefited. Business generally has been hit an almost crippling blow as layoffs and bankruptcies sorted out the 21st-century men from the 20th-century boys. And more change is to come.

PRODUCT QUALITY

One of the positive results of all this change – for customers at least – is a level of product quality and sophistication of production beyond what was imaginable hardly 20 years ago. Things don't break down in the way they used to. Reliability in cars, for instance, is now a minimum requirement rather than a marketing plus. Once quality (and indeed price and availability) ceases to be an issue, we tend to take it for granted.

Total quality management (TQM), propounded by Edward Deming and inspired by Japanese practice, helped to make this turnaround in quality possible. The quality movement spanned several years and continues in different guises. It has contributed much to the relatively high technical quality we have come to expect, such as in cars and electrical goods.

But the 'quality movement' is only one example of the changes forced on business by customer-focused competitors. In earlier, less competitive, growth periods, responses to financial feast and famine were more likely to have been of the centralize/decentralize variety. Although this changed the organization chart, changes were cosmetic when compared with the radical changes that we have become familiar with more recently. As well as the 'quality movement', as we have seen, these include business process re-engineering and management delayering.

Before product quality became paramount, changes were fairly standard in nature. Generally they took the form of responses, rather than planned, strategic initiatives. The solution was usually centralize, decentralize, or reorganize in some way. The response, moreover, was usually to problems to which there was no ready answer but about which something serious and far-reaching had to be *seen* to be done. This was as much to mollify investors concerning half-yearly performance as to serve the customers on whom, in the end, everyone's fortunes depended. In the context of survival, which the pace of change threatened, structural changes that did not affect direct customer value that could translate into sales and profits were not enough. After all, car buyers would not keep buying rust boxes if a competitor offered antirust treatment and a warranty thrown in, whatever internal changes a supplier made. More substantial solutions were needed. First, in the real quality of products, and second in the real service that customers increasingly expected. Quality was usually applied to the technical quality of goods and features, rather than the quality of service, and the total product 'package' bought. True to the age, business concentrated on product rather than people – at least the people who buy. Its emphasis was on manufacturing rather than marketing.

RE-ENGINEERING

More recently, process re-engineering, the movement popularized by Michael Hammer, became the 'in' solution. This involved a whole new way of doing business, in deed, not just in word. Change was mainly bottom up rather than top down. Commitment of top management was sometimes lacking. Their backing waned when implementation schedules slipped, budgets were exceeded, and the quality champions failed to demonstrate early bottom-line results and rising stock values.

Re-engineering change affected *horizontal* processes. These were the chains of systems directed to serving customers rather than vertical management structures for the convenience of the business. It is this degree and depth of change that marketing has to be measured against, when faced with the same business challenges.

But re-engineering, like 'total quality', is often half-heartedly under-taken, and is now increasingly questioned as the panacea it purported to be. Michael Hammer admits in his book *The Reengineering Revolution* that 'reengineering has not been an unqualified success. There are numerous reports in the press of reengineering failures'. Nonetheless, re-engi-neering is an example of how radically companies have had to react to the new, canny, consumerist marketplace. More specifically, to a new kind of customer. Rather than a mass consumer statistic, a real, individual customer, with his or her own perceptions, feelings and expectations.

EMPLOYEE EMPOWERMENT

'Empowerment' had its day as another contemporary buzz concept. Again, a laudable concept, especially insofar as empowered staff were empowered to serve customers without the inertia of a large organization, the fear of being too 'visible' and the risk of being blamed for making inevitable mistakes. But empowerment, all too often, turned out to be no more than lip service on the part of staff and top managers alike. Even worse, devolved responsibility enabled ever-leaner companies to squeeze impossible levels of productivity and accountability out of their people.

Ironically, staff were 'empowered' in droves to take early retirement or seek new pastures. This was a 1980s perspective on power and empowerment more Machiavellian in character than enlightened 'human resource management', under whose aegis empowerment had blossomed. Most significantly, as we weigh marketing in the balance, empowerment was another *reactive* response to the pressures of competition and change, rather than an active, indigenous marketing policy to serve customers better.

RIGHTSIZING

Change has had its price. Expensive, temporarily disruptive attempts were made to respond to it. Radically different company practices followed. Most were accompanied by massive downsizing and delayering (or even more euphemistically, although quite seriously, 'rightsizing'). In its train came almost universal job insecurity, the loss of the company's 'memory' lodged mainly in middle managers' heads. Not far behind came record business failures.

The most notable victims have been the hitherto thriving species known as middle management. These are – or were – the populous tiers in between the few that really had to manage and those (mostly lower paid) who did the real work of creating customer value. The middle management fate was borne by any person or function that could be culled or contracted out to save, in as short a time as possible, non-productive expense. Put another way, anybody or function that could not articulately justify their existence in a dog-eat-dog world.

Typically, salespeople, and other functions that could clearly demonstrate their 'bottom line' contribution to value and revenue, were spared. But the wider marketing function was more vulnerable, particularly when centralized or run as a cost rather than profit centre (or when they couldn't prove otherwise). Many disappeared without a legacy of measurable contribution to the business.

To be fair, business in general has responded to all manner of change. Change has included product obsolescence, changing social tastes, regional and international economic recessions, and competition resulting from the deregulation of markets and freer worldwide trading. *En masse,* we have come to live with continuous change, just as some countries learn to live with endemic hyperinflation. But something has to give. 'Survival' in a free market has its own meaning at the level of the individual company, or even a particular industry. Many have gone under. But for every corporate change loser there are winners. These are typically smaller, nimbler-footed enterprises that thrive on the very change and uncertainty that defeat larger, less responsive firms. Or brand-new industries such as are spawned by telecommunications and computer technology – that is, businesses that are themselves part of the driving force of change.

Not surprisingly, even the more efficient companies can get out of kilter. One symptom is the tendency for environmental and ethical concerns to lag behind the pace of scientific and technological breakthroughs. Values become clouded, and the very purpose of the business is called into question. A fashionable industry can be marred in the public eye with a few PR crises. The public response in Britain to BSE and GM food crops, for instance, had the potential to change farming as much in two years as in the two previous centuries. At some point, everything becomes secondary to short-term profit or political success – even environmental issues that the general public have long since taken on board.

Amidst all this, traditional marketing models struggle to meet the challenges of 21st-century products and customers. Marketing is in the balance. Let's assess how it is coping with all this change before considering a new, more effective, mind to mind marketing paradigm.

CANNY CUSTOMERS

The purpose of business is to get and keep customers. That is the business of marketing, and – more importantly – the business of everybody in the company. On the face of it, the pace of change has resulted from technological breakthroughs, such as in computing and microtechnology. In fact, only market demand can bring about such change. In other words, customers at large call the tune. Many a wonder product has had to wait a decade or so until the customer was ready. Many products never reached a retail counter. According to the 'marketing concept' customers have to get satisfaction at the right price. At the heart of change are real people with a free will.

Today's customers are knowledgeable, demanding, articulate, and increasingly informed. So marketers, who specialize in customer satisfaction, find themselves right in the middle of all these changes. That's both a blessing and a curse. With the right ideas and tools, marketers can impact the way we buy, sell and live our lives in the 21st century. Or they can fuel the frustration and hatred of customers who resent non-service in all its forms. Most of all, marketers need to understand customers, in order to win and keep them.

THE IMPACT OF TECHNOLOGY

Although admittedly still a baby among business disciplines, marketing has produced no great paradigm insights on a scale such as has graced the physical sciences or the ubiquitous information revolution. In the case of the physical sciences, rather than playing with rhetoric, it seems that scientists are on the threshold of discovering the very equation of life. Most of us have not recovered from the shock of quantum mechanics (things are different while you are looking at them, which means they are two things at the same time – author paraphrase) that has turned so much orthodox thinking on its head. In the case of IT, information that may have taken a lifetime of painstaking research is no more than a telephone call and a few key words away.

MCDONALD'S AND MICROSOFT

These great advances have not been confined to the learned journals. On the contrary, every aspect of our lives is affected by the march of science and technology. And this, perhaps, is what makes even the short history of marketing seem so lacklustre, and especially lacking in so-called paradigm advances and 'moments of truth'. It would be exciting to hit on something as big as the discovery of penicillin to the world of medicine, or the transistor to communication and computing. We have got McDonald's, of course. But producing fast, standardized junk food is more an example of quality-controlled mass production than marketing. That was a production and distribution coup – no fundamental marketing changes were involved, at least as concerning the customer. Any marketing involved is old-fashioned marketing from

1960 anyway (like considering the customer), simply carried out better than the nondescript competitors. So we search in vain for a marketing paradigm shift.

Bill Gates and Microsoft – surely a marketing success story – might qualify better in terms of a paradigm impact. But again, the push was led by technology rather than marketing. I don't recall the market researchers of the 1970s screaming for the fantastic information and entertainment products that wide-band communications and the silicon chip have since made a reality. Even far more recent market research missed all that. Moreover, it was surely production technology that helped miniature computers overtake science fiction, as capacity soared and costs plummeted. Just as the technology of the Model T production line changed the private motor market – and the world we know – for ever.

PARADIGM MOMENTS OF TRUTH

Sadly, for true marketing professionals, this toddler of a management discipline cannot take the credit for creating a global village or the blame for destroying the planet. It has never reached that league. The Boston Matrix quadrant diagram has had little impact outside the world of the marketing guru, the management consultant and their enthusiastic supporters. Clive Sinclair's dream of a throwaway calculator, or Bill Gates' absurd notion of a personal computer on every desk (as e-folklore has it), has probably affected us all more than whole textbooks of marketing matrices and models. Even a daring political declaration – to land a man on the moon – can call the scientific and technological tune. So what can marketing produce in these expectant peri-millennial times? What's new and what might have an effect that will last? Is it possible that already changes in marketing thinking are happening that will affect the way we live in the 21st century?

Physicists and biologists juggle with cosmic and genetic wonders that seem to promise the secret of life. Whole, awesome libraries of knowledge are at our fingertips. Nor have these great advances been confined to the learned journals. On the contrary, every aspect of our lives is affected by the march of science and technology. And this, perhaps, is what makes even the short history of marketing seem so lacklustre by comparison; so devoid of what have been called 'paradigm moments of truth'.

NON-MARKETING PERSPECTIVES

This book takes another look at marketing in a fundamental way. I am not concerned about refining or revising what we have. I don't set out, for instance, to add, as others have done, 5 or 25 Ps to the 4P marketing mix model that gets my attention in the following chapter. Nor do I postulate about how marketing might react to the Internet and other changes that are bound to affect our lives in the future. That's the sort of adaptation that does not demand or expect paradigm changes. Any function or body of thought, from law and accountancy to the bicycle and the typewriter, will eventually have to come to terms with its contemporary world, however wild the kicks or loud the screams. I am more concerned with how marketing might make its own active, creative contribution to business, organizations and our everyday lives.

It is tempting to chronicle the shortcomings of multi-million dollar market research and the howlers that gurus, business schools and 'excellent' companies produce in such profusion. I got enough stick as an accountant to leave me conscience-free of offending other professional camps. Such knowledge at least might reassure the lone businessperson of his or her instinctive creativity and common sense – which is what the best marketing is all about. You don't realize how good you are until you realize how useless others, with less excuse than you, happen to be. I resist the temptation to quote howlers however it adds to the prose. For inevitably there are pockets of creativity and innovative thinking that prove any broad indictment wrong. Examples of excellent marketing are there for the finding, just as are so-called excellent companies. The latter, however, turn out to be all too ephemeral and the neat theories to which their excellence is attributed turn out to be non-transferable. I hope that among the examples of excellent marketing, not confined to companies of any reputation, let alone those labelled as excellent, there are models of marketing innovation that will be readily transferable and instinctively recognized as common sense.

Drawing on the greater access at company rather than industry level that the information revolution has opened up, I have searched for the good and positive among the motley initiatives carried out under the general banner of marketing. More specifically, I have searched for omens – significant examples of marketing innovation that might augur well for mainstream marketing in the coming century. I have looked for twists and trends of 'paradigm significance'. Most of all, I wanted to find the seminal ideas from which businesses around the world could implement profitable change.

THE ROLE OF OUTSIDERS

One of the first mistakes I made was to search the marketing literature. I should have remembered that it is rare indeed for major thinking changes to come from within a well-defined field of scientific, political or professional thinking. To the chagrin of the experts and 'establishment' thinkers, the reverse is the case. Professional rationale can stifle and blinker when that's all there is around you. Like-minded (through qualification, experience or a common organization culture) teams, whatever their pedigree, suffer similar creative handicaps.

The greatest advances usually start out as the heresy of outsiders (or prodigal insiders considered as outsiders). The longer a body of thought has prevailed, the less chance there is for the *status quo* to be upset – however much the world has changed around it. Too many reputations are at stake. Whole careers may stand on what overnight is exposed as nonsense or irrelevance. All the 'sensible' possibilities have been considered and discarded already ('I've been in this business long enough to know…'). Even the more credible outside contributions will have been courteously sidelined. It's the unusual associations that are summarily discounted, or not even imagined, that matter in the creativity stakes.

At minimum, a paradigm change demands a new perspective. New associations can take on special meaning – sometimes of Eureka quality. The mind synthesizes and creates synergy out of the disparate pieces of information unconsciously thrown into the idea pot. Insights such as these usually come from functional foreigners – outsiders, be they other professionals or lay people. I'm not sure how my own professional background in financial management and management development might contribute in the more glamorous world of marketing. Or my lay interest in popular psychology, neurophysiology and linguistics. Either way, at least I qualify as a marketing outsider, and that is what counts. The outsider has a head start in his or her freedom to ask silly questions, and not being shackled to 'received wisdom'.

Having said that, just being a lay thinker does not mean that you are a creative thinker. And creativity is the name of the game when you are in paradigm mode. In 'moments of truth', a hundred left brains cannot compete with a single, penetrating, childlike insight. You need insight plus common sense wherever you are coming from.

As it happens, pockets of marketing thinkers now seem to be questioning the whole mass culture that has built up since Henry Ford made so convincing a practical case. At one end of the spectrum, even when so-called global products are marketed, whether fast food or motor cars, local tastes and cultures are considered and allowed for. Differences are recognized, even if just between markets, such as countries, rather than individual customers. But, cosmetic catering for taste apart, both marketing and production remain very mass. The individual is not catered for, unless he or she happens to conform to the specification of the segment into which he or she has been scientifically slotted. At the other end of the spectrum, you can order jeans or a BMW customized to your actual needs. By using computerized production techniques you can stay 'mass', but be flexible and responsive also. At last the actual customer, rather than a demographic caricature, has come into the equation. Mass customization does not always mean a one to one relationship, of course, let alone a mind to mind relationship. But it signals the demise of mass marketing as we have known it and augurs well for the tomorrow's customer.

TOWARDS THE CUSTOMER

I hope to show that this direction – towards the customer as an individual – is the right one, but that there is a long way to go. So far, marketers, and even market researchers, have not dared to go beyond behaviour into the recesses of the customer's mind. The camera-wielding lodgers record outward *behaviour* but cannot account for the feelings, beliefs and values upon which such behaviour is based. Even more enlightened market research still stops at the eyes, ears, nose and mouth, as though these clever organs were responsible for the decisions and the motley feelings and mindsets upon which purchases – whether recurring or so-called impulsive – are based. Every behaviour has its explanation in the neural network of the human mind. And such a precept extends well beyond customers and marketing – it's a universal people thing. So however sophisticated we become at analysing effects (behaviours) we will be no nearer understanding causes. Even a child can imagine the massive unseen roots of an oak tree and understand, in simple terms, the process of growth. But it seems the unseen mind is too much for the scientific researcher to cope with. To Skinnerian thinkers (next paragraph), observing outward behaviour seems more scientific anyway than the brain, which looks increasingly messy and incomprehensible the closer we look.

For example, the Skinnerian time and motion study of the 1950s and 1960s was a joke to the informed workers who knew the whys as well as the hows of every task or behaviour and could adjust them to achieve the desired job timing, and, more important, bonus end result. Yet the latest in-home observations of market researchers have the same blind spot about what goes on below the 'ground level' of outward behaviour. They don't know why Sarah stopped eating peas. That it was nothing to do with the colour or flavour the laboratories were spending millions to get right. Cleverer researchers know that John buys on impulse. But they don't know what triggers his impulse, let alone how to create such an impulse in a promotion message to clock up high margin sales. Yet it so happens that John's impulse buying is as predictable as a pensioner buying his or her daily newspaper once a simple mental pattern is identified.

READING MINDS OR MARKETS?

Marketing is now starting to pay more attention to the individual rather than geographical and demographic statistics. Unfortunately, although going in the right general direction, mainstream marketing is still preoccupied with analysing customer labels, and, even worse, the most general, irrelevant demographic data. Those who have advanced to observing actual behaviour are preoccupied with historical transactions (purchase data).

The next gaping knowledge hole is what the customer sees, hears and feels that produces this critical buying behaviour. How do they *sense* the world? How do they sense a product or a brand? This is the stage at which we begin to get into the other person's shoes, in order to see, hear and feel what they do. But key decisions are made in the mental 'back room'. That's where we *interpret* what we sense, test it against past experience and the values and beliefs they have produced, perceive what this world is about, and decide how we should act. As we shall see, even this subterranean process is multi-layered and hierarchical. Colours, sounds and words (the stock-in-trade of mass advertisers) can quickly change an ephemeral feeling, for example. However, attitudes and beliefs, on which important decisions and – not least – supplier and brand loyalty are based, are of sterner human stuff.

Beliefs and brains

You can change a person's non-self belief – such as 'sugar is bad for your heart' (rather than a self-belief 'I'm useless') if you know just what the belief is and you appeal both to logic (left brain) and emotion (right brain) in getting your message across. Other beliefs, such as 'politicians are crooks', might be more of a challenge. But again, once identified, they are amenable to a marketing-type message – as is the classic buyer's 'objection' once the experienced salesperson teases it out.

A self-belief sits at a higher (or deeper) level in the hierarchy of perception and you will need more than a multi-million pound advertising campaign to convince Shirley that she is not ugly, Fred that he is not tone deaf or Gill that she is not allergic to just about everything. But these techniques have so far not penetrated marketing except at the heavily interpersonal end of selling – a subset of the marketing process. 'If we didn't think of it, it can't be very good' is the usual response to innovative thinking, and such a sentiment is certainly not confined to the marketing function that happens to be my present focus. But sooner or later, however entrenched the mindset, common sense (as it always seems in hindsight) prevails and a paradigm change is inevitable. The trick is to bring the change forward a decade or two and spare a lot of customers what their predecessors have had to bear.

Non-marketing people like myself don't mind turning marketing on its head, or even replacing it with something different. After all, it's happening elsewhere. Where does computing stop and telecommunication begin? And what does 'publishing' mean as the World Wide Web reveals its awesome influence? It's good if you have no axes to grind. But it's better if you are steeped in your subject like Einstein or Poincaré but are childlike or anarchistic enough to think outside the mental boxes you have so painstakingly constructed. We need marketing to change from the inside so that we don't waste the brains.

CUSTOMER-FIRST TRENDS

The customer drives quality, cost, service and competitiveness. In the end, the humble customer determines a firm's very survival. There is a danger, however, that the changes in technology and customer expectations are running ahead of traditional marketing thinking and practice. Some trends, such as miniaturization to almost molecular level, and from tangible products to invisible information ('atoms to bits', as it has been described), are awesome. Together with other parallel change trends they demand a whole new marketing paradigm.

We have already met a few of these trends. Here are some of the trends and issues that modern marketing needs to come to terms with:

- manufactured product to service;
- tangible goods to intangibles such as insurance, financial services and tourism;
- consumerism and customer rights;
- product features to benefits;
- empowerment and decentralized leadership;
- mass production to 'mass customization';
- falling costs of computer power;
- mass marketing to relationship and database marketing;
- global markets to niche segments;
- niche market segments to individuals;
- vertical management to re-engineered, horizontal, customer-led, process management;
- competition to strategic alliances;
- atoms (of tangible product) to bits (of information);
- interest in what customers do to what they think and feel.

You may recognize some of these from inside your own company and industry. Although familiar with them to different degrees, we cannot fully understand the impact of these fundamental changes. Even less can we predict how they will affect marketing in this new century. The issues and questions themselves are not easy to define. Solutions, in the form of clear, customer-focused marketing strategies, are even more elusive. Fortunately, common 'customer' threads run through these otherwise disparate trends.

After obsessive focus on quality and re-engineering, some companies have come to realize the importance of a long-term customer relationship over and above an excellent product or service. But this involves a new marketing 'paradigm' or operating model. For a start, the short-term focus of investors, entrepreneurs and business managers is called into question. So are marketing approaches that fail to understand how the customer thinks. Such approaches have little success in achieving the long-term loyalty of unpredictable customers. Such an approach, however, is just what competitiveness, profitability and survival increasingly demand.

These are macro trends that will affect far more than marketing. But lots of other changes are taking place, any of which might affect customers and the way we do business. For instance:

- A shrinking day. Quality time will be more and more valuable. That means people will not do what they find unpleasant – whether shopping, housework etc. Brands may take on further significance, not for prestige, but for the convenience of getting a known quality and consistency.
- Connectedness. This will be mainly evident in the e-mail and www community. This community will develop between suppliers and customers as well as between friends and people of like interests. Paradoxically, this mass Internet resource will be used for niche markets. People will be looking for a very limited range of services and products and information. This is very different to TV viewers, say, bombarded with shotgun advertising, most of which is not only not of interest, but annoying into the bargain.
- Body and soul. Strange things are happening. People stuff themselves with junk food yet are obsessive about exercising. They will stay at home more to shop, work and meditate, but they will expect more of the outside world in terms of entertainment and travel. This entertainment factor will need to be part of the retail experience. It will no longer just be shopping. Campbell Soups claim that not only can its products save us time but also they can renew our souls. 'Mm! Mm! Good for the body. Good for the soul' says their promotion.
- Individualism. People know what they want. A woman is no longer a woman for marketing purposes. She is an individual with unique needs, interests and ideas. For instance, a badminton player and rambler. Children are also individuals, and also influence the buying habits of parents and peers heavily. By age 10, a child in the USA visits on average 270 stores a year. Individualism already affects fashion suppliers, but this could extend widely to ethnic, children's, special interest needs, and the needs of the greater numbers of self-employed people.

MARKET RESEARCH METHODS

A swing to real customers is also mirrored in market research methods. Focus groups have replaced the less personal socio-economic methods. In the heady mass marketing days, market research subjects anonymously responded to surveys designed by non-customers. Customers can now express themselves in their own way and actively contribute to the development of a product or service. Heresy of heresies, customers might think of better ideas than the consultants, R&D people and scientific mass-market researchers. Although a long time in the coming, a woman can have a say in the design of a kitchen or a child in the design of a toy.

This market research trend continues. For instance, camera-wielding researchers now 'live' with a subject family for weeks on end to establish actual rather than theoretical buying and product use behaviour. That's a long way from the C2 or 'over-50 female' level of segmentation. The search, however, is for that mystical yet real person that represents a few million others. A 'customer' to whom the market can cater without losing its economies of scale or abandoning its well-proven mass marketing and production methods. Quite simply, you need real customers to construct a scientifically valid ideal, or modal, customer – the icon of mass marketers. And even a modal customer has a modal mind, and a psychographic profile. With a mind to mind strategy you identify and sell to real customers from the start.

MARKETING MYTHS

Levitt later referred to his '1960 manifesto', 'Marketing Myopia', as a kind of 'corporate consciousness-raising'. Nine years later, in his book *The Marketing Mode* he acclaimed it had done its intended work. At a corporate level, maybe. And 'consciousness' rather than practice. But at the vital customer interface, and with all the new marketing rhetoric, little changed. 'The customer is king' was a myth.

SELLERS WITH ATTITUDE

Specifically, the seller's *attitude* changed little. Change was cosmetic. It involved internal change, such as customer service words and policies, rather than external change. Customers were not so easily convinced, nor were their perceptions altered. Underlying management and staff values and prejudices were of hardier stuff. Slogans became more succinct or catchy, and customer's charters added extra comfort. But the reality of customer attitudes was and today still is quite a different matter. Rhetoric has run ahead of what customers instinctively know is 'reality'. Suppliers don't often mean what they say and they do what they do as a business necessity rather than a delight. But canny customers see the join. And their perceptions count for everything, including corporate growth and profitability. Customer supremacy, for most, remains a myth.

Customer-first smiles

Attitudes reign, whether of seller or buyer. Witness, for example, the unprintable subvocalizations of the hotel worker as another unwelcome patron finally exits the automatic doors. Note how the professional, plastic, customer-first smile is erased with relief as a malcontent shopper turns to leave. And did you spot the knowing smirk of sympathizing colleagues? Actions speak louder than words, but *attitudes* speak louder than even well-practised customer-first mannerisms. The nuances of body language betray deep-rooted mindsets and tell a different story. The story that the customer is not, and never has truly been, king. That's the reality and that's the challenge for 21st-century marketing.

Sound bite rating

The customer revolution of the 1960s was thus no more than an ideal – a good idea. But 'The customer is king' has a useful sound bite rating. It created a new life form for consultants, business writers, marketing professionals, academics and management gurus. The idea gained popularity and respectability. A generation of business schools amplified and analysed Levitt's wisdom. A thousand AGM president's speeches quoted lofty customer-centred mission statements. In due course a big enough platform in business schools and the marketing establishment meant that customer sovereignty could no longer be openly challenged in orthodox management circles. Sadly, there was no dramatic change in the way customers were actually treated. The reality fell short of even the 'corporate consciousness' Levitt thought had been achieved, let alone the practice of the new consciousness. Reality fell short of what the customers he championed deserved.

CUSTOMERS WITH FEELINGS

As it happens, the species 'customer' has itself changed since Levitt's article. The turn-of-the-century customer is no longer just a demographic statistic, a mystical modal entity created from countless question-naires. No longer just a database entry, a Visa card number and expiry date. He or she is a unique person with feelings, hopes and fears. The customer expects, and increasingly demands, to be treated as a person with rights and minimum expectations of companies, products and services.

Company marketing professionals and their CEOs don't just need to *know* this ('corporate consciousness'), but need to know what to do about it. Specifically, to know their customers' minds. In today's competitive environment this can be the key to growth and survival. Customers as a species are themselves evolving fast in a fast-changing world. And that means a changing role for marketing. What role will that be in the coming years and decades? Can it and will it keep pace with the continuing technological and social changes that have been so widely prophesied? And will the change be by evolution or revo-lution? To keep it simple, will marketing take account of customers' feelings?

NOTHING NEW

Levitt's idea in 'Marketing Myopia' was hardly novel, even with hind-sight. It is no more than common sense. Who other than the customer paid for the products that made the profits, even before the liberated 1960s? In token fairness, some successful businesses did recognize, although all too few, that their profits lay in customer satisfaction rather than product excellence. But *service* excellence remains a minority phenomenon. The big challenge lies in excelling in customer understanding and satisfaction.

A couple of factors, however, offer hope:

- Information technology has meant that one to one managed customer relationships are feasible. Even small companies can become world leaders through access to information, and by applying database technology to individual customer 'intelligence'. Those with products and services amenable to Internet cyber-marketing are especially well positioned.
- The traditional marketing mix is losing its canonical status and marketing is being reinvented to meet contemporary business, and we address this in the next section. Marketing change of a paradigm nature is in the air.

THE MARKETING MIX

Marketing as we now know it started around 1960, not least due to Levitt's popularization. The 4Ps became the universal model, or paradigm, for marketing policy and practice. The test for this simple model is against the needs of 21st-century customers and marketers.

The four elements of the traditional 4Ps 'marketing mix' are Product, Promotion, Place and Price (Figure 1.1).

PRODUCT

'Product' includes services. The main change in this element of the mix is the move away from physical product to services and invisible, information-type products – as the term has been coined, from 'atoms to bits':

- Will the nature of product change?
- What will this mean for customers and marketers alike?
- How will the product be *perceived* given the customer's expectation of choice and quality, if not service?
- To what extent is customer satisfaction (or dissatisfaction) due to the tangible product performance or the sales and after service experience?
- Put another way, what is the customer's get it–use it–fix it experience?
- How do customers weight their feelings about benefits against the facts about features? How do they rate the pleasure or pain of being a buyer and customer?
- How can you change their perception by what you say and do?

Figure 1.1 The marketing mix

The big marketing change will be to start finding products for customers rather than customers for products. You will meet the Total Product Concept in Chapter 2.

PROMOTION

Promotion includes selling, but as we consider the role of the customer's mind, promotion covers much more. I have referred to the significance of the trend towards relationship and one to one marketing, and how this will affect promotional strategies. Adopting the principles and skills of NLP set out in Chapter 3, the marketing message can be better promoted. An important question is the extent to which NLP techniques, already successfully applied in person to person selling, can apply to promotion more generally. Specifically in database marketing, but also in sensory-based advertising, covered in Chapter 6, and promoting a consistent corporate 'personality', covered in Chapter 9.

PLACE

'Place' is an alliterated dumping ground to include markets and distribution. How will place, or product distribution and availability, be changed along with all the parallel technological advances? What, for instance, of the world of publishing, in which traditional distribution channels, along with the very nature of the product itself, are changing beyond all recognition? The Internet, of course, has already become a key feature of this 'place' element, and we can hardly imagine how this will develop in the immediate few years. The big question is whether this will become another major marketing channel or whether it will turn the 'place' pigeonhole on its head, and require totally new marketing concepts.

PRICE

The effect of all these changes is just as dramatic on pricing. Already we have come to live with an almost throwaway-price calculator, replacing weighty machinery that once only large wealthy companies could afford. Computers themselves follow the same dramatic, helter-skelter price curve which shows little sign of slowing. Hence, the question, how do you price 'bits' of information which, through the Internet revolution, have become so accessible at hardly any cost? Who adds value and who pockets the profit? What benefit does the customer enjoy?

The 4Ps marketing mix models the production-led marketing philosophy of the first generation of marketers. It spawned marketing as a function, a profession, a branch of management 'science', a department or division, and a main board appointment. But did it put the customer first? People, for one, are conspicuously missing from the 4P paradigm. So how will the four-element marketing mix stack up for 21st-century marketing? Let's check its pedigree. We don't want change for change's sake.

MIX AT THE CROSSROADS

The idea of the marketing mix was introduced by Neil Borden in the 1950s, developed from the notion of the marketer as a 'mixer of ingredients' reconciling the various means of competition and the need to make a profit. Comprising the above main elements, it was soon labelled the 4Ps.

Earlier models existed, but these did not have the same universal impact on business. For example, the 'organic functionalist' approach advocated by Wroe Alderson and 'parameter theory' developed by the Copenhagen school in Europe. Over the years these were all but abandoned. Earlier approaches still, such as the commodity, functional, and geography-related regional and institutional schools suffered the same fate. None of these had the popular impact of the simple, 4Ps marketing mix.

But rather than rendering the 4Ps as just another fashion, these intellectual but transient precursors only highlight its robustness over a generation, and the remarkable way in which it created modern marketing. Marketing, and the 4Ps, have met a number of crossroads over the years. In due course, however, the 4Ps marketing mix model became an accepted part of academic research and marketing practice and simply taken for granted.

THE HOLY QUADRUPLE

In most cases this remains the same today. The concept has been referred to, for instance, as the 'holy quadruple of the marketing faith, written in tablets of stone'. For academics and researchers questioning such truths, careers could be at stake. When additional marketing variables were propounded, for instance, they were liable to attack in subsequent publications so never managed to topple or even amend the sacred quadruple. As a result there has been a neglect of empirical study into key marketing variables and how they are understood and actually used by marketing managers. Structure dominated process. Students of marketing were simply given a toolbox and not encouraged to question the underlying concept and in particular the process nature of marketing relationships. Worst of all, the real needs and desires of the customer were not high on agendas.

THE 4Ps CANON

The idea of a discrete list of factors has always been suspect, whether defining the attributes of a leader, an 'excellent' company or a concept such as marketing. By its very nature it never includes all the variables nor fits all the circumstances. And the longer the ideal list becomes, the less useful it is in practice. The variables themselves in due course become obsolete or of little relevance. Sadly, even helpful additions to the original 4Ps canon have not survived, perhaps because they did not start with P, thus upsetting the comfortable alliteration. Hence, advocates of the 'service' variable – a strong contender – failed. Even 'People' – perhaps because it is so ubiquitous in the whole field of marketing rather than a neat, functional, segment – did not attain the canon.

Viewed in a more modern context it is perhaps as well that the service tag never stuck. Businesses have struggled hard to get their people to think of customer service as the responsibility of the whole workforce, and not a separate function or, worse still, department. As it happens, the same can be said of the original 4Ps. These, when almost universally adopted in the early 1970s, spawned marketing functions and in due course main board marketing directors, mainly in larger companies. Marketing was soon professionally institutionalized. Remarkably, much of its prestige stemmed from the neat, unassailable foundation of the 4Ps model that was so much in tune with contemporary models, especially quadrant matrices, from 'management science'. Along with finance and production directors, the new genre of marketing directors in due course occupied CEO chairs. Marketing had come of age.

Any criticism of the 4Ps canon is unfair on Neil Borden, as the model is an oversimplification of his original concept. His list had 12 elements and it was not intended to be a definition. Moreover, as he saw it, the elements of the list would probably have to be reconsidered in any given situation – *à la* 'situational leadership', where a leader changes his or her style depending on the situation. McCarthy reformulated Borden's marketing mix in the shape of the rigid foursome, where no blending of the Ps is explicitly included. So either he misunderstood Borden's intentions, or his own followers misunderstood his. So, although the blending of the four elements is discussed in the textbooks (such as in Philip Kotler's popular *Marketing Management*), this was never an explicit dimension to the model. Nevertheless, the theory thrived along with business school programmes and marketing careers. Customers had little place in the marketing corridors of power. The 4Ps, with its heavy product bias, reigned.

THE COPENHAGEN SCHOOL

In fact the earlier parameter theory was much more developed than the 4Ps version of the marketing mix. In the late 1950s researchers of the so-called Copenhagen school used the idea of action parameters from von Stackelberg in the 1930s, and from this Arne Rasmussen and Gosta Mickwitz developed the 'parameter theory'. This was a dynamic marketing mix approach linked to the popular product life cycle in which the parameters were integrated by means of different market elasticities (in short, clever stuff). Mickwitz also connected the demand and supply sides in his theory, using an economic rather than behavioural approach. The theory never received much international attention and was overtaken by the simpler and more teachable 4Ps. And the short list of four no doubt seemed to fit typical business situations of the 1950s and 1960s, when marketing itself was a novelty and mass production called the tune. After all, marketing as a business discipline had not existed a decade earlier, nor the 'customer first' notion.

THE DIRTY LITTLE SECRET

The 4Ps model applied especially in the North American environment which featured consumer packaged goods with huge mass markets, a competitive distribution system and well-developed, commercial mass media. But even in this environment there have been doubts about the 4Ps. For example, Reg McKenna, a respected marketing consultant and writer, concludes a discussion about the decline in advertising in North America, the flagship of traditional marketing, which ran: 'the underlying reason behind... (the decline)... is advertising's dirty little secret: it serves no useful purpose. In today's market, advertising simply misses the fundamental point of marketing – adaptability, flexibility, and responsiveness.'

This may overstate the point. It is, however, in line with a more recent trend to turn the anonymous masses of potential and existing customers into interactive relationships with well-defined customers. McKenna's 'adaptability, flexibility and responsiveness' are more in character with individual customers than market segments and a static 4Ps theoretical model. Whatever the historical reasons, and despite opposing voices, the 4Ps became and to a large extent still is the dominating paradigm both for researchers and marketing practitioners – no less than an anachronism in the 21st century.

EXORCISING THE 4Ps

So with all the excitement of 'Marketing Myopia', and acknowledging that marketing is still a baby among business disciplines, it none the less has little to offer beyond the 4Ps. Not that this ubiquitous model was its first and only theoretical base. On the contrary. As we have seen, others have come and gone and some live on, although none with the timeless charm of the 4Ps. The indictment is not that this model has not served us well. Rather, attuned more to the Industrial Revolution than the information revolution and reflecting the product-led marketing of the 1950s and 1960s, it offers us little in what is supposed to be the enlightened era of the customer.

The 4Ps marketing paradigm is hallowed ground indeed and should be rubbished only with caution. Few marketing thinkers are ready to attack the pretty alliteration on which they cut their professional teeth and which they ardently practised and preached.

POST-MYOPIA MARKETING

The textbooks since 'Marketing Myopia' still suggest that the 4Ps model is *the* theory of marketing. But contemporary theories have arisen since the 1960s and these further help to trace the trend in marketing. In particular they monitor where the customer stands in the mind of contemporary marketers. These parallel ideas support the growing emphasis on individual customer relationships, and confirm the significance of 'relationship marketing'.

None of the contemporary ideas I discuss in this section gained the popularity of the 4Ps marketing mix, but each contributed towards more customer-centred marketing. Each took us a little nearer to understanding the customers and the interfaces between them and the marketers. Each brought us in the direction of a customer–supplier relationship and away from a buyer–seller transaction. Each brought us nearer to the *mind* of the customer.

PART-TIME MARKETERS

The 'interaction/network' approach to industrial marketing, for example, was originated in Sweden at Uppsala University during the 1960s and has since spread to many countries. Within this model, between the parties in a network, various interactions take place, where exchanges and adaptations to each other occur. A flow of goods and information as well as financial and social exchanges takes place in the network.

In such a network the role and forms of marketing are not very clear, and certainly cannot be allocated according to four discrete elements. Importantly, all exchanges and interactions have an impact on the position of the parties in the network. The interactions are not necessarily initiated by the seller (or marketer, in the marketing mix paradigm) and they may continue over a long period of time – reflecting the more recent emphasis on long-term customer relationships.

In the network, the seller, who at the same time may be the buyer from another seller in turn, may employ specialists such as sales representatives and market analysts. But in addition, hosts of people in functions which are outside traditional marketing boundaries, including research and development, delivery, customer training, credit management and so on. These other members of the network nevertheless have a vital part in the success of the 'seller'. So they are central to the marketing process. The term 'part-time marketers' was coined for such people, and these typically outnumber the full-time marketers many times over. Gummesson, the main proponent, concludes that: 'marketing and sales departments (the full time marketers) are not able to manage more than a limited portion of the marketing as its staff cannot be at the right place at the right time with the right customer contacts'.

This gave a sound theoretical base to the adage that 'marketing is too important for the marketing function'. In reality, apart from sales-people, the part-time operating marketers, spread throughout the company, are the only true marketers. So this approach spread respon-sibility widely and (unlike the marketing mix, as we have seen) did not foster functionalism and departmental empire building. It was theoret-ically more robust than the 4Ps mix. It better reflected the actual customer interfaces, the missing People element, and the longer-term nature of customer interactions. But still the customer was not an *indi-vidual* person, let alone with a mind of his or her own. Marketing still meant *mass* marketing.

MARKETING OF SERVICES

The Swedish model was mainly directed towards industrial marketing. But in the early 1970s the marketing of services started to emerge as a separate area of marketing with concepts of its own. In Scandinavia and Finland especially, in what has become known as the Nordic School of Services, researchers recognized that the marketing of services could not be separated from overall management. This again reflected a wider, supra-functional definition of marketing, rather than the narrow, four-part marketing mix. In North America the marketing of services also gained importance. But here it remained to a much greater extent within the traditional boundaries of the marketing mix, albeit with some creative ideas.

Perceived quality

For example, Gronroos brought quality back into the marketing context by introducing the concept of *perceived* quality in 1982. What the customer *thinks* entered the equation, not just what the supplier thinks, and this could be translated into objective product quality. He also added the concept of the *interactive marketing function*. This covered the marketing impact on the customer during the consumption or 'usage' process. This is the after-sale period when the consumer of a service typically interacts with the systems, physical resources and employees of the service provider.

Once again, the relationship factor emerged. In France, Langeard and Eiglier developed the 'servunction' concept to describe this system of interactions. These approaches all stressed that the employees interfacing with customers are not considered, by themselves or their managers, and certainly not by the full-time professional, to be marketing people. But 'part-time marketers' they certainly are. So the nature and scope of marketing had to change.

THE MARKETING CIRCLE

A further development brought us nearer the present focus on relationships. Gronroos developed *the customer relationship life cycle model.* Originally called the marketing circle, this covers the long-term nature of the relationship between the firm and its customers. Although managing this life cycle is a relationship marketing task, the term was not used at that time. Once again, as he saw it, in establishing and maintaining long-term customer relationships, the part-time marketers, not the full-time professionals, fulfil the true marketing role. The emphasis was on real person to person interactions and relationships, rather than the abstract 'relationship' between a company, or its marketing function, and the 'market'. But still customers were anonymous, and part of a group, just as were the part-time marketers that served them.

Each of these marketing movements added in some way to the importance of the customer in the marketing concept, and the importance of a relationship rather than one-off transactions. They also starkly highlighted the limitations of the 4Ps model. But they still paid little attention to how customers think, other than what they think about *our* product (the seller's). That is, how the customer will respond to our product or service, rather than how can we respond to the wants and aspirations of customers. This chasm of understanding as between the supplier and customer required an equivalent paradigm change in the way suppliers marketed. The focus of this had to be customer perceptions: the mind of the customer.

These approaches have commanded varying degrees of interest during the reign of the 4Ps model. They clearly view marketing as an interactive process where relationship building is a vital cornerstone. They are, ironically, somewhat related to the earlier systems-based approaches of the 1950s, before Levitt's 'Marketing Myopia'. The marketing mix paradigm, on the other hand, is a much more clinical approach in which the seller is the active part and the buyer and consumer passive. No personalized relationship between seller and buyer is supposed to exist, other than with professional sales representatives – a small minority of 'marketers', as we have seen. This does not fit the reality of industrial and services marketing and the proven results from managing key accounts. Nor does it begin to reflect marketing as a one to one relationship with individual customers. The parallel approaches since Levitt's 1960 article, however, reflect an important trend towards customer relationships as central to the marketing process.

THE RISE AND FALL OF THE MARKETING FUNCTION

Marketing is too important for the marketing department. The 4Ps model makes managing the marketing mix temptingly easy to organize. The function is separated from other activities and specialists are charged with analysing, planning and implementing the various marketing tasks. Market analysis, marketing planning, advertising, sales promotion, sales, pricing, distribution and product packaging all became marketing 'operations'. No surprise, then, that a marketing *department* had to take care of all this, sometimes with the help of outside specialists, for example for market analysis and advertising. The marketing department took on the now prestigious marketing *function*, and the crucial responsibility (indeed the *raison d'être* of the business) for fulfilling customer needs and desires. Other staff were spared the unenviable job of satisfying customers.

FUNCTIONALLY ALOOF

But what has become an organizational approach weakens real marketing even further. The onus for customer service is taken away from the firm as a whole, which becomes less customer focused. The marketing department becomes functionally aloof yet powerful. And even though specific activities such as market research and advertising are customer focused functionally, this can never replace true market orientation (an attitude and culture rather than a function) on the part of the whole organization.

Departmental marketing empires arose that were isolated from design, production, delivery, technical service, complaint handling, invoicing and all the other activities upon which the customer relationship depends. Worse still, they were alienated from the customer. Managing the marketing mix entailed *mass* marketing, and mass marketing did not entail a relationship with real customers. Marketers rose to the top without meeting customers, who to them were segments and stereotypes. Along with finance and production, another functional pillar had been erected with its own professional standing, career opportunities and bureaucratic baggage. Its foundation in management science, however, was no more robust than the 4Ps marketing mix.

Although practically obsolete and usually counterproductive, functionalism, departmentalism and centralization live on. And whilst accounting and treasury functions may have had statutory, economic or functional reasons (like pooling cash) for some centralization, marketing, even with the 4Ps, had no such justification. As it happens, some marketing functions have lost their central power through the delayering, rightsizing, process happening all around.

ENLIGHTENED LATTER-DAY MARKETING

More enlightened companies, on the other hand, have scaled down, decentralized, dispersed or disbanded their marketing people in a positive attempt to place the function where it should be – with every manager and employee. Even the term marketing has been dropped in some companies because of its departmental connotation. The new emphasis is on customer service and quality through the whole 'chain' of business. Structure has given way to process. Theory has given way to the pragmatics of competition and customer demands. Something had to replace the flawed structural model. The latter-day emphasis has moved to long-term customer relationships and relationship marketing.

THE TEST OF A MARKETING PARADIGM

So much for the 4Ps marketing mix idea and the ubiquitous function it spawned. How does it stand the test?

- The limited marketing mix was production-oriented, rather than marketing- or customer-oriented.

- The model did not cater for interaction between the elements, either in nature or scope. The categories, in any event, are not mutually exclusive.
- Besides the inherent weakness of any list approach (like the traits of a good leader or manager), there was never any formalized definition of what characterized a marketing 'element'.

These were fundamental theoretical flaws. Where marketers actually thought about the process, a 'catch-all', 'other' category of non-fitting elements inevitably grew – a typical sign of the gap between theory and practice.

However obvious these theoretical flaws happen to be in hindsight, there has been little change in mainstream marketing for over a decade. Given the extraordinary technological and social changes, the inertia of marketing over the period cannot be overemphasized. Nor the urgency for a better paradigm. Marketing has been slow to think in terms of a different world. Nevertheless, its functional influence continues. And, after subjection to universal delayering, its departmental status.

We cannot say how companies and economies might have fared during the short history of marketing if Levitt's customer manifesto had been actually implemented. Yet it is from *outside* marketing that stark comparisons arise. The tragedy is that there have been no quantum insights in marketing on the scale that has graced the physical sciences or, especially in recent years, the so-called information revolution.

Every aspect of our lives is affected by the march of science and technology and the information revolution that now fuels it. And this, perhaps, is what makes even the short history of marketing seem so lacklustre by comparison; so devoid of paradigm moments of truth. Marketing is a baby among business disciplines, based on a weak and ageing paradigm. The search is for a new paradigm – a better way to satisfy customers with goods and services and stay in business.

2

The customer in mind

'If it ain't broke, don't fix it.' The question for us is whether modern marketing principles and practices are 'broke'. More specifically, how have corporate marketing functions fared during this period of change and in the light of the important trends I identified right at the beginning? Have they kept abreast of the changes? What about the customers they serve? How have they been served? Is mass marketing compatible with the sort of service and relationship that customers increasingly expect? What form will marketing take in this new millennium? Is marketing, as we know it, broken beyond repair? Is it ready for replacement? What sorts of principles and practice will satisfy both the needs of firms wishing to sell and customers wishing to buy?

In Chapter 1 we saw that the marketing pronouncement 'the customer is king' has not become a reality. In particular, we saw that the marketing function has not kept pace with advances in technology, and that mass marketing would not satisfy the 21st-century customer. In this chapter, in the light of the above sorts of questions, in each of the following sections we will consider some important topics that we need to take account of in a modern marketing strategy:

- how customers think;
- understanding customers' values;
- understanding customers' needs;

- the meaning of a product;
- how sellers see things;
- mind to mind marketing;
- market positioning and segmentation;
- customer satisfaction.

HOW CUSTOMERS THINK

You have to answer some fundamental questions if you are to succeed in marketing:

- Who are your customers?
- What's on their minds?
- Where can they be reached?
- What are they buying?

The 'who' and 'where' questions have been well addressed by marketing over the years, so, for our present purposes, I will not add to them. The 'what' question is becoming more and more feasible to answer with the proliferation of checkout data capturing and online commerce. The big challenge is 'what's on their minds?'

This is the weakest link for most businesses, yet it carries a very high rating when comparing with the other demographic and transaction data. It's the key to the customer's buying hot button, and the basis for any relationship and loyalty. It can even outsmart transaction data as it will incorporate customers' aspirations as well as historic buying patterns. In other words, what would the customer like to buy (and probably will next time round or soon)?

Going to the bother of understanding what goes on in your customer's mind is probably the best evidence of 'the customer is king' in practice. It has not been fully recognized, even by 'dyed in the wool' one to one exponents, who often treat detailed transaction data as the pinnacle of customer information.

Understanding how individual customers think is probably the ultimate marketing challenge. Every customer is different. Our unique life experience produces beliefs, values and ways of thinking that make your behaviour different to mine and the next person. We are motivated by different things. We make decisions according to different criteria, feel strongly about certain things, and are comfortable behaving in a certain way. In short, we each use our own mind. And the same applies to sellers – themselves customers and ordinary people. The dual, mind to mind challenge for marketers is to understand their customers' minds, and their own mind also.

ALL IN THE MIND

We have seen that customer thinking includes their attitudes, beliefs and feelings. This includes what they think about your company. Not just your products and services, but the company people they come into contact with in the buying and after-sales process. It includes how customers perceive the words you use, the brand images you communicate and the personality you project. These perceptions determine the customer's buying (or not buying) behaviour and his or her relationship with you as supplier. Hence their loyalty and profitability. Sadly, given the remarkable advances in production and information technology referred to earlier, there is little new originating from the world of marketing in this important area of the mind of the customer. It is this we need to fill.

There are few areas of science and technology that have advanced in very recent years as dramatically as the study of the human brain and the mind. This has revealed the sheer complexity and awesome power of this visually unattractive organ. It is estimated, for example, that the human brain has more potential neuronal connections than there are atoms in the known universe. At the same time, these advances in neurophysiology, assisted not least by computerized scanning technology, reveal something of the unique, subjective process (if not yet the content) of thinking as it happens. Real-time thinking – a window on the customer's mind.

The process is complex, to say the least. And because we don't understand it, it doesn't feature much in how we consciously communicate, solve problems and make decisions, let alone run a business. We know generally that people act in a certain way when we do or say certain things. But even that is confined to people we 'know'. In any event that is about all we have to go on when we want to persuade them to buy and be loyal customers. Unfortunately, each customer acts differently, and, even worse, does not act consistently for any apparent reason. In short, we don't know what happens to our marketing message once inside the black box of the mind (if it gets there).

Fortunately, however, we don't need to understand the human mind fully to be able to use it or get somebody else to use it, any more than we need to understand electricity to get the benefit of a dishwasher. How a person thinks, in terms of their thinking style, is central to how they behave. Knowing what happens in their mind – even without knowing why or even how – can be of enormous benefit, not least in selling and marketing.

In fact it is possible to identify the values, beliefs and mindsets that underpin behaviour. We can determine the characteristics of how a person translates the material world around them into the thoughts that make them uniquely who they are. We will cover this when I address NLP in more detail in Chapter 3. Individual customer knowledge is of less use in the context of mass marketing than in a one to one relationship. In mass marketing the individual customer is ignored and replaced by a standardized or modal customer. Even here, as it happens, an understanding of the human mind is an asset. But, in the case of individual customers, understanding how they think is the key to a successful relationship and business.

STANDARD THINKING

I said earlier that every customer is different. In another sense we are all the same. 'Human nature' is repeated timelessly from person to person and indeed from culture to culture and nation to nation. More specifically, we exhibit a range of standard thinking characteristics. For instance, we do what will give us – or what we *think* will give us – pleasure rather than pain. That is universal. We interpret things around us consistently according to our view of the world and what we *think* is important.

The sensory inputs and the behavioural outputs themselves are variable, of course. But the 'system', or process of thinking, is surprisingly understandable and consistent. When you identify an individual customer, these macro thinking characteristics – sometimes called Meta Programs – are more predictive and relevant than demographic data such as a person's postal address and income. In fact, these mental programmes are crucial when it comes to establishing a long-term, loyal customer relationship and creating a competitive edge.

Fortunately, for practical purposes, this range of 'standard' thinking characteristics can be classified into a dozen rather than hundreds. So the resulting psychographic segments are large enough for most marketing purposes, even when selling mass product globally. At the same time they are simple to apply when fostering one to one relationships. They offer new ways to communicate with your customers and a new basis for market segmentation.

META PROGRAMS

Here is a list of Meta Programs for the moment. Some will be familiar, and all are described in some detail in the following chapters:

- logical;
- intuitive;
- towards;
- away from;
- visual;
- auditory;
- kinaesthetic;
- internally motivated;
- externally motivated;
- risk taker;

- cautious;
- knowing;
- doing;
- having/getting;
- being;
- necessity;
- possibility;
- matcher;
- mismatcher.

This is a selection only, and appears a longer list than it is as it includes 'opposites' – people at different ends of the same personality scale, such as logical/intuitive or matcher/mismatcher.

There is no standard list of 'Meta Programs'. In this book I have included enough to form the basis of an effective psychographic segmentation strategy. However, you will not meet so many examples that you are spared the important task of identifying further types from your own customer base. In short, you need to understand the principles that underlie this new way of understanding and serving your customers.

From the descriptions of some of these Meta Programs in Chapters 5 to 8 you should be able to think creatively of applications in your own industry and market context. The thinking characteristics themselves are of the extroversion–introversion type (although I have not used these here) and will be all too familiar. The novelty is simply in applying these to the marketing concept. Or, in marketing-speak, in *positioning* your company or product and *segmenting* your market on the basis of chosen psychographic as well as demographic and behavioural characteristics. That is the new mind to mind marketing perspective.

UNDERSTANDING CUSTOMERS' VALUES

Understanding your customer's mind means identifying their values. These are what each person considers important. Values therefore have an effect on all our behaviour, including buying. They affect relation-ships, including with suppliers of goods and services. The above list of thinking characteristics largely reflects people's values, such as the importance of doing over knowing, the need to feel right about some-thing before committing (included in the kinaesthetic sense), or the importance of avoiding (or taking) risks. In other words, our personality traits reflect what we think is important. We can usually justify them. Put another way, values are worth their weight in customer loyalty.

Values open up a little-understood Pandora's box of the human mind. From one point of view this may be the last thing that rational business people want to get involved with. From another point of view values are one of a handful of customer 'hot buttons'. If you can identify and 'press' them in your promotion and service, you will gain competitive advantage.

First, you need to understand a few basics about values. These are initially addressed as customer values, but you will probably be able to make analogies with corporate values – the seller's mind – as you think about each characteristic.

SLOW-CHANGING VALUES

Values are not like feelings, which tend to be ephemeral and volatile. They are formed over a period, and it usually takes time to change them. Sometimes a person will stick to certain values until the day they die. You can handle this value feature in different ways. One rule might be not to change your customer's values, but to reflect those values yourself, in your mission, culture and operations, and take account of them in all your communication. It follows that you will seek to serve customers with broadly similar values, just as you might serve a niche segment of customers interested in a particular product or service.

However, although values are slow to change, they do change over the years. This happens, typically, in conjunction with lifetime events, such as getting married and having children, getting a job promotion, or through the influence of a boss, colleague or friend who has a special influence in your life. We also change our values throughout life as part of the process of getting older and, hopefully, wiser.

Viewed in this light, it might make sense for sellers to take an active part in the *formation* of customers' values as part of a lifetime mind to mind strategy. The cosmetics company Avon has several values, for instance, the most well known being women's issues. Each value has to be communicated just as does a brand. 'Cause marketing' mainly builds on existing values, just as brand promotion addresses basic human motivators. But promoting values can also change values. The common factor, however, is recognizing the importance of how the customer thinks – including his or her values – and, one way or another, building that into your strategy. You will make mistakes, of course, but in the long run you will make less if you have a consistent one to one, mind to mind marketing strategy.

VALUES IN CONTEXT

People's values sometimes depend on the context or situation in which they have to make decisions and choices. For instance, the values a person applies when purchasing on a business to business basis, as part of their job, might be different to how they buy personal and family items. For example, a person might strangely change their values depending on whether they are spending their own money or someone else's. Or their own values may subserve the company's. In other words, as an employee, a person takes on board his or her employer's values, perhaps as in a written mission statement or customer charter.

The values in business buying might be anything from hard economics to ruthlessness, with a narrow cost or bottom-line focus, and over a short time horizon. Values in buying, say for one's children, or a hobby or special interest, might be quite different. Price may be secondary, and the product quality viewed over the long term might determine the decision. 'Nothing is too good for our Johnny' is the sort of sentiment we might meet in this case, rather than 'a bed is a bed' or 'you're just paying for the big name'.

Similarly, personal buying decisions may be more holistic in one situation than another, taking into account a far wider range of factors in parallel. For example, you may have 'in mind':

- the rights and wrongs of a decision;
- the effect it might have on other people (good or bad);
- the indirect results of the action;
- the 'peace of mind' factor;
- the conscience factor (can you live with yourself?);
- the opportunity cost (other things you could have bought instead); and so on.

This illustrates the scope of mind to mind considerations, but also the common sense of identifying important values and communicating in that 'language'.

VALUES AND BEHAVIOUR

Values affect our behaviour in all sorts of ways, again depending on the context. We tend especially to incorporate our values into large, important purchases such as a house or car, and to durable and 'image' goods such as clothes, holiday travel and books. In other words, things that reflect our identity and personality, and might affect how others perceive us. On the other hand, we tend to take value shortcuts with commodities, repeat consumables and suchlike. In fact the same phenomenon might occur in company purchases, say as between a computer installation, building, or boardroom table, compared with stationery, or ordinary office tables. Clearly, the sales message will differ depending on what a commercial or industrial customer, in this case, is actually buying – status, image, peace of mind, or just a bargain. What we do, including what we buy, is, knowingly or unknowingly, influenced by our values.

VALUES AND DEMOGRAPHICS

Values may not correlate with a customer's socio-economic status, postal address, sex or education. So it is safer to treat them as psychographic traits, or segments in their own right rather than in conjunction with other non-mind data. Two adjacent households may have identical demographics but be worlds apart in their values. The big question for marketers is what kind of data is the most significant when it comes to influencing buying decisions and loyalty? All behaviour has an emotional element, and buying in particular is usually more emotionally than logically based. So values will drive behaviour more than non-emotive statistics or value-free logic.

However, a demographic statistic can sometimes take on an emotional character. Postal address and income, for instance, insofar as they are important to a customer, will affect their values and thus their emotions. This illustrates the importance of identifying values, on whatever they are based. In other words, you need to understand your customer's mind. Track *what is important* to your customers, and you will start to understand the mysteries of what they do and don't do.

ELICITING VALUES

Although values are important, they are important in a context, rather than as abstract personality characteristics. And you need to be able to apply this 'value elicitation' process to yourself before applying it to customers. It helps first to think about different areas of our lives, as a checklist. We have already referred to the difference between a work and personal context, for example. The areas commonly used for this purpose are:

- work/career;
- relationships;
- family;

- personal growth;
- health and fitness;
- spirituality.

By choosing an area of life with which you can associate your everyday behaviour, you will find it easier to identify values. Remember that values are simply what is important. Thus, 'what is important about your work?' will elicit more than 'what is important to you?' These are just broad categories, of course. The answer to this question might be 'meeting people', 'getting on in the world' or 'providing for the family'. This narrows the area of life to consider, which concentrates the mind further, and will probably elicit more values. Thus:

- What is important to you about meeting people?
- What is important to you about getting on in the world?
- What is important to you about providing for your family?

Questions can be designed according to whatever subject interest is used. For example:

- What do you expect in terms of after-sales service?
- Why is that?
- How do you know you have done a good job at (joinery, teaching, keeping fit, etc)?
- Why did you choose your (car, house, job, hobby, training course, partner, etc)?
- Tell me about a (job, task, house, car, person) that gave you trouble.

Any subject of interest that a customer has divulged provides a basis for eliciting values. That is because we apply values throughout our lives, and not just when buying or relating to a seller. However, once you get down to specific applications of value, prescribed questions, in the form of standard questionnaires, may not be practicable for one to one data gathering. You will have to 'use your mind', just as you need to when forming and maintaining a personal relationship, even though we all have the same basic human instincts. Sometimes you will need to be ingenious and creative. In every case, when identifying values, you will need to be courteous and considerate of the feelings of the customer.

The above 'what is important' process will be used, typically, in face to face elicitation of values. Each main life area can be pursued in the same way, and a short list of values will soon emerge. For instance, the 'providing for my family' answer gives a value in the family life category. Main values will keep cropping up and will span most areas of a person's life. The life categories are just used to stimulate the mind to relate values to actual behaviour in different situations.

For mind to mind marketing there is a further consideration. The customer relationship will not necessarily be face to face (although it would be, say, in a hotel or restaurant, or in professional practice). That means that the opportunities for getting value responses – at least interactively – will be more limited. Or, more to the point, you will need some ingenuity.

The channel itself will lend itself to different approaches. Telephone has few restrictions other than being able to read body language. Direct mail and online communication will be more restricted to the written word. Choice of channel is thus a marketing consideration. Any subject of importance to the customer can be used as a vehicle for eliciting values. If he or she has made a high value purchase, that can be the topic. For example, 'what is important to you about a house/car/computer/training course', and so on. An existing purchase commitment, or known customer interest (deduced from the communication context, such as an online search), will provide fertile values material.

Similarly, information obtained from registration or membership data provided is usually a legitimate subject upon which to base simple questions. Of course, you are not, ostensibly, asking for 'values' – personal information that a customer might be reluctant to divulge – but simply asking questions for marketing purposes as is widely accepted.

THE CORPORATE COUNTERPART

Customer values usually have a corporate counterpart. That is, supplier companies can seem like a certain kind of customer. Put another way, there is such a thing as a quasi-mind. This is illustrated in so-called left-brain organizations, which, in their bureaucracy, order and attention to detail, mirror a left-brain-dominant person. But you will find, just as easily, a wacky company, a caring company and a cautious or negative company. In other words, a corporate counterpart of common human traits. Customers will recognize and relate to a corporate mind, or personality. At the same time the company can deliberately create and change its 'mind' for strategic marketing purposes. 'Corporate personality' is covered in Chapter 9.

UNDERSTANDING CUSTOMERS' NEEDS

We cannot understand the customer's mind without taking account of some well-accepted, universal human needs we all have to some degree. These include basic survival necessities such as food and shelter, but here I have chosen a few human needs that affect marketing, and the buyer–seller relationship.

FRIENDSHIP

We generally like to have friends – people we enjoy being with, with whom we trust and share our thoughts and lives. The characteristics of a friend appeal to the human mind, and tell us much about what customers want of their suppliers. Friends are dependable. They care for us. They are always there. They trust us, and we trust them. We are alike in many ways, probably more in values than in appearance. They are tolerant. They understand us. We get on well together. Friends have empathy.

These characteristics, although essentially human traits and qualities, also apply to inanimate things and organizations. Anything from a blanket or old chair to a car or a house can be a 'friend'. So can a favourite airline, a corner shop, or McDonald's. At least we *act and feel* as though they are friends, which amounts to the same thing. Friendship, and other human characteristics, can be incorporated into a mind to mind marketing strategy. For instance, a company can be dependable by simply getting its act together and doing what it promises to do. It can be friendly by remembering your name and your preferences. And as we have just seen, it can exhibit a corporate personality that embraces the 'friendly' or any other human trait. It doesn't take rocket science, but such a simple strategy can generate remarkable customer loyalty.

Similarly a company, like a good friend, can seem to be 'always there'. This is in the sense of being available, when the customer may want them (more or less round the clock) rather than when they decide to open their doors. This offers special advantages to e-commerce and telephone banking, just as was the case with ATMs which also helped to transform banking. Or a supplier can *care* – not just demonstrate caring behaviour in their service, but by adopting a caring attitude, and fostering it throughout the company. Again, just as would a friend. And that doesn't cost a lot of money. It just requires a change of mind, which anyone, managers and front-line workers alike, can adopt if they accept its importance.

Friendship characteristics can similarly be incorporated into a company's culture, mission and day to day operations. Even more, characteristics such as 'likeness' (of values, interests or feelings) can be adopted once you have the important individual customer profiles upon which to base your communications. For instance, you can express 'caution', 'logic' and a conservative approach in a sales message and be perceived as 'like' by your customer or potential customer, sharing their personality traits. This is a 'matching personality' strategy, and an important feature of mind to mind (or personality to personality) marketing.

None of this happens consciously. The customer simply finds the message more sensible, realistic, attractive etc and for that reason is more likely to act on it. Or simply because it seems a 'friendly' company. The mind of a trendsetter can similarly be accommodated in a 'like' mind communication. In practice a slight adaptation of the promotional wording will usually do the trick. In other words, mind to mind communication doesn't mean changing your mind (the supplier) for every customer. The relationship is created incrementally, and values are not stated explicitly. Some customers perceive Marks & Spencer as being 'with it' when it comes to fashion and others see them as 'fuddy-duddy'. The difference may be a generational one, or just a function of how different we all are. Or it may be the physiological fact that we each have two brains that process in different ways and one may be dominant. The diverse reasons need not matter, if the supplier can reinforce a positive perception by mirroring what is important to the customer. Simply, the supplier has to seek honestly to put the customer first, as any true friend would.

COMMUNICATION

It's good to talk. Human beings have an innate need to communicate with fellow humans. Most of the world's ills, at a personal, domestic, social and global level, can be traced to a breakdown in communication. Marketers, more than others, should not fall into this age-old trap. What causes most anger when trains or aeroplanes are delayed or cancelled? 'Not being kept informed.'

It has often been found that a stronger relationship exists between a customer and supplier after a heated complaint has been satisfactorily resolved than in the case of so-called satisfied customers. One factor is that complaints allow a supplier to exhibit aspects of its personality that it may not have had the chance to communicate, so that there is a greater meeting of minds. But, just as likely, the simple process of communicating – by telephone or person to person, and maybe repeatedly over a period – forms the bond. A similar, strange phenomenon happens in the relationship between hostages and their captives over a period as they are in close communication. There can be a meeting of minds, even in an ideological sense, and a coming together of the kinds of values we considered earlier.

This important factor further explains why mass marketing cannot create the necessary relationship upon which customer loyalty is built. Without individual knowledge of the customer, no line of communication can be opened, let alone rapport and mutual understanding created. Having said that, the effectiveness of communication is not measured by the number of words spoken. The best relationships, including between close friends or a married couple, don't rely on the volume of communication, but on its quality and nature. This is akin to the 'she's always there' friendship factor.

An open communication *channel* is therefore perhaps as important as the communication itself. In other words, the sense of control you get by knowing you can say what you feel if you need to. Road rage is often due to the absence of this basic ability to communicate, even when so physically close. That's probably why mobile telephones have become a way of life for millions. Communication channels (perhaps several, such as telephone, e-mail, interactive world wide web, fax, person to person, mail) are a crucial part of any one to one or mind to mind marketing strategy.

EXPRESSING EMOTIONS

Feelings play a bigger part in the mind and all our behaviour than was thought up to just a few years ago. Even decisions and behaviour we think of as objective or logical probably have an emotional element.

Indeed, it is the unconscious operation of these emotions that make them so ubiquitous and powerful a part of our lives. To feel is a universal need, and this is important in a mind to mind, seller–buyer context. A word, for instance, can trigger emotions out of all proportion to the part the word plays in, say, an overall sales pitch, advertisement or promotion. In most cases there is no way of tracing the source of such emotion, just as with a fleeting smell that revives a childhood memory, or the sound of a long-forgotten song full of personal meaning.

However, some words or phrases, called 'sensory predicates', reflect a person's sensory preference – whether visual ('I see what you mean', 'that's clearer'), auditory ('I hear what you say', 'that sounds fine') or kinaesthetic ('I feel that…', 'hold on to that idea'). Appropriate sensory predicates that reflect the customer's preference (more about sensory preference in Chapter 6) will make any communication more effective. Inappropriate sensory predicates are no more than linguistic pot luck, and may be counterproductive as well as a waste of effort.

JOINING AND SHARING

Another universal need is to belong to a group, be it a family, club, country or whatever. This may involve strong relationships, although they need not be personal. This is the sort of relationship that often develops between customers and other customers, as well as between customers and suppliers. Owner clubs, such as Jaguar and Harley Davidson, can create strong, cult-like relationships and do a lot to strengthen the product or corporate brand. But any common interest will bring people together, whether physically, or more commonly now, through Internet Usenets, chat sites and such. When the interest is a brand, such as Harley Davidson or Apple Mac, a company stands to benefit enormously from the shared associations and free, word-of-mouth referrals. There is usually an inbuilt loyalty to the product, so this sense of belonging is another route to important customer relationship objectives. It is no coincidence that membership of groups involves some form of registration and a one to one relationship with the sponsor or corporate brand. The common interest is an ideal basis for exchanging mutual information. Valuable databases can be built up, and members receive useful information about their special interest both from the company, and, more likely, from fellow group members.

Sharing implies mutual commitment, loyalty and strong relationships – the holy grail of relationship marketing.

This sharing and belonging tendency also embraces causes, such as environmental concerns, animal protection and charitable organizations. The cause, interest or product association offers a route to the mind of the customer and his or her values (what is important). People can be very enthusiastic about their special interest and contribute heavily both in frequency and value of purchases. They tend to be loyal and freely give ambassadorial support for the company and its products. We all have this special belonging need to some degree and this offers another route to the individual customer's mind.

The sharing and belonging phenomenon can happen remotely, without personal contact. E-mail and the Internet are good examples. An online weight loss service, for example, offers personalized weight loss and diet programmes weekly by e-mail. New visitors complete a profile outlining daily and weekly exercise and diet habits, and state where they wish to improve. The service provides advice about the right programme to achieve a person's health objectives. For a fee, you can have a personalized 12-week programme, which is more customized than the usual community programmes. When run as part of an online group, even the peer pressure element – an advantage of Weight Watchers and similar programmes – can be added to the experience, to increase the success rate. Cross-selling opportunities (for a bigger share of the customer) are obvious. Specific dietary products to reflect personal needs and preferences, as well as exercise hardware and clothing, are on offer.

Women.com is an online community site that offers editorial content and e-commerce services. It has surveyed its visitors for years and has demographic and psychographic profiles both for its own use and for advertisers. As well as getting information on buying habits ('have you shopped for anything online recently?') they ask agree/disagree questions such as 'I'm usually the first in my peer group to try something new'. That's a start at finding out how the customer thinks, and is valuable data that can apply to all sorts of purposes. Unlike actual product-by-product purchase behaviour, such personal information will remain valid over time. That's the advantage of psychographic information over even the most detailed, up to date transaction data. Understanding whether customers are risk-oriented, family-focused or career-minded, for example, can open a door to the customer's mind. The club or membership setting makes it easier to create such a rich database.

THE MEANING OF A PRODUCT

A 'product' or 'service', such as a chair or a holiday, is a perception in the mind of each customer. Marketing is about selling products and services, so it is important to understand how the customer sees these, and how this will affect the way we have to communicate with them.

PERCEIVED CUSTOMER VALUE

'Perceived customer value' is a crucial measure of marketing success. This is the product or service quality, in its overall sense, that customers expect, at the right price. Each customer will attribute different characteristics and scope to a given product. Each will have different expectations, partly based on his or her past experience. Nevertheless, that's the package they are buying. So their perception is crucial information to the marketer.

AT&T found that changes in real, technically measured changes in product quality are followed about three months later by changes in the customer's perception of those products. Changes in perceived quality, on the other hand, are followed a mere two months later by relative changes in market share. They also found that their perceived price competitiveness as a company was worse than competitors'. So managers were given the flexibility to price at a level that matched the customer's idea of reasonableness.

When 'total product' is valued, price may be considered very reasonable indeed, or low (although not many customers will volunteer the information). So there can be immediate bottom-line economies by measuring perception factors and marketing accordingly. In fact, the customer's perception may be quite wrong, and any objective price/quality evaluation would put you ahead of the competition. That's interesting, annoying information, but it doesn't win you customers. Somehow you have to address the customer's perception, and not reality. CRM doesn't do this *per se*, but a mind to mind strategy will reach this important depth of customer understanding.

Skoda cars, the butt of jokes, have borne their dated image of poor quality for years. In fact, Skoda has long outpaced competitors in most aspects of quality and in crucial industry J D Power rankings, as well as in top motor sport. But changing customers' minds means more than communicating technical data, such as service frequency, 0 to 60, body treatment and such. It means transferring a whole new image of the car and the company. That is difficult at the best of times, but impossible if you haven't spotted the importance of what goes in the customer's mind, rational or otherwise.

Perception is everything. So a strategy to communicate and manage customer perception is the grand mind to mind project. It is as important as, or more important than, a strategy for technical quality excellence. A paradox, perhaps, but not the only paradox in customer-driven business.

THE TOTAL PRODUCT CONCEPT

Theodore Levitt, of 'Marketing Myopia' fame, and a leading authority on marketing, wrote about the 'Total Product Concept', and the many invisible attributes that go to make up a product or service in the eyes of the customer. Although a model centred on the product, the Total Product Concept tells us a lot about what goes on in the mind of the customer to affect their buying behaviour.

The following describes the elements of a product that Levitt identified (see also Figure 2.1).

The generic product

This is the rudimentary 'thing' the customer is buying. It's the basic product – like a hi-fi, funds to borrow, bulk steel, vegetables or whatever. For the customer to perceive you as not supplying the generic product you have to be pretty hopeless. 'You call this a steak?' is the sort of instance when this basic threshold is not met. At this low level of customer satisfaction you are usually in the area of a full refund

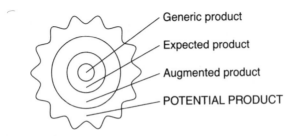

Figure 2.1 The Total Product Concept

or litigation. Whether for a product or service, this tends to be the tangible aspects of the 'total product'. For instance, a room and a bed in the case of hotel service, and the actual food in a restaurant. Its significance for marketers is:

- It's a threshold only that you simply have to meet, and will not produce satisfaction or loyalty. You are safest if the customer's mind is not even drawn to the generic product.
- It is often a small part of the total product the customer is actually buying.
- It's the part that can easily be matched by even a novice competitor. So it's of little value in a competitive world, even though you can't begin to compete without providing it as a minimum.

The expected product

The expected product includes the generic product, as a minimum, but extends to whatever the customer expects. This varies from customer to customer, industry to industry and depending on conditions. For instance, you would not expect Egon Ronay, five-star cuisine at 40,000 feet in the sky – at least not in economy class. Nonetheless, expectations extend well beyond the generic product. We expect delivery, extras, service, a warranty and anything we consider part of the purchase.

Customers base this, not least, on the sort of service they have come to expect, whether from the present supplier or a competitor. Some customers would not expect a lawyer, for example, to dress in torn jeans, even though he or she can probably well fulfil the generic product of legal advice, as evidenced by a certificate on the wall. The same might apply to the location and condition of his or her office. In failing to meet a potential client's expectations – whether reasonable or not – the lawyer will fail to win and keep the client. Even commodity-type products considered generic by nature, such as wheat, steel or petrol, will be differentiated in the mind of the customer, one way or another. For instance, by the clean toilets at a petrol service station and the fresh rolls at the forecourt store. Apart from the wide, real product differences that specialists recognize, the customer's expectations regarding overall service and every aspect of the buyer–seller relationship will form part of the expected product. When the customer expects more than the generic product – which is usually – you can only sell successfully when you meet those expectations.

The augmented product

Marketing goes beyond giving the customer what he or she expects. It has to produce a profitable sale and a satisfied customer. Fulfilling customers' expectations is an entrance level only to successful business. Better if you can offer more than he or she expects, and has become accustomed to receiving. That introduces the surprise element, so important in winning and keeping customers. That complimentary extra course at the restaurant, for example (if you don't usually get one), augments the value of the product in your mind. Or the car air-conditioning that, as this month's special, comes as standard.

The trouble with augmented products, from the seller's point of view (customers love them), is that they soon fall into the 'expected' category, which incrementally reduces the value to the customer. So successful marketers have to keep continuously abreast of customers' growing expectations, including those induced by competitors, and thus stay ahead in their product offerings. At the same time, the generic product itself grows (a heater used to be an extra in a car), so the basic level of customer satisfaction is, at best, a movable feast.

What used to be an optional extra in a car is now standard across the range. So, sooner or later, if you don't provide these as 'basic' the customer will reasonably ask 'do you call this a car?' This is the 'do you call this a steak?' restaurant equivalent question. It means you haven't provided the generic product and don't deserve to be in business. 'Augmented' is the perception of the customer, of course. If a lawyer correctly judges that by dressing casually he or she will create better rapport with a certain prospective client, torn jeans (or whatever) will be perceived as part of an augmented 'total product'. In other words, it will be a marketing plus for that particular customer.

Thus, what in the mind of one customer fails to reach expectation, exceeds expectation in another. Your own fancy product enhancement might not make any impact, so you could have saved your time and effort. On the other hand, you may have under-priced in terms of exceeding expectations. That's the sort of customer rationale we call marketing, although it's a little-known phenomenon among corporate marketers. Successful salespeople and other front-line staff know this well and have learnt to accommodate customers accordingly. No surprise that communicating a 'product' hinges on a mind to mind approach to the customer. No surprise that focusing on the product in the marketing mix does little for the customer, and, in the end, marketing success.

The potential product

In the coming months and years, product augmentations that will surprise customers and add to their expectations will continue to proliferate. These constitute the potential product, for which there is no limit and which we cannot begin to imagine right now – or we would be augmenting the product already.

The potential product may stretch the generic product out of all recognition ('this isn't a car, it's a lounge on wheels!', 'this isn't a house, it's a palace'). In the total product diagram on page 67, potential product is represented by a wavy line, as it has no limit. The whole circle, and each concentric element, grows, like the expanding ripple caused by throwing a pebble into a pond. Marketers cannot stay still for long without risking an unsaleable product or service, let alone customer loyalty.

One survey ascertained the factors that make customers return to a Web site:

- very entertaining;
- attention grabbing;
- extremely useful content;
- information tailored to a user's needs;
- thought provoking;
- visually appealing;
- imaginative;
- highly interactive.

This underlines what we already know about the importance of a one to one relationship, individual attention and interactivity. It also illustrates the total product concept. From the descriptions it seems that the product or service – whatever it is – is lost in the many intangibles of the 'total product'. The findings also make clear to marketers the direction they need to go in to augment the product in the minds of customers. Each of these areas offers marketing opportunities. A new, pleasing attribute will tap the unlimited potential of the most seemingly mundane product.

The total product concept is central to mind to mind marketing. It simply describes the customer's perceptions as to what they are buying. Successful marketing depends on getting this right, rather than just on tangible or outwardly measurable features. Unless you know the mind of your customer insofar as his or her expectations are concerned, you will not be able to create satisfaction and loyalty. So, incorporating the total product concept into your marketing requires not just a one to one approach (mass marketing simply does not fit the bill), but also a mind to mind strategy.

MEASURING PERCEIVED VALUE

To measure customer perceived value you have to identify what quality really means to the customer. 'Quality' is the total product – complete with intangibles, exceeded expectations, consistency, a 'good feeling' or whatever. Part of your strategy will then be to find out which of your competitors (or potential competitors – they are not always obvious in a fast-changing marketplace) are performing best on each aspect of perceived quality. You then have something to measure against. For instance, if speed of response is important, you can measure it – for example, three rings of the telephone or 24-hour despatch. If fulfilled responses (query answered, refund executed etc) are important, then these can and must be measured objectively. The same can apply to repeat purchases, extended range of purchases, value of individual purchase, and purchase value over a period.

Customer response measurement was developed by direct marketing and is now a widespread feature of CRM. Value, whether qualitative or quantative, is part of the customer's perception and thus a non-negotiable aspect of mind to mind marketing.

HOW SELLERS SEE THINGS

Marketing is as much about the seller as the customer. In particular, it involves how the seller sees things, their understanding of customers and their attitude towards them. As with customers, a company's *perception* – of themselves, the customer, the product etc – will largely dictate how they communicate.

EVIL CUSTOMERS

Sadly, suppliers don't think about how the customer thinks, even in the fundamental sense we have just seen of what 'product' they are actually buying, let alone their personal needs and desires. Some don't think it possible to probe customers' minds in any such way. Some profess to 'know' their customers well enough anyway.

Behind corporate closed doors the customer is often considered as rude, unreasonable, unpredictable and worse. Fathoming his or her mind is (say many marketers) for psychiatrists, not marketers. Even customer-focused companies don't usually see beyond 'standard' customer behaviour such as historical purchase transactions. So the beliefs, attitudes, personality and individual thinking style of the customer get scant attention. Customers may as well be soulless robots. Some are considered alien, others intrinsically evil. Most are considered unreasonable, over-demanding and ungrateful. In fact, even when professing a customer relationship strategy, few suppliers know their customers.

With such ignorance, marketing solutions range, not surprisingly, from hit-and-miss to counterproductive. The supplier seems to speak a different language to the customer, and vice versa.

BLACK HOLES

Some suppliers try sincerely to see things from the customer's perspective, but don't have the know-how to do it effectively. Hence the precipitous, often desperate 'special promotion' reactions to down-turns and competition. Even in the few cases where customers are intently observed (*à la* in-home, 'lodger' researcher), they are not understood. Hence what may seem, both to customers and front-line staff, to be change for change's sake. Intense activity, however, especially if on an activity in vogue that features the customer, usually appeases top management and major stakeholders. Any kind of activity can cause a temporary diversion, and top managers are more gullible than most. But the source of marketing success – the mind of the customer – remains as unknown and remote as a galactic black hole. Large corporations are particularly vulnerable to this blind spot in customer understanding. And the stronger the internal structure or bureaucracy of the company, the less chance outsiders have – including customers.

Research has shown that even the most loyal customers can switch to a competitor brand on a whim. What depresses marketers (smart enough to realize this), investing so much in the brand, is that they don't know why. In most cases they don't get round to asking – at least to asking the customer. But that is a price to pay for not having a relationship with the customer that promotes such honest feedback.

In all too many cases market researchers ask the wrong questions anyway. They don't understand the customer's *mind*, so there is not much hope for their corporate clients. In particular, they probably don't understand the relevance of that *level*, or *dimension*, of communication – a deeper level than catch-phrases and a single, mass-market message. If they do, they probably don't have the know-how to penetrate and affect the customer's perception. That's not marketing, as marketers know it. So customer perception goes by default, which explains the enormous gap between how customers and suppliers see the same things. Customer satisfaction, if it happens, happens by accident, attrition or luck.

THE FREEWAY OF 'BEST PRACTICE'

Any changes are worth trying if in the end they reflect what the customer really wants. Positive thinkers (in no short supply in sales and marketing) tend to react to market problems according to 'best practice'. That is, what so-called excellent companies do. By and large 'leading companies' apply the same buzz concepts and management solutions. Consequently, with the worldwide availability of information, 'best' practice turns out to be 'me too' practice. Everybody tends to do the same thing. That doesn't create competitive edge, especially as industry information becomes more readily available.

Business schools have majored on analysis and rational management, but also tend to apply their brains to existing best practice. They usually choose well-known companies for their case studies – sometimes sponsors or clients. But marketing best practice, at best, reflects yesterday's market intelligence. It certainly doesn't provide a competitive edge. The Internet, for instance, provides an almost limitless source of information for the intelligent marketer, whatever the size of company and its market share. So the fast lane of the freeway is jammed with 'excellence'. Creativity and originality – of the sort that delights the customers – are at a premium. Few 'best practice' companies have the courage to find their own routes away from the familiar highways of received wisdom. Tomorrow's top companies are leaders rather than followers and rarely reflect 'best practice' of today.

Competitive edge demands creative, profitable ways to satisfy the customer. Marketing is not about unloading goods and services but about making a profit and staying in business. And certainly not about following the leaders, whatever their pedigree. That means no less than continuously outsmarting the competition. It's a *mind* game. Marketers need to *think*, and to think 'outside the box'. You will need to focus on how your customers think and feel rather than analysing your own internal world. And, most importantly, think yourself, in a more creative way.

MIND TO MIND MARKETING

The 1990s were labelled the decade of the brain. That reflects some astonishing advances in the world of neuroscience, and a revival of interest in all things concerning the soul, spirit and consciousness. The problem is sometimes just one of keeping up with the flow of new information. There is no lack of novel lines of thought that could apply to a flagging function such as marketing, or any shortage of ideas for a business. Creativity doesn't pose the biggest danger. Increased knowledge within different disciplines, and the specialization it spawns, does more to enlarge the barriers between the proliferating schools of thought. So, for example, heart surgery doesn't gain from space research and textile processing doesn't benefit from mining technology. Thus we fail to see the big picture when that is what is needed, and we are all impoverished in the process. We don't have the richness of data upon which creative associations and the resulting insights are based.

The mind versus brain dilemma persists, of course. Whichever we are referring to, the subject is too important to ignore. The kind of marketing problem we face cannot afford to wait for the final discovery of the customer's soul, any more than space exploration can wait for the grand unified theory of the cosmos.

Marketing can benefit from an understanding of the human mind, whether from the mass or individual perspective. It helps to know, for instance, that we have universal desires and instincts that translate into economic decisions. For instance, we like or we don't like. We buy or we don't buy. That's the 2.4 children type mind, and it can be refined in the sense of the child's, accountant's or woman's mind. But at the other extreme it also helps to know that Mr Johnson particularly likes big cars, is very 'label conscious' and never buys unless the smell is right. That's the unique, individual mind that offers so much to relationship and database marketing, and is part of the mind to mind dimension of marketing.

BRIDGING THE MIND GAP

Mind to mind, however, suggests a mind at both ends of the communication or relationship. The marketing professional also has to think, perceive and become involved in the relationship. Marketing is communication, and communication is not just saying the right words or painting the right picture. It requires mutual understanding. It has to bridge the mind gap. A long-married couple often acquire uncanny mind-reading skills and possess the very two-way understanding – about fears and desires, preferences and tastes – that direct marketers would kill for. Similarly, true empathy, which is the basis for good communication, does not need to take decades, but can happen within days of two strangers falling in love.

The secret is that the communication goes beyond externally observed behaviour, message or medium, and becomes a mind to mind communication. The top salesman or -woman can instinctively think like the customer. He or she somehow knows how the customer feels. So the words to say and the way to say it become almost obvious. A salesperson can be 'all things to all men', and we all tend to adjust unconsciously to better relate to people, such as children and old people. This illustrates how some form of mind to mind communication happens all the time. The challenge for marketing is to apply these skills to whole markets, rather than just in interpersonal situations.

The sort of 'customer intelligence' I propose does not need long sales and marketing training. Because the communication is two-way, and uses the same 'language', the customer naturally warms to the salesperson and confides in him or her. In the process, the customer openly transmits all the non-verbal signals that betray even unconscious intentions. The communication is bilateral, not unilateral. It involves two minds. And the mental interaction produces a magical synergy. With empathy come trust, loyalty, credibility and affection. 'I think I would have bought it at any price, I don't know why. Wasn't he a nice man?' sums it up. That synergy is the unexplainable buzz that both selling and buying produce, and it can best be described as a mind to mind rather than person to person – let alone seller to market – phenomenon.

The mind to mind concept is most obvious when applied in a one to one personal situation. But it doesn't take much imagination to apply it to relationship or database marketing, which is what this book is essentially about. Interpersonal communication is well covered in mainstream NLP literature. It can similarly be applied to the large, growing field of conventional direct marketing (including via the Internet). But to illustrate any paradigm significance, I will also explore applications that will apply more generally to marketing, rather than in specific selling or promotion.

As well as reflecting a fundamental change in marketing, the mind to mind concept also reflects the current explosion of understanding of the human brain, and the parallel distaste of large, faceless supplier organizations. It adds 'heart' as well as 'mind' both at the supplier and the customer end of the marketing relationship. Compared with Henry Ford's 'any colour provided it is black' of mass production, or even the elusive modal customer that scientific market research seeks to create, mind to mind marketing opens up a whole new world of customer relationships – a whole new way of doing business. It offers a marketing paradigm for the 21st century.

NEUROLINGUISTICS AND MARKETING

Besides advances in neurophysiology and related sciences, there has been a parallel development: neuro-linguistic programming or NLP. This has been called 'the study of subjective experience', and involves personal excellence, and communication both with oneself (self-knowledge) and others. It is concerned with identifying and modelling individual thinking 'strategies' in order to reproduce 'excellent' behaviour, and the achievement that goes with it. It has made a particular contribution towards interpersonal communication, with remarkable success in sales, training and coaching. At the very subjective end of science, and as yet not very amenable to orthodox scientific method, its origins are more in psychology and linguistics than neurophysiology.

NLP offers a disarming level of common sense that is sadly lacking in entrenched scientific and professional disciplines. More to the point, for practical businesspeople, it is a remarkably effective tool for understanding and changing human behaviour. For present purposes, it can contribute to marketing insofar as marketing needs to major on the customer as an individual. It focuses on 'how', and practical results or 'outcomes'. It wisely avoids the 'why' kinds of questions of physical science or traditional psychology.

But this is not to berate its pedigree of theory and research. Among other things, NLP has developed a robust model of human perception that helps us to predict and if necessary change behaviour. And it applies as much to how customers behave as it does to any other human behaviour.

Although increasingly used in psychiatry and therapy, NLP has many applications extending to business, sport, education, training and personal development. I have written in some of these areas and, as a businessman, have tried to open what seemed like a 'soft' subject to the world of pragmatic business people, including many top corporate bosses. I applied some of the concepts of NLP to corporations, rather than individuals, in the book I co-authored with Paul Temporal, a leading international marketing consultant, *Corporate Charisma* (Piatkus). This showed how to create a corporate 'personality' as a fundamental requirement to attracting loyal customers. It is summarized as part of Chapter 3. A more general introduction to NLP can be found in my book *NLP in 21 Days* (Piatkus).

The mental approach, and NLP methodology, well reflects the present trend towards one to one or 'relationship marketing'. The customer is *known* as a unique individual, just as in the days of the corner shop, and marketed accordingly. As we saw, traditional marketing has largely involved mass production directed towards a mass market. The new marketing paradigm I propose replaces this with a 'mind to mind' relationship, in which the customer finally is king, in attitude and belief, rather than ideology and rhetoric. It will benefit anyone who is concerned with attracting and keeping customers.

THE BENEFITS OF MIND TO MIND MARKETING

The benefits to a company of a mind to mind approach will depend on the particular context and circumstances. What results in excellence for one company may not mean the same for another. At the same time, the feasibility of introducing mind to mind marketing may hinge more on the willingness of management and staff to change their culture and attitudes than on the technical task of gaining and using special customer data. In any event, I have not included any slick three-stage techniques that will offer instant change. One of the important messages I want to get across is that in an ever-changing environment, static techniques or standardized 'McDonald-like' practices – whatever their track record in another country or company – will not be valid marketing tools for long-term, one to one customer relationships. Practices from a mass marketing era may thus be obsolete. If not, don't copy them anyway. There is probably a USP (unique selling proposition) – such as a long-established culture – you won't be able to emulate. Rather, you need to ask more pertinent questions both inside and outside the company. 'Questioning insight' will be of greater value than off-the-shelf models if you want to create ongoing customer relationships.

Just like customers, organizations and professional functions have a tendency to settle into ruts. Marketing is no exception. Sometimes no less than a whack on the side of the head is needed to stimulate the sort of change needed. A whole new marketing paradigm has to be identified, which I develop throughout the book. However, you can benefit (as well as your customers) from *any* further understanding about how your customers think. It can even make for better advertising copy in an unashamedly mass-market approach. So you can quickly convert what you learn as you read into practical benefits for you and your company. As you gain a thorough understanding of the simple mind to mind marketing principles, you will learn how to:

- attract new customers;
- understand your customers better;
- create extraordinary, long-term customer loyalty;
- match your own corporate personality with your customers;
- find the customer's buying 'hot button';
- gain a bigger share of your customers' total spending;
- create a distinct market advantage;
- create a 'personality' that cannot be copied;
- conduct your own profitable market research;
- change the perceptions of your customers about you and your products;
- change the attitudes of staff to be genuinely customer-focused;
- get a powerful brand message across;
- surprise and delight your customers;
- appeal to both reason and intuition;
- know when to communicate with pictures, words, symbols, colours, stories;
- make intangible benefits tangible to the customer – at no cost;
- save at least half of your advertising budget;
- be forgiven by the customer when you make mistakes;

- create a 'customer-centric' culture;
- boost employee morale;
- extend your customer base without (necessarily) extending product range;
- provide focus and direction for all your advertising and PR;
- lock into the atoms to bits revolution – convert atoms to bits.

This is an ambitious shopping list of benefits. It is up to you what eventually you take away in your corporate basket. In most cases you will have to use your experience and specialized knowledge of your business in applying the ideas in the book. And you will need to think imaginatively. A creative, thinking company can thus become as unique as each customer, and thus maintain a competitive edge. That way you can't help but be one step ahead.

I can't begin to guess at your particular needs, any more than either of us can know the *content* (as opposed to traits and processes) of the customer's mind. But the bottom line is simple: the rapport that comes when you and your customers are 'on the same wavelength' results in a 'meeting of minds' and the special loyalty that follows. Your ultimate success therefore depends on this 'mind to mind' relationship. You can achieve such a relationship using the technology of NLP you will learn in this book.

MARKET POSITIONING AND SEGMENTATION

We can't address marketing without covering the traditional marketing topics of positioning and segmentation. Not only do these concepts form the core of mainstream marketing but they also have special significance when adopting a mind to mind approach.

POSITIONING

As far as positioning is concerned, however you seek to position yourself or your company, your real position will depend on what your customer thinks – for whatever reason and on whatever basis. It is a function of each customer's mind. Your 'position' is based on the customer's perceptions. Your positioning strategy must be based also on your customer's thinking. In this sense you are (among others) at the mercy of your customer. 'Position' may comprise no less than his or her beliefs, values and feelings, and how the customer uniquely interprets what you do and say.

These perceptions tend towards *personal* attributes, such as 'kind', 'considerate' or 'trendy', even when applied to inanimate products or an impersonal corporation. In other words, they *personalize* a company or brand. This adds a major emotional element to the customer's perception, on top of any logical reasons for buying. It represents both an opportunity and a threat for marketers. Friendship and enmity, pleasure and pain, are fuelled by emotion. For the serious marketer, 'mind positioning' also forms a basis for loyalty and a long-term relationship, and the profitability that goes with it.

Once you know something about the way your customers think – how their perceptions are formed, and what it takes to change them – there are things you can do to influence this perception. This involves no less than the *process* of thinking. This includes how values, beliefs and attitudes are formed and changed, how we 'frame' or interpret words, events and circumstances, and how states of mind, such as motivation, happen. It includes what we term thinking strategies: the unique processing of thoughts to bring about the desired outcomes, or desires, of – in this case – the customers upon whom your success depends. Market positioning in the 21st century demands such a mind to mind approach and the new skills that go with it.

This aspect of marketing has not changed. It is, however, appreciated more of late and is less product- and service-focused than seller-focused (*our* position, as though we, rather than the customer, created it). What has changed is our understanding of how customers think and the process that creates a 'position', or perception, in his or her mind. Hitherto, companies have sought to *position themselves*, rather than *be positioned* by the customer, which is what matters.

SEGMENTATION

When it comes to segmentation, the issues are more profound, and not so familiar to marketers who deal in mass-market segments such as geographic and demographic. In terms of conventional (mass) marketing, it boils down to whether these Meta Programs (listed on page 55), when adopted as market segments rather than individual customer traits, are valid predictors of buying behaviour. Or, at least, more so than, say, demographic or geodemographic data. In other words, do they constitute valid, economic segments? If they do, and if you can segment your customers in this way, you will start to solve the dilemma of which 50 per cent of the advertising budget is wasted, and which half produces the sales. More than this, you will learn not just how to *measure* successful advertising (which direct marketing does quite well), but how to do it better from the start. This means communicating with your customer on the basis of knowledge rather than ignorance.

Already companies are benefiting from more directed (mass) marketing. This doesn't imply a one to one relationship, but simply means defining segments better. The Range Rover Mk II, for example, was probably the first major automotive product to be launched entirely by means of *directed* marketing – that is, direct marketing to potential real customers rather than customary mass advertising. This has only become possible as databases have become more sophisticated.

In terms of one to one and mind to mind marketing, however, segments as we have come to know them have little significance. Customers are simply not segments. The 'segments' of interest are inside, rather than outside, the customer's mind. So mass segmentation of that sort is an anachronism in a customer relationship context.

Psychographic segmentation

Psychographic segmentation may involve matching your strengths and weaknesses as a company with identified customer characteristics. Even in a one to one strategy it means responding to the customer as a total person rather than the buyer of a specific product or service – in effect treating the customer as a 'segment of one'. Matching your customer base may in turn mean that you may have to change what you *do* and what you *are* – your very identity or corporate personality – as well as the message you communicate. In a more conventional mass-market strategy, it may mean positioning yourself to serve a psychographic segment (or a few) rather than choosing a segment to match whatever you happen to do as a supplier.

All sorts of change can result from adopting a 'mind to mind' relationship with your customers. Once you create this understanding and relationship, however, *what* to communicate is no longer a mystery. Once you know what turns a person on, you don't need to be a psychiatrist to get the buying behaviour you want. The clever work has already been done.

Segmentation and CRM

Segmentation is one of the key features of most CRM policy. But this is only part of the story, and represents the vestige of mass marketing, in which customers had to be grouped, whether by hundreds or millions, but were not treated as individuals. The danger with segmentation techniques is keeping them simple enough so as not to be confusing, whilst at the same time relevant to how and what should be communicated. In fact, the need is for more psychographic than demographic information. Psychographic information, in turn, needs to be standard and validated, rather than the proliferating 'folk' classifications we have already met. Too many classifications of segmentation will confuse rather than clarify the picture of the customer. And even the most accurate modal customer will not represent a real person – the new, 21st-century customer.

CUSTOMER SATISFACTION

Marketers, customer service managers and managing directors have been concerned with customer satisfaction for years. Customers have been even more concerned, and for longer. Under a mind to mind marketing paradigm the idea of customer satisfaction has to be carefully redefined. The aim, as we have seen, is customer loyalty, and profitable lifetime share of the customer. Unfortunately, satisfaction does not always equate with these marketing aims. Customers admitting to being satisfied or very satisfied are prone to switch loyalty, apparently without reason. In fact, customers do not act without reason, even if the reason, or motivating cause, is outside their consciousness. But that reason lies in their perception, and requires an understanding of how they think. Satisfaction may well be a useful, interim, yardstick of success, but only if is redefined in these terms. Happy customers don't keep you in business, loyal ones do.

Ask customers to tick off all the things they expect in a product and services and they don't miss many out. On reflection, every aspect of the sale, pre and post purchase, is important. However, we know that in practice customers don't 'reflect' on a purchase in the way they complete a theoretical questionnaire, but act according to their personal thoughts and feelings, and in accordance with their perception of the total product. No surprise, therefore, that statistically they are *dissatisfied* by a fairly short list of factors – not by everything they claimed was important.

DISSATISFIERS

For instance, a 'dissatisfier' may be an out of stock item, no paper towels in the hotel room, a delayed flight, and so on. Reasonable and even catastrophic product failures are soon forgotten if the accompanying service is prompt and courteous. Dissatisfiers, on the other hand, are often the core element of a product or service, such as the accuracy of a bill or normal product performance (ie the generic product we met earlier). These don't 'satisfy', but their absence will certainly dissatisfy.

Customers have long memories when it comes to dissatisfiers, especially when they are not efficiently corrected and the right, apologetic attitude shown. That doesn't mean you always have to perform at 100 per cent. Increasing performance from 99 per cent to 100 per cent (a major challenge to any company) will not bring about a proportionate improvement in customer satisfaction. The rule with the generic product and service is to always reach the minimum threshold, but then to apply your ingenuity and creativity to the 'higher', less tangible aspects of the total product. Specifically, focus on the positive things that will reach, and remain at, the 'top' of the customer's mind. These are the things they talk to their friends about, and use in your favour when standards are not so good.

Positive satisfaction, as distinct from the avoidance of dissatisfaction, is best achieved in the less tangible aspects of the total product, and the relationship aspects of the transaction. These particularly include how the customer perceives having been shown respect and empathy, and generally 'treated' – regardless of the ostensible product or service.

WHOM SHOULD WE SATISFY?

If satisfaction is the aim, a pragmatic question arises: whom – which customers – should we satisfy?

- The presently loyal ones?
- The new ones, from whom we want to get repeat purchases?
- The most affluent ones, with the greatest potential lifetime spending power?

- The most profitable ones, as measured, not just by the product they buy at different margins, but by the channels they use (telephone, online, etc) that have different costs per dollar of sales?
- Frequent low value buyers?
- Infrequent high value buyers, attracting lower average transaction and overhead costs?
- Potential customers, such as first-time online site visitors, whom we want to get on board?

The point here is that it is better to choose the criteria for which customers you want to treat best, which ones you could do without, etc, rather than aim for something as indefinable as 'satisfaction'. It is reasonable to assume that long-term loyalty is a good indicator of satisfaction anyway. Having said that, it has been found that there is a big difference between 'satisfied' and 'highly satisfied' when it comes to loyalty. Highly satisfied customers are several times more likely to remain loyal. This underlines the importance of augmenting the total product as we saw earlier, by going the extra mile, and pleasantly surprising the customer. Once loyal, a customer will be prone to satisfaction. That is, the relationship, as well as individual transaction experiences, influences his or her perception. Conversely, creating a relationship, by interactive communication and portraying the right attitude, will gain loyalty. In other words, the relationship, however it is formed, is crucial to successful marketing and long-term business.

SOLVING CUSTOMERS' PROBLEMS

Customers want solutions. To have a solution you must know the problem. To know the problem you need to understand the customer. Specifically, what goes on in his or her mind. That includes the unconscious mind, as, whether buyer or seller, we are not always aware of problems that, even to outsiders, are staring us in the face.

Sometimes you need to identify the problem behind the problem behind the problem. Do you want a drill bit, or a hole in the wall, a shelf or somewhere to store your books? To gain all this customer intelligence and satisfy their needs you need to know your own strengths and weaknesses. In other words, know your own mind. There is no shortcut to insight and understanding. You cannot market well without using your imagination. You cannot satisfy your customers without knowing their problems, and what will satisfy them.

- Satisfaction is a precondition for loyalty, but not necessarily a predictor.
- About 40 per cent of customer dissatisfaction is caused by the customers themselves. This may explain the frustration of marketers but is no cop-out for not putting the customer first.
- Find out what your customers expect. Then work out ways in which you can exceed their expectations. You may also need to manage expectations, just like politicians do.
- One problem experience can reduce customer loyalty by 30 per cent. Loyalty here is repurchase intention.

If you ask customers what's important to them they will give a logical, socially acceptable answer. In one detailed airline study, price, comfort, keeping to schedule, leg space, food etc that 'happy sheets' identified did not identify the real problem. The real market damage was caused by dirty washrooms. In most industries fewer than one in 20 complain anyway, so you have to find out in other ways rather than wait till you lose customers.

- Did you have a problem during your last transaction (flight, hotel stay, etc)?
- If so, what was the problem?
- Did you contact any member of the staff for help?
- Were you satisfied with the response?
- Will you purchase other goods and services or recommend our company?

People have more than enough problems. Solving customers' problems is one route to satisfying them. But you need to know what's going on in their minds anyway.

3

The NLP mind model

Neuro-Linguistic Programming is a revolutionary approach to human communication and personal development. Some people call it 'the art and science of personal excellence' or 'the study of subjective experience'. It offers state-of-the-art skills in interpersonal communications and practical ways to change how you think and behave. Millions of people have benefited from its simple principles and techniques, building better relationships, establishing a new level of confidence and achieving personal success in every aspect of their lives.

Here I extend its main focus on interpersonal communication and apply some aspects of NLP to mainstream marketing functions and better understanding the customer. In this chapter I introduce some aspects of NLP and outline some of the ways it can help you to build customer relationships and loyalty. I show how its principles and techniques can be applied to a relationship marketing strategy, and how it will, in turn, form an important basis of a mind to mind marketing strategy.

NLP PRESUPPOSITIONS

NLP offers a number of principles or presuppositions. These are not inviolate laws such as apply in the 'hard', physical sciences. Rather than being 'true', NLP presuppositions can be considered as *useful*, but none the less fundamental principles. If you *assume* they are true, you will get a better perspective on things and achieve what you want. Here are a few I have chosen that have immediate relevance to marketing.

Presupposition: *The map is not the territory*

The map here refers to our individual perception of reality as we 'represent' the outside world through our five senses. This map is our *subjective* reality, and not the reality or 'territory' of the outside, material world. We can only make 'sense' of that world through personal 'filters' of past experience, beliefs and values.

This presupposition underlines the importance of *perception* when dealing with customers. As we have already seen, perception is everything. It is the customer's map of the world. Nothing makes sense to your customers other than as they 'see things' through their personal, unique mental filters. So marketers cannot afford to base their marketing strategy on their own (the supplier's) 'map' of reality. They have no greater claim than the customer on understanding the territory of the real world. Communicating with your customer is all about bridging this mental chasm. It's a mind to mind, or map to map, relationship.

Presupposition: *You cannot not communicate*

In a marketing context this presupposition highlights the fact that a company, or any member of its staff, will always communicate *something* to customers, whether intended or not. Even when silent, for instance, we may be communicating something to a partner, friend or colleague ('he's in a mood', 'she's ignoring me', 'he's upset about something', and so on).

Similarly, a company will itself be perceived by customers and potential customers – as well as by staff – in some light or other. This often happens by default. Put another way, you don't need to *do* anything for your customers to form a perception of your company and products. But you *do* have to do something if you want to affect and manage those perceptions.

Presupposition: *The responsibility for a communication is with the communicator*

This is a corollary to the previous presupposition. Marketers, as communicators, have responsibility for getting the right message across, and for its effects. You can't blame the customer, or potential customer for not listening, or not understanding. If you do, not only will your business not gain any advantage, but also you may continue with ineffective, wasteful communications, which will soon become counterproductive. It's your job to communicate understanding and meaning, rather than just a message. Whatever the message, you need to take responsibility for the response, or outcome of what you communicate to customers and potential customers. Their perception – the effect on the customer's minds – will determine their response, and your success or failure. You cannot afford to leave it to chance.

COMMUNICATION GROUND RULES

From these presuppositions we can set a few valuable communication ground rules to apply to relationship marketing:

- We all see things differently, because of our different mental maps.
- We need to understand the customer's map of reality if we are to communicate effectively.
- This determines not just your marketing message, but the whole basis of the business – to satisfy the customer.
- Whatever you communicate has to reach the customer's mind in as close as possible a state as it left yours. This means establishing a mental bridge – a mind to mind relationship with the customer. In this way you can influence the customer's *perception*.
- You need to communicate consciously and positively rather than let a wrong message get across by default.
- Whatever you say or don't say, your customer may read something into it and perceive you and your company accordingly. In any event you can't do nothing, at least if a competitor is projecting a more acceptable message and fulfilling it in the mind of customers.

So the task is to manage customer perception. It's hard. But not as hard in the long run as if you get the wrong message across.

NLP helps us to understand the structure and process of thinking. We then have a better chance of designing and communicating appropriate messages and creating the right perception. These presuppositions can be applied to many marketing situations using a little common sense. Just asking the critical questions they implicitly pose will increase your chances of success. For example:

- What does the customer think about our products and company?
- How can we influence their thoughts and feelings?
- What questions would best elicit what is going on in their mind?
- How can we persuade them to give us the information we need?
- How can we change our existing image as a company or brand?
- How can we identify customer 'hot buttons'?

Good questions get you well on the way to answers. Nothing demands as much questioning insight as the human mind.

SUBJECTIVE EXPERIENCE

NLP has been called the study of 'subjective experience'. It attempts to model, or give a structure to, experience. This is illustrated in what has become known as the NLP model. As Figure 3.1 shows, our understanding of the world is based on sensory inputs. These reach us

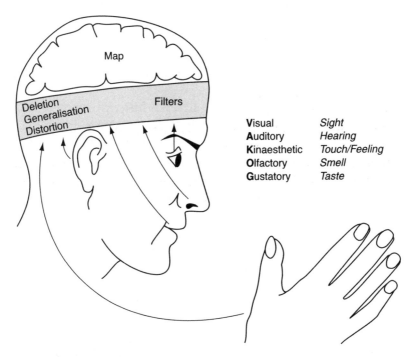

Figure 3.1 The NLP model

through our eyes, ears and other sensory organs. These sensory stimuli are 'interpreted' and acquire meaning as they pass though various mental 'filters'. The way we process or filter this data, via millions of electrochemical signals, determines what we 'think' or understand. These filters are formed from our beliefs, values, attitudes, experience and the many 'life rules' we accumulate throughout life. With them we generalize, distort and delete lots of the reality or territory we see, hear and feel. We access consciously just a tiny fraction of the available information. Nevertheless, amazingly, through a remarkable system of mental guessing and approximation, our world (literally) 'makes sense'. So, by and large, we survive with our fellow beings.

Without this remarkable sensory process, the external world, or 'territory', is nothing but colourless, meaningless energy waves. These mental filters make us who we are. They provide our unique 'subjective experience', and consciousness. So each customer is far more than a number with no less a unique identity than a multinational supplier firm. According to the NLP model, shown as Figure 3.1, every person is different. The process makes it that way. Whether as psychographic segments or individuals, you need special understanding and skills to communicate with your customers.

SEEING WITH YOUR BRAIN

In this sense you don't see with your eyes but with your brain. This happens in any event, of course, when you visualize in your imagination without seeing externally – when you daydream, for instance, or are preoccupied with thoughts other than your present physical situation. It is not hard to accept that external and internal representations involve much the same process, and use the same sensory raw material of sight, sounds and feelings. We can sometimes hardly distinguish one 'sensory world' from the other, for instance when waking from a vivid dream. The same filtered representations form our memories, and the whole *basis* for imagining, thinking and perceiving.

All this has immediate relevance to the marketing message. You cannot assume, for instance, that a standard visual or auditory message will have the effect you want. Different people perceive the same inputs differently. The same words and events have a completely different effect from one person to the next. A product can be loved or hated with no logical basis. People are simply different. NLP helps us to understand these differences and take account of them to communicate better.

The NLP model illustrates the structure of this highly subjective process. The bottom line for marketers is that only what registers finally on the cortex, after negotiating myriad personal filters, will be of any positive significance: subjective experience. In other words, for present marketing purposes, what your customer actually perceives of you, your product or your message.

MENTAL SEGMENTATION

We cannot know the content of customers' minds, nor the myriad personal filters that result in their perception. But we can begin to understand the *process*, and make allowances for the way we communicate. The contents of your customers' minds are infinitely varied – what they see, hear and feel moment by moment, and the way they filter all these sensations. However, each person displays certain, fairly standard, broad thinking characteristics. These are high-level thinking traits or patterns by which people can be classified, such as optimism and pessimism or introversion and extroversion (to quote the simplest of examples for the moment).

These thinking characteristics can be equated to internal or *mental* customer segments, as compared to characteristics such as income, address and hobbies we could use, or demographic and behavioural segments. Unlike impersonal demographic data, these thinking patterns reflect the personality and attitudes of your individual customers. They include their emotions and motivation, so are a more powerful factor in the buying, loyalty and relationship process.

Several of these thinking characteristics are described over the following chapters. Once these are identified, you can predict how different customers will interpret different messages. They act as a kind of high-level language of thought. They offer a route to the customer's perception. By influencing perceptions, you will influence behaviour and be more effective in carrying out your marketing objectives. From a traditional marketing viewpoint, these mental characteristics, or psychographic groupings, also form a basis for market segmentation. More importantly, individual customer thinking styles will be your prime information when establishing a one to one relationship marketing strategy.

CREATING EXPERIENCE

Through NLP you can start to understand 'subjective experience' and the mental maps of your customers. Where necessary, you can *change* this 'experience' or perception through a properly directed marketing message and supporting behaviour. You can thus create experience, and a different future for you and your customers.

Typically the change starts in you rather than the customer. And this doesn't require a new plant or advertising agency. Even a marginal change in the *attitude* of the supplier will evoke a different response in the customer. This applies in any communication. You unconsciously transmit your attitude, along with all the subtle body language and voice tone signals. This determines the other person's perception and response. You affect the other person in far more than the conscious 'message' you convey.

These sorts of seller–buyer interactions are largely unconscious. Moreover, they are so subtle that conscious, outward behaviour, however well trained and polished, may not bring about the desired outcome. The customer may see things differently. Hence the importance of, not just understanding the mind of your customer, but aligning your own mind in a way that better reflects your customers. It's an interactive, mind to mind process. Sometimes we get this wrong. But the marketing sin is not realizing the effect you have on your customers – not communicating at the level of the mind.

BETTER MARKETING WITH NLP

Having introduced NLP and the NLP model, I will now summarize some of the ways that NLP principles and techniques can contribute to better marketing. In particular, some of the principles involved in developing long-term, one to one relationships with customers. Consider, as you read, how you can adapt these ideas. Ask, what familiar marketing concepts will need to change? What will I need to do differently? In this section you will learn about:

- understanding your customers;
- identifying buying and other strategies;
- influencing customer behaviour;
- psychographic segmentation;

- customer database technology;
- brand appeal;
- creating customer perceptions;
- congruent customer communication;
- customer aspirations;
- corporate personality;
- creative marketing;
- goal setting;
- marketing linguistics.

Each of these marketing topics is considered from the perspective of the NLP model and presuppositions described above. They are treated briefly, and give further background to Meta Programs, the main contribution from NLP, which are introduced in the final section of the chapter and most of the remainder of the book.

UNDERSTANDING YOUR CUSTOMERS

You can understand your customers by identifying their ways of thinking, or 'Meta Programs'. Sensory preference (visual, auditory, kinaesthetic), for example, can be identified and used to create rapport with customers. This has been found to be significant in every culture and in people of every age and demographic type. So, unlike 'swinger' or 'plodder' – the sort of categories coined by market researchers and advertising professionals – sensory preference can be used standardly with customers or groups of customers. There are techniques to measure sensory preference as well as right- or left-brain dominance and other common thinking traits. Even where a basis for measurement is less obvious, however, these universal (or 'meta') programmes can be of value to anyone who wants to understand customers better.

IDENTIFYING BUYING AND OTHER STRATEGIES

As well as these Meta Programs, or broad thinking characteristics, NLP has developed ways of identifying the specific mental 'strategies' that underpin a person's behaviour. For instance, you can elicit and 'model' (or replicate, if you wish) detailed strategies such as for speed reading, concentrating on the job in hand, 'thinking on your feet', doing mental arithmetic, playing ten-pin bowling, and scores of other skills or talents. But, of special significance to marketers, customers also have consistent buying and decision-making strategies, such as the Convincer strategy in Chapter 7. You can use these personal strategies as the ultimate marketing hot button.

Most of the methodology involves one-on-one communication, between the NLP modeller and the model, the salesperson and customer, the therapist and client, or whoever. It requires skills in 'reading' total physiology or body language and voice tone, as well as understanding the nuances of language itself. This individual, interpersonal emphasis reflects the therapy origins of NLP. Such skills can be applied, for instance, to group work and in-depth market research interviews, uncovering further dimensions of customer understanding.

Greater standardization, in particular, will mean wider applicability and research validity. The search for the elusive modal buyer, or perfect segment representative, will, if no easier, now be more focused. It will be based on customers' rather than sellers' perceptions. I include examples of how to elicit specific strategies, and the whole subject of modelling, in my book *NLP in 21 Days* (Piatkus).

The application of NLP to wider marketing functions such as branding and positioning was addressed in *Corporate Charisma* (Piatkus). But more creative thought is needed on the part of marketers themselves if they are to utilize the presuppositions we met earlier. One of the purposes of this book is to stimulate such thought.

INFLUENCING CUSTOMER BEHAVIOUR

More than anything, NLP offers a new model of *people*, including customers. It is based on the five senses as the internal counterpart of all external experience. It sees our unique history of perceptions, beliefs, attitudes and values – or *interpretations* of experience – as the basis of how we act and react today. However, NLP also offers practical ways to *change* experience, including the past – that is, how we *perceive* the past, which also affects the present. We can change the habitual filters or mindsets that normally determine what we do and achieve. That's what selling and persuasion have done for millennia, of course. The difference now is that we can purposely design our marketing messages based on the Meta Programs of individual customers.

Any people-oriented discipline such as marketing can gain from this new understanding and the skills that accompany it. The technology is not confined to better communication, but includes wider behavioural change. Change is focused on customer perception, from which behaviour follows. So NLP offers a powerful tool for influencing buying behaviour and the whole customer–supplier relationship. What happens in the mind becomes behaviour.

PSYCHOGRAPHIC SEGMENTATION

There has been a lot of attention in recent years given to psychographic as compared to demographic segmentation. New personality type models regularly appear. Here are examples of psychographic customer classifications that have been used commercially:

- actualizers;
- achievers;
- believers;
- experiencers;
- fulfilleds;
- makers;
- strivers;
- strugglers;
- status seekers;
- swingers;

- conservative;
- rational;
- inner-directed;
- hedonists;
- techno-boomers;
- techno to go-users;
- techno-teamers;
- techno-critical;
- techno-wizards.

Using such descriptions, market researchers create modal customer types. Along with the name label, each has a description of the customer it typifies.

Psychographical market segmentation will no doubt continue apace, reflecting the characteristics of customers' thinking as well as their behaviour or demographic characteristics. But this can extend well beyond the broad, non-standard personality types used to date. Any of the Meta Programs defined in NLP is a potential psychographic descriptor. I have used only a selection in this book to illustrate their power in creating a mind to mind relationship. A simple Internet search will produce scores.

These, of course, whatever the research base, are subjective and not standardized. NLP Meta Programs help to standardize such psychographic distinctions. Moreover, they are particularly powerful predictors of behaviour, exposing important cognitive (thinking) and emotional (feeling) motivators in the customer's mind. I have already referred to sensory preference (such as visual, auditory, kinaesthetic) and left–right brain dominance. Based primarily on neurophysiology rather than more ephemeral social or cultural differences, these categories are more robust as a basis for long-term market segmentation. A person is likely to retain, say, left-brain dominance and visual sensory preference as he or she moves geographically and socio-economically from orthodox segment to segment.

Later in this chapter I summarize the main NLP Meta Programs that can be used to gather customer information for relationship marketing, and to use as psychographic market segments.

CUSTOMER DATABASE TECHNOLOGY

By identifying individual thinking characteristics, relationship marketers can understand their customers better. They will know the questions to ask, the possible different ways of perceiving a product or service, and what are their customers' 'hot buttons'. NLP success has been mainly in face to face consulting and other communication, such as in therapy, training and coaching. However, Meta Programs can be adapted to direct (or remote) database marketing. In this case, the medium or channel (such as mail, telephone or online) rather than content and type of customer data will change.

There is no limit to the potential information about each unique customer. This can range from the effect of colours, words and symbols, to a person's willingness to try something new or what value they place on product reliability. But the basic structures, or mental processes, apply universally – that is, they apply to people. Once we become aware of the 'inner cosmos' of the human mind, relevant database questions and methodology will not be far behind. With good questions, answers will be inevitable. If you don't look beyond outward behaviour, you are unlikely to see anything else.

Database technology has been one consequence of ever-cheaper data processing power. Using the new type of customer information NLP techniques can identify, this is the opportunity to raise database marketing to new heights.

BRAND APPEAL

The communication models and techniques of NLP can be applied to advertising and brand conception and management. Marketing promotions will thus be both more sophisticated in terms of the sensory messages communicated, and more effective. We know well the marketing power of images, music and other sounds, as well as smells and tastes and the strong emotions they evoke. But a lot of such sensory promotion, in the form of conventional, mass (what I have called shotgun) advertising is again hit and miss. The tendency is to bombard the senses and, at best, to treat the customer as a single, standard kind of person.

As well as customer sensory preference, examples are given in Chapter 5 of how advertisers can appeal to the logical and intuitive sides of the mind to reflect how each side of the brain processes inputs differently. Each of the Meta Programs described in Chapters 6 to 9 offers opportunities to communicate with customers more effectively through branding and advertising messages. This takes a lot of the chance factor out of marketing, simply by being more directed and using the 'language' of the customer.

The personality and feelings that a brand evokes can be identified and then used actively as part of the brand message. In Chapter 9 I explain also the importance of corporate and brand personality in the mind to mind relationship, covered in depth in my book *Corporate Charisma* (Piatkus).

Once you are aware of these common personality features, you can apply a consistent brand policy and establish an overall corporate image. Psychographic niche marketing will become possible as we identify 'thinking niches' more accurately and learn how to respond to them in the messages conveyed.

CREATING CUSTOMER PERCEPTIONS

Product and service 'intangibles' have long been recognized as major buying factors. We have already met Theodore Levitt's 'Total Product Concept'. This illustrates how customers have expectations well above the generic product or service, or what is *ostensibly* being bought. Rather, their perceptions involve a whole variety of intangible benefits upon which purchase decisions and product loyalty are based. By identifying some of the structure of perception, and in particular customers' Meta Programs, NLP takes the mystique out of this well-known marketing reality. Marketers need no longer confine themselves to the tangible product, observable service and measurable standards – all vulnerable to competitor emulation. Reality will be based on the *customer's* reality. Getting inside the customer's mind will mean more rapport – a mind to mind relationship. That means a better relationship, mutual loyalty and more business.

CONGRUENT CUSTOMER COMMUNICATION

The sophisticated techniques of person to person communication can be deployed in all the important situations in which the customer interfaces personally with the supplier company. So whether the hotel receptionist, the service mechanic or the salesperson, all face to face communication can benefit from what has become known as the art and science of personal communication. Customer service training, for example, can now extend far beyond observable behaviour and words – the right 'script'. The staff's own beliefs, attitudes and perceptions of the customer will all form part of the change process. Specific NLP belief change processes are now well validated, but little used in a marketing context. Change at this depth, on the part of the supplier representative, will ensure that there is congruence in body language and every part of the direct customer interface.

Even infrequent direct contact is important. In these 'moments of truth' impressions are made and love or hate emotions occur. Based on the NLP presupposition we met earlier, 'you cannot not communicate', either customer contact will be deliberately focused on creating a specific and lasting corporate image, or perceptions will happen by default. The latter will mean weak or inconsistent messages, or inconsistency between the message and behaviour – between what you say and what you do. Customer-specific, 'managed' communication will multiply the response. The secret is congruence between:

- what you say and how you say it (message and modality);
- what you say and what you believe and feel (your attitude);
- what you say and what you do ('walking the talk').

CUSTOMER ASPIRATIONS

For example, a lot of buying is based on *aspirations* rather than present lifestyle and status. Aspirations are in the mind – another cause. Only mind to mind marketing can unlock these motivations and convert them to ongoing sales. Even so-called impulse buying turns out, once it is understood as a process, to be a consistent mental 'strategy'. On each occasion behaviour follows the same order or syntax of sensory responses to sights, sounds, smells or any particular advertising media. That is, mental strategies are, for the most part, consistent and reliable. So what appears impulsive or irrational has its own innate sense or purpose, even though the buyer him- or herself is not consciously aware of that reason or purpose. Using NLP methods, you can now 'elicit' such customer strategies truly to understand and cater for their buying habits.

NLP offers a way to understand the customer as an individual. Rather than just observing outward behaviour, there are techniques for understanding how they think, feel and are motivated. As it happens, except in the field of person to person selling, these communication techniques, well proven in other areas, have hardly touched the important world of marketing. One of the purposes of this book is to extend these models and techniques to the marketing of products and services.

The benefits of one to one as compared with mass communication are obvious in the sense of better rapport, two-way understanding and forming a relationship. NLP has been used with great success, for instance, in face to face selling. The uses of mental models at a higher marketing level are, however, far from obvious.

CORPORATE PERSONALITY

A customer's perception can apply at a corporate as well as product level. He or she buys a product package (the Total Product Concept we have met), and part of that package is the supplier – its people, culture, friendliness, reliability and so on, as *perceived*. Thus you can emulate the personality type of your chosen customer segments to 'be like them' and thus create rapport and a relationship. In their earlier years, companies like IBM and Federal Express gained enormously from their distinctive corporate image, or personality, quite apart from individual product perceptions. Company loyalty can reach cult levels, in the case of both employees and customers. Chapter 9 specifically addresses the corporate, supplier end of the mind to mind customer relationship.

Usually a corporate personality evolves over a long period, sometimes linked with a charismatic leader. Rarely does a company's present market position result from a positive, conscious corporate image strategy – even when an intended image strategy is in place. All sorts of factors influence how customers perceive supplier companies. A big enough personality, such as Fred Smith at Federal Express or Lord Sieff at Marks & Spencer, can have a dramatic effect both on the internal culture of the businesses and also on public perceptions. Leaders come and go, of course. And each new personality will be comfortable in a handed-down culture.

By establishing and managing a unique and truly corporate personality, to which every person in the company adheres, a single and long-term message can be got across to the customers. This, however, involves more than corporate branding. In the long run, a business has to live up to whatever image it communicates. It has to 'walk the talk', or it will be seen to have an inconsistent split personality. So it may need to change its identity, or personality, whilst at the same time effectively communicating it to customers.

Little attention was paid to this aspect of corporate image in the earlier days of mass marketing. But just as the customer has become more 'personified', no longer just an anonymous number or inconvenience, so it is with the corporation. To establish any sort of a human-type relationship – the kind that evokes loyalty and strong, human emotions – the company has to have its own *mind*. And preferably a mind that reflects the minds of its customers. We are now well aware of the significance of top-level, consistent, corporate image branding. We can identify and deliberately manage the characteristics we wish to live out in the company culture. We can then communicate to staff, customers and the world. There is no such thing as a corporate mind, of course – a company is just a legal entity. But there are hundreds or thousands of *employees'* minds, as well as managers' minds, and of course the leader has his or her own thoughts. These have a very different weighting, or influence. A well-televised CEO can soon affect the customers' perception of a company. But collectively, through their behaviour and actual contact with customers, one or a thousand individuals become the corporate 'mind'.

Paradoxically, at this important level of direct customer interface, more junior 'coalface' staff may well play a bigger part in creating the customer's perception. But whatever the relative influence of human beings, through a unifying vision, mission and values, these disparate minds can be synthesized into a consistent corporate culture and personality. And that, however it is treated on the balance sheet, is an invaluable asset to any business.

CREATIVE MARKETING

As well as models and techniques for better communication (which is what marketing is all about), NLP offers different 'reframing' techniques. Reframing allows us to see or 'frame' things from other perspectives, and get new angles on or insights into otherwise familiar situations. Creative thinking has always been crucial to marketing success but this adds a new dimension. Continuous creativity will ensure competitive advantage. Such reframing techniques have been used in answering the key 'What business are we in?' marketing question (addressed in my book *NLP for Managers*, Piatkus), as well as product, service and other customer issues.

Creativity has historically been associated with new product development and technological change. One to one trends offer new areas for lateral customer- rather than product-centred creativity. The question becomes: How do you access your customer's mind? How do you win their attention and get their agreement to divulge personal information? What can you offer them as part of the mutual loyalty exchange? What will you do with all the disparate information you obtain? How can you surprise your customer at every contact? We have hardly begun to apply our creative marketing minds to understanding the customer.

GOAL SETTING

NLP takes a more holistic approach to goal setting than that typically used by businesses. This can help in understanding the customer's 'outcomes', desires and wants – all subject to the perceptual filters I have described. This includes a major unconscious aspect that other communication models completely ignore. Most buying behaviour, for instance, cannot be explained by logic alone, or by any conscious thinking process. Underlying unconscious 'intentions' may be crucial to buying behaviour. These add a new dimension to marketing theory and practice.

Of more left-brain significance, and perhaps more familiar to business people, the 'well-formed outcome' principles developed by NLP can be used by marketers in setting their own marketing and business goals. These are also covered in *NLP for Managers* (Piatkus).

MARKETING LINGUISTICS

NLP has a lot to say about language and its power in communication. Sensory-based 'predicates', for instance (such as 'I see what you mean' and 'I hear what you say'), can be used both to identify and respond to a customer's sensory preference. The communication impact of metaphors, analogies and stories is also well accepted. The best sales-people and advertising copywriters know intuitively how to use language to great effect. But in most cases they do not understand the mental processes that bring about the customer reaction, and especially the NLP model described earlier in the chapter – processes that translate neural 'firings' in the brain into 'like' or 'dislike', 'love' or 'hate', buying behaviour or defection to a competitor store. Given such ignorance, marketers cannot replicate success from one advertising campaign to another, let alone from one customer to the next.

Milton Erickson, the outstanding hypnotherapist, has become famous for his ambiguous, or 'artfully vague', language patterns. These can have a dramatic but unconscious effect on the receiver, and indeed have been found to be the key to top sales performance (although an unconscious, or 'natural', skill) as well as in therapy and counselling-type communi-cation. But, without an understanding of the structure and power of such language patterns, these devices would not get far with a 'left-brain' executive who has to commit to and logically justify advertising expen-diture. That is part of the fundamental marketing change needed.

At the other extreme, precise, 'meta model' language can be used to elicit customer perceptions that otherwise would remain labelled as the vagaries of human unpredictability. Again, these models are long since validated, but have had little impact on the world of marketing, preoc-cupied as it is with more tangible media and short-term focus. As well as the models themselves, these processes involve hands-on skills, which could open whole new dimensions of customer understanding and communication. These are covered in *NLP in 21 Days* (Piatkus).

META PROGRAM SEGMENTATION

In this section I will describe some Meta Programs. You will have met some at least, although the terminology may be new. In every case, these are familiar ways of thinking, not least from the point of view of positioning or segmentation that marketers are familiar with. In some cases advertisers and marketers have already tried to address these characteristics in some classical campaigns. However, few companies have applied them to CRM database strategies, and this is where you will gain benefit in communicating with your customers, and where you can gain a competitive edge.

My chosen list of Meta Programs (chosen, that is, for mainstream marketing purposes) is far from comprehensive, although you will have plenty of ideas to work with. The greatest bottom-line results, however, will come when you explore further how your customers think and creatively respond. I'm not pretending that I know your customers. Nor should you be too certain that you know them yourself. But provided they are human beings, you may find that, once you understand and start to apply mind to mind communication techniques, they are not as enigmatic and unpredictable as they have seemed in the past.

Ways of thinking at this level change very slowly and are remarkably consistent. Many are at the level of beliefs and attitudes that have long been gauged into our mental landscape. It usually takes something special for a person – customers included – to act and think differently. Consequently, *changing* these so-called Meta Programs is the hard way to market. *Understanding* and *responding* to them is not only more feasible, but brings extraordinary results. If the customer truly comes first, so does his or her values, beliefs, tastes and any other perceptions.

CLASSIFICATION APPROACHES

There are two approaches to classifying according to Meta Program. One approach is to use the various classifications and types of mental strategy or Meta Programs as a basis for segmenting customer markets. Each of these offers insight into how your customers think. Insofar as groups of customers have similar thinking styles or personalities, they can be segmented just as for other differences such as age or income. In fact, these thinking characteristics are usually more significant, or predictive of behaviour, than familiar demographic factors. For the moment, just being aware of these stark differences in two outwardly alike customers will concentrate the mind, enable you to respond better, and help you to focus your messages.

The other approach is to use the categories as a market research basis to determine where individual customers lie in their personal thinking preferences, or position along a continuum.

META PROGRAM COMPARISONS

Most thinking characteristics can be described as a continuum, with some people fitting one end, some people the other end, and others in between. One lesson is the remarkable difference from one person to the next in how they view the same outside world or people and behaviour. A bigger lesson for most is that our own view of the world is not the universal one – or at least the one espoused by intelligent people. You will recall the first presupposition we met, 'the map (your view or my view) is not the territory (of reality)'. Some of these major psychographic differences from person to person resulting from Meta Programs or thinking strategies are:

1. The logical (left-brain) thinker as against the intuitive (right-brain) thinker. This whole subject is now well researched and has a big place in learning, self-development, creativity, and so on. Except at the level of advertising (appealing to both heart and mind) it does not form part of traditional marketing segmentation. Various questionnaire-based instruments can identify this basic personality differentiator, which is sometimes labelled hemispherical polarization. Other research has resulted in a four-quadrant classification, but still based on the different ways we process thoughts in different parts of the brain. This is covered in Chapter 5.

2. The towards (pleasure) rather than away from (pain) person, and vice versa. The universal pain/pleasure motivators are used in selling and product promotion. But these are no more than universal human traits, and how different customers behave in respect to pleasure and pain is neither understood nor identified. For example, we are all subject to pleasure and pain motivators, but which do we more readily respond to – the pleasure of buying or the pain of not buying? In any event psychological factors, when they are considered, are more likely used to gain a sale than to establish a lasting customer relationship. *Share of market* rather than *share of customer* is still the emphasis. A similar, very limited application of the above right-brain/left-brain difference also applies. Neither is treated as a psychographic segment requiring its own *marketing* as opposed to promotion or selling strategy. This inherent difference in approach – as powerful as the great optimism/pessimism, half-full/half-empty divide – may be a far bigger buying factor than the age or disposable income of a potential customer.

3. The predominantly visual person who responds to external images and can easily internalize visually. This and the following two sensory types are addressed in Chapter 6.

4. The predominantly auditory person who will listen to a message and perhaps think more in words than pictures, often running internal dialogue. A good listener, on whom visual and gimmicky sales techniques may be wasted: 'Just tell me, in plain English.'

5. The predominantly kinaesthetic person who is influenced both by physical sensation and also perhaps less tangible inner feelings rather than pictures or words. He or she wants to feel and experience the product.

6. The internally as against externally motivated person. The people who do not seem to need outside recognition but, in effect, measure themselves against themselves. They don't care about what the Jones's think. The popular advertising copy that runs 'Imagine what they will think... 'is wasted or even counterproductive on internally motivated people. They set their own standards and measure against them.

7. The risk taker as against the more cautious conservative person. The pioneer-cum-leader as against the more sheep-like follower. The 'try anything new' person as against the 'is it tried and tested?' person.

8. The person who wants to *know* – the specification, how it works, the small print, the features. This and the following four types form the so-called Life Content model, which is covered in more detail in Chapter 8.

9. The person who wants to *do* – 'when do we start?', 'just let me try it', 'what do I have to do?'

10. The person who wants to *have* or *get* – 'what do I actually get for my money? What will I acquire, possess, own?' How can you emphasize tangibles for such people if you are a hotel, travel operator, training or insurance company? What will the customer 'take home?'

11. The person who wants to *be*. 'What will this make me? How will I feel differently? Will this make me a golfer, writer? Will I be content, happy, fulfilled?' The idea of 'being' something (free, young, happy, etc) applies, of course, to all sorts of branding and product messages.

12. The person who wants to *relate*. 'What will so-and-so think? Will they be happy? Will they like me, respect me more? Will this purchase impress them?' This is the externally motivated person described above but one concerned with personal relationships rather than image at work or in the world.

13. The person who thinks in terms of necessities – what they should or must do – rather than possibilities – what they can do. And vice versa. This is covered in Chapter 8.
14. The person who sorts in terms of what things have in common, rather than in terms of differences and exceptions. And vice versa. This is also covered in Chapter 8.

These are just examples of important differences in the way we think, in buying or any other behaviour. Each is a potential market segment, simply because many millions of people fall into the category. This type of segmentation is clearly more relevant to successful marketing than geodemographic data which cannot begin to identify how these perceptions may differ.

There has been a move away from demographic to psychographic market research, or in simple terms, from quantitative to qualitative data. But psychographic research has tended to use simple personality type or lifestyle classifications. These may be based directly on Jung's basic continua such as logical–intuitive, introvert–extrovert. Or they may reflect modern customer types, using caricatures or stereotypes, such as 'swinger', 'techno', 'plodder' etc, which are easy to visualize and remember. However, there is no hint of a standard approach. Even when there is agreement on categories, there remains the problem of standardly measuring what are essentially qualitative characteristics. Differences are as much in the eye of the researcher as in the mind of the customer.

These are very early days in the application of 'mind technology' to marketing. Much of the success of NLP has been in a one to one inter-personal context where major changes in both behaviour and beliefs are routinely achieved. Consequently, selling is an area of marketing that has been affected substantially. My challenge has been to apply the principles of NLP beyond selling and customer service to the central marketing function, and thus introduce state-of-the-art communication technology to whole customer bases. Having already predicted the dethronement of mass marketing, as we know it, this mind to mind paradigm is all in the context of a one to one relationship marketing strategy.

Surprisingly, perhaps, some of the ways people think, once iden-tified, turn out to be consistent and predictable. In fact, customers are often far less volatile than the corporate 'minds' that serve them (for example, they don't suffer from organizational politics and periodical restructuring). So while customers are different, and indeed unique, they stay remarkably true to their personal beliefs and 'mindsets'. Once you know 'how they tick', customers are not so belligerent. We are creatures of habit. Market intelligence of this mental sort is the stuff of customer loyalty. It is a must for any relationship marketing strategy. Get it right, and you will gain extraordinary competitive advantage.

4

Creating relationships

A car wash sole proprietor started tracking by computer the frequency of his customers' purchases, using the car licence tags to identify them. He soon discovered that two-thirds of his customers came in only once or twice a year. The remainder, who washed their cars more than twice a year, accounted, moreover, for two-thirds of the business. So he created new incentives to increase the number of visits. For example, he gave discount coupons to customers who came back within two weeks. Frequent customers were given special attention and persuaded to buy extra services such as waxing or undercarriage washing. By answering a few questions – that would add to the growing computer database – customers could earn further discounts. To add the extra relationship touch, as soon as the licence number was keyed in as a customer drove in, his or her name would appear on the screen so that he or she could be greeted personally. The car wash business soon outperformed the competition and built up a strong word-of-mouth reputation for outstanding, friendly service. Simple, but exhibiting many of the key characteristics of relationship marketing. And illustrating the true, customer-centred nature of business success.

Similar examples crop up in different industries. For example, a small company delivers any sort of goods to its customers, charging a percentage on the value of a delivery. Orders are phoned or faxed weekly. The company provides a storage unit, complete with refrigerator and freezer, typically housed in the garage so that deliveries can be made when customers are not at home. During the testing phase it was found that customers bought on average 3,600 items a year, spending more than $6,000. Recommendations and special offers are then based on actual transactions, so the hit rate of promotions gets increasingly better, along with customer loyalty. A nominal fixed charge is made for the service, but it can easily be envisaged that as relationships develop and individual customer purchase value increases, service premiums could be reduced or abolished. The whole basis of the business is the customer rather than the product (just about any product will be supplied) and a long-term relationship.

A hospital and care home bed management company rewards its customer managers based on increasing share of customer, rather than selling to more hospitals. The aim is for share of customer rather than traditional market share.

THE BIG PLAYERS

Few big-name companies have achieved anything approaching individual customer relationships. The exception is in the case of business to business key account relationships with which salespeople are familiar, but which typically apply to a handful of top customers. Special one to one relationships exist between some large suppliers and large intermediaries. For instance, between a grocery food group such as Unilever or Procter & Gamble and large retailers such as Wal-Mart, Tesco or Carrefour. Even though the products concerned are fairly standard, other terms of business such as delivery, information and other services are individually customized and long-term relationships established.

When it comes to the end customer, no such relationship exists. However sophisticated their databases and transaction data, retailers such as Sainsbury's and Tesco and banks such as Barclays and Lloyds TSB cannot accommodate two-way relationships with their hundreds of thousands of customers – however loyal and long-standing they are. So, whatever special loyalty rewards are on offer, the end consumer remains no more than an account number that can automate a name for personalized mail and throw in the odd bit of 'intelligent' data.

RELATING ONLINE

E-businesses are generally ahead of the relationship game when compared with high street businesses. This partly reflects a medium amenable to instant, two-way communication and an interactive relationship. And it partly reflects the fact that online businesses are usually not so tied to the traditions and infrastructure of their physical world counterpart organizations. This 'green field' advantage may also apply to the e-commerce divisions of existing well-known corporations, especially those allowed some independence and who have bought in appropriate technical expertise.

Examples of e-commerce leaders are Cisco, Ford, GE, Dell and Visa. Such companies use the Web not just to relate to customers, but also to relate to suppliers, and to provide 'downstream' after-sales service. Ford's suppliers, for example, are informed immediately each customer places an order. With such a symbiotic relationship, customers and suppliers alike penetrate deep into each other's companies as synergies are identified and trust builds up. Cisco, a manufacturer of Web equipment among other things, outsources all its manufacturing, and is recognised as an 'advanced intermediary' between manufacturers and customers. RS Components in the UK, a major electronic parts intermediary, and Marshall in the USA, provide tens of thousands of their business customers with a wide range of product information and technical support. Chemdex, with nearly 200 suppliers and offering nearly half a million laboratory products, does a similar job for research chemists. Their Web site has become far more than an online order taker, using procurement software, for instance, for online buying to suit customers' corporate purchasing policies. These sorts of tools and the inherent interactivity of online commerce don't just promise better service, but form the basis of long-term customer relationships.

Home shopping is an online growth area that fosters individual customer relationships, and where existing big names can expand into cyberspace. Dell, for example, sells about $5 million a day via Dell.com. Tesco Direct and Tesco Mother and Baby are examples in the UK. Amazon.com and Amazon.co.uk, initially selling books but now capitalizing on their outstanding market lead with other products, are perhaps the best-known examples. But the meaning of 'shopping' is changing. Amazon customers can share reviews and communicate with authors in a way impossible in even the largest high-street bookstore. The DIY chain B&Q has a Web site of some 500 pages, including product listings and step-by-step guides for DIY enthusiasts, as well as store directory and location maps. This is an example of working synergy between a traditional retailer and its online counterpart. Success on both fronts, it has been shown, is a realistic business goal.

Partnership is one of the features of online success. IBM has an online home shopping experiment with Somerfield, in which 2,500 staff can get same-day delivery on orders placed before noon. The partnership approach is spreading to service operations. Home Depot is a DIY retailer that offers Web site advice to builders and domestic customers. It will act as a clearinghouse, for instance, helping builders to locate subcontractors. Or it will provide help for trades people to estimate jobs, and delivery information to help minimise their inventory.

Whilst some of these successes are linked to database technology and a strong Internet presence, they mostly boil down to old-fashioned good service – something any astute business can emulate – rather than a truly individual relationship, and even less a mind to mind customer relationship. None of these companies exemplifies one to one marketing, even though they are better prepared than most for the transition.

Auctioning is another online development that has added 'perceived value' by taking advantage of online real-time transactions and a large customer base. Suppliers can dispose of surplus stock, for instance. Adauction.com is an auction leader that sells off spare online advertising space.

So-called 'yield management' and automated purchasing are other developments spawned in cyberspace. For example, Coca-Cola is reported to be testing machines that adjust pricing according to the weather. But such an example of technology in marketing is no one to one omen. Market-led pricing reflects no more than a traditional mass-market, supply and demand economic model. However, automation of this sort doesn't preclude individual customer relationships. You can still give your best customers special prices, whatever the weather. Online suppliers simply command a better armoury of goodies with which to foster special relationships and the profits they bring. The auction–information–clearinghouse roles of a few leading Web sites have changed the nature of 'shopping', as well as the hitherto one-way, anonymous relationship of companies with their customers.

Web-savvy companies such as I have cited, unlike many online start-ups, not only make a profit, but they strive to make their suppliers profitable also. That way they get paid on time and benefit from a long-term relationship. They may well integrate upstream design processes to further boost each party's bottom line. Such a partnership makes end-customer satisfaction a more realistic proposition than it ever could have been in a world of physical and psychological barriers.

The Web makes a variety of novel services available to the smallest businesses and individual customers, not just to those with purchasing power or big names. This is where the true potential for widespread customer relationships lies.

A random selection of Web users was surveyed on behalf of the Peppers and Rogers Group about their Internet habits and preferences. No surprise, it found that customers want to be treated as individuals. They not only like personalization on the Web sites they visit, they expect it and get annoyed when they don't get it. It also found that customers understand that personalized Web sites require them to provide personal information and they are willing to provide it as long as their privacy is protected. Practically all the respondents had registered with a Web site and provided personal information. The ones who liked personalized features were the ones on the Web for eight or more hours a week – a group that comprised 63 per cent of the sample. Eighty-five per cent had purchased online during the past six months. Seventy-three per cent wanted a Web site that remembers basic information about them and 50 per cent were willing to share personal information to get a personalized online experience. Nearly two-thirds were annoyed when asked for personal information they had already given. Not surprisingly, users were concerned about the privacy of their personal data. About 60 per cent agreed that a privacy statement was necessary before they would divulge personal data. Interestingly, relatively few online suppliers show a simple privacy statement. Clearly, customers are keen to establish relationships, and are willing to divulge personal information. All this supports the growth of CRM and is a good foundation for eventual mind to mind interactive relationships.

These examples illustrate the sophistication of databases and their increasing value to customer and seller alike. The Web in particular is exploding with a range of customer-centred benefits and functions:

- consistency across all access channels;
- self-service options that reduce costs and allow round-the-clock service;
- a shift in the ratios between transactions and enquiries;
- greater trust in online security;
- increased opportunity to cross-sell and up-sell;
- increased knowledge of the customer, enabling individualized support;

- focused promotions/market offerings;
- personalized service by customer value;
- support based on their customer preference;
- customized service models;
- increased customer comfort and loyalty;
- improved first call resolution.

The customer relationship, whether car wash or e-retailer, is a dynamic process. New ideas continuously enhance the value of supplier information, and the element of surprise for the customer. The relationship 'bottom line' is simple and powerful: identify your best customers and develop new incentives to get them to return repeatedly.

The failure of many e-commerce start-up ventures may have hidden the fact of the bottom-line benefits of online business as compared with conventional outlets, not least the facility to establish lasting customer relationships. Online banks such as Egg, for example, are able to compete well with high-street banks, and even with their telephone banking divisions that bring their own economies. By avoiding human and physical infrastructures, such as branches and call centres, cyber-based businesses can move into profit unsaddled by the vestiges of a very different way of doing business. Meanwhile, several big-name corporations suffer ongoing losses in online enterprises they nonetheless cannot afford to abandon. Others have taken quickly to the cyber world. Interflora, for example, the international flowers/greetings company, charges close to half the normal price in the case of online orders. As with the highly competitive interest rates of 'real' online banks, this illustrates the tangible cost advantages of online business done well. Lego is another company that has quickly developed a massive online presence. This is far more than a short-term sales or market share advantage, or the savings of avoiding the hefty costs of orthodox mass advertising. Lego have clearly added real value to the 'total product' as perceived by their young, evangelistic consumers. The investment is in relationships, and 'lifetime value of customer'. Cyberspace technology simply provides the opportunity and tools for old-fashioned customer-first marketing.

THE SIMPLE RM MESSAGE

Having reached the one to one stage you have hardly begun to understand how your customer thinks as a person. But by *treating* him or her as a person, and showing your interest, you have made an essential start. Just going to the bother of knowing what each customer buys will earn your respect and a competitive advantage. How many suppliers show *any* sort of personal interest in their customers? There is no limit to the way the relationship can develop.

Fast, consistent, quality service is what the customer primarily wants, and this is increasingly a minimum, non-negotiable requirement. A special relationship will enhance customer satisfaction, but a minimum threshold level of service has to be achieved. The relationship will convert short-term, transaction-by-transaction satisfaction into long-term loyalty. This is the one to one relationship we have already met, and the basis of the mind to mind marketing paradigm I propose in the book.

The mass, anonymous buying experience customers have been conditioned to expect will be tolerated less and less. So some suppliers – particularly in service businesses – will be forced out competitively, even though, on the face of it, they are price competitive. The message is simple:

- Build the business on the idea of repeat sales.
- Aim for 'share of customer', over a lifetime.
- Add value continuously to create the special relationship.

Because of ingrained attitudes, what is simple is unlikely to be easy. And nor will it happen overnight. However, more and more business leaders agree that customer relationships are the key to success that in previous years could be achieved by excellent products alone. Moreover, notwithstanding the long-term horizon of Lifetime Customer Value, businesses are already clocking up profits in return for their one to one marketing policies.

THE BUSINESS OF CUSTOMER RELATIONSHIPS

A company has three kinds of businesses, each fulfilling a unique role, and each essential for long-term success:

- The customer relationship business is concerned with finding customers, and building relationships. This can happen at many different points, such as between salespeople and customers, through customer service contact, online communication, queries and complaints resolution, and so on.

- A product innovation business. This conceives attractive new products and services and gets them to market.
- An infrastructure business. This builds and manages facilities for high volume, repetitive tasks such as manufacturing, storage and distribution, and accounting, as well as communication with customers.

These are not separate businesses, of course, but core processes, which are interdependent and cross-functional. Traditionally these core processes have been combined in one company as a single, legal entity. That's because the level of interdependence is such that it would cost more to consolidate the operations if they were divested to three companies. However, the economics of such a position change over time, and not least as bigger external changes happen all around. Change is therefore needed, not just in the way customer relationships are handled, but in the way that product development and infra-structure are geared to the new demands of customers.

The objectives of each kind of business, or division, are never iden-tical. Manufacturing will favour a limited range of products, while a long-term relationship might mean offering customers what they want rather than what you happen to have. Similarly, an infrastructure opti-mized for new product development may not suit CRM. Customer relationships require a long-term, incremental, information-based approach. Product innovation, on the other hand, is basically a project business based on speed of delivery. Infrastructure business is based on catering for the whole company's needs, and depends on routine, predictability, standardization and the economies of scale these produce. Customer relationship business responds to the unique needs of customers, customization, and a variety of support and services for different value customers.

This three-business distinction is especially important when one or other (in this case relationships) is given special focus. They don't easily reconcile, and are likely to be counteractive if you don't appreciate the distinction and what each business is trying to do. For instance, you can't reconcile scope (customer relationship), speed (product inno-vation) and scale (infrastructure) in a single business entity. If you do, you can't do it optimally. Somebody loses, and it tends to be the customer. The relationship business, which concerns us here, will not succeed except within this three-business context.

SUPPLIER PARTNERSHIPS

The growth of e-commerce has been characterized by strategic partnerships and synergistic relationships that no longer adhere to traditional organizational models. Amazon.com, for instance, can exploit its customer relationship scope by adding a wide range of products to its books and videos. But that doesn't mean it has to stock everything or develop an infrastructure that can do everything. It relies strategically on equal partners.

Yahoo is another key player increasingly focusing on the customer relationship. Many may see Yahoo as a search engine. But that function is in fact provided by another company, Inktomi, which has expertise in parallel computing, enabling it to search millions of Web pages simultaneously. Inktomi, in this partnership, provides the innovative product. Yahoo has also forged relationships with AT&T, which manages a large part of Yahoo's infrastructure – the other key area of business. Yahoo may not yet be typical, but it is indicative of the way business is being transformed. The new emphasis is not just on long-term customer relationships. Strategic, creative supplier partnerships not only share belief in one to one customer relationships, but also add synergy to the process.

INFOMEDIARIES

Yahoo is an 'infomediary'. Its power lies increasingly in the customer information it obtains and manages, and the value this represents to Web content (product) and infrastructure suppliers. It appears that the level of synergy surpasses that achieved by the manufacturing mergers (sometimes later demerged) to which we have become accustomed.

These fundamental business changes extend well beyond the new Internet services. Traditional car dealers, for example, will increasingly give up their customer relationship business. Online infomediaries, with a broad range of independent information across manufacturers, will become the repositories of the information on which their marketing success depends. Customers want to know which car will meet their needs, what it will cost and when it can be delivered, what will it cost to insure, service, etc, and maybe information about a car phone, a financial package and so on. The powerful, new infomediary will control all this and more – in other words, the customer's personal transportation needs. The power lies essentially in the customer information, and the relationship and loyalty that can be forged.

Manufacturers and dealers will no longer be able to control the important customer interface. By attempting to do so they will be less quality and cost efficient in doing their respective part – making good cars (product business) and running on-the-ground showrooms and service facilities (infrastructure business). 'Do one thing and do it well' might sum up this business philosophy.

This does not mean that all the power goes to the customer relationship specialists. Whoever can consistently produce quality, competitive cars, service, insurance, financing, accessories, etc will attract the business. Independent infomediaries simply point customers their way, if it is consistent with putting their customers first and giving them the best. The rest, who don't do one or more of these three business functions well, need to worry. But you can't blame the Internet for everything. Good business is good business through any channels and whatever the technology. Below-par businesses should have already been worried anyway under the above traditional, three-legged-stool business paradigm.

RELATIONSHIP RESEARCH

The importance of customer relationships is backed by market research. A 1999 survey of e-business executives found that their number one area of concern was finding the right technology to get better measurement (metrics) of customer and marketing ROI. Ten months on, the same survey showed the number one concern was understanding the profiles of their Most Valuable Customers (ranked number seven in 1999). Where simple site data was once considered sufficient, one to one customer information is now seen as a basic marketing requirement. The second top area in 2000 was understanding the value of e-marketing versus traditional marketing (up from number 20). Fifth was understanding which offers are most relevant to each customer segment (up from number 12).

These changes are dramatic over such a short period, indicating increased CRM awareness, especially among Internet businesspeople. But they also track the evolution away from mass, through niche (customer segments) to true one to one, customer relationship marketing, which I will now specifically address under the topic of relationship marketing.

RELATIONSHIP MARKETING

Customer relationship marketing is one of the vital three businesses that every enterprise is engaged in to some degree. As we have seen, it is the aspect of business that has been singularly lacking during the years in which marketing has been a business function. Importantly, it is the aspect of business that will be the critical test of marketing in the coming years.

CRM DEFINED

Relationship marketing is one of those areas of business activity that are widely discussed and attempted in various forms, yet which are least understood. It has been described as follows: to establish, maintain and enhance relationships with customers and other partners, at a profit, so that the objectives of the parties involved are met. This is achieved by a mutual exchange and fulfilment of promises.

It has emerged mainly in the field of industrial products and services, rather than FMCG marketing, but is spreading ever more widely. 'Relationships' tend to be long-term, and individual, or 'one to one'. The main aim is loyalty to a product or company brand. As we saw earlier, loyal customers are of more value than happy ones. The process can be divided into attracting customers, then building and maintaining a mutually beneficial, profitable relationship.

'DRIP IRRIGATION' DATA GATHERING

There is a growing awareness of the importance of CRM but early attempts by many companies have not been too favourable. In one survey about two-thirds of respondents rated their programmes as either 'ineffective' or 'marginally effective'. Most revealing is the fact that some thought they were actually driving customers away by processes the customers thought irritating. This underlines what the better operators have known all along – the importance of getting the information-gathering process down to an incremental, reward-based art rather than a mass database procedure. 'Drip irrigation' is the term used, in which information is obtained a little bit at a time, and in return for perceived benefit of some sort, such as a freebie, greater customization or a special standard of service.

Even more fundamentally, customer satisfaction has to be in the mind of the customer. Just because a supplier thinks he has satisfied the customer does not mean he has succeeded. Creating customer loyalty requires a special understanding of the customer (hence the need for a more mental approach) and know-how of the principles and processes. Success is only measured from the customer's point of view. Even today, a generation after 'Marketing Myopia' and 'the customer is king', not many businesses have got this right.

As we have seen, customer relationship marketing (CRM) can be measured against age-old marketing criteria for success. It has not re-invented marketing, but reminded us how it should be done – with the customer at the centre. Marketing is about creating customers that you can sell to at a profit. CRM is about doing this better, and in particular over a longer-term horizon based on customer loyalty and a mutual relationship. Even mind to mind marketing is still marketing. It uses, however, a very different model or method in bringing about marketing aims.

ACID MARKETING TESTS

There are several acid tests for marketing success, and it will be useful to fit customer relationships into the context of these. A few simple questions suggest what is important, and, in particular, the central role of the customer:

- Do you create a flow of potential customers? Even when majoring on existing customers, repeat sales and long-term loyalty, you can't afford to stop getting new ones. However, your method of achieving this might change out of all recognition. A well-managed customer relationship strategy will typically result in a stream of word-of-mouth referrals – and that's the kind of customer you want to start a relationship with. Your effort and investment should be weighted towards existing customers.
- Are you positioned high in the customer's mind? Branding is as relevant today as ever. It means getting a place (position) in the customer's mind – preferably at the 'top'. However, as we have already seen, the communication vehicle – such as an interactive Web site or infomediary – may be as heavily branded as the products and services it communicates. Who comes to mind when you want a particular kind of book delivered to you quickly? Who

comes to mind when you think of a sci-fi writer? These 'top of the mind' associations will determine who gets your business. What better way to keep that position than by giving consistently top-class service and the odd pleasant surprise, and treating each customer as a special person?

- Do you give as well as take? You will need to give valuable information, over and above the product or service you are ostensibly selling. Amazon, for example, gives book reviews and author and publisher information of the sort you will not get in other online book retailers (e-retailers), let alone in a bookshop. And it will direct you towards the sorts of books it learns, from your clicking behaviour, that you are interested in. That's part of the total product, of course. And it's the total product that customers buy, based on perceived value, however they might describe it, or indeed whatever they are consciously aware of. The point is that now product expectation might include any interactive exchange element – giving and taking.

- Are you different? CRM differentiates you in the customer's mind. Mind to mind marketing can position you no less than uniquely. Do your customers and potential customers identify your unique difference?

- Have you a strong hold on the marketplace? Amazon is building fast on its market-leading position, diversifying from books and videos into a whole range of products. However, it achieved its leading position through its CRM strategy, backed up with consistent delivery service. At the time of writing it is still clocking up losses. However, this probably underlines the importance of the need to establish market dominance, the long-term nature of customer loyalty on which the business depends, and the need to invest at hitherto unheard-of up-front levels to achieve that. The likely eventual profitability that will arise from such market dominance is apparent from Amazon's multi-billion stock valuation, notwithstanding the demise of other e-commerce hopefuls.

- Do you keep customers? To date, and by a long way, CRM does this best – better than product quality. It is all about putting the customer first, and this underlies all the other characteristics of marketing and business success.

In the remainder of this chapter I will say more about the scope of relationship marketing, and some of the familiar marketing functions and topics that play an important part in successful customer relationships.

Each of these familiar marketing topics has its own RM (relationship marketing) significance. Each will, in some way, contribute to the transition to a relationship, mind to mind strategy, and will form a section of the chapter as follows:

- customer loyalty;
- mass customization;
- customer profitability;
- interactivity;
- database technology;
- direct marketing.

CUSTOMER LOYALTY

Customer loyalty has declined at an alarming rate owing to competition and a proliferation of products and services. Customers usually have a bewildering array of choices and are more promiscuous, being indifferent to two or more brands per product category as opposed to being loyal to one.

The impact of direct marketing has upset long-term loyalties. Of all people, grocery retailers such as Asda, Sainsbury's, Tesco and Safeway have persuaded customers to switch their savings from the big-name banks. Insurers such as Standard Life and Prudential Egg have managed to do the same. This is now a feature of diversification accompanied by the revolution in communication technology. Marketers are therefore shifting their focus from customer acquisition to customer retention. Rather than aiming for market share, relationship marketing focuses on 'lifetime share of customer'.

Retailers in particular are rewriting the rulebook. Carrefour in France has moved into the motor market, and Tesco in the UK did a promotion involving the sale of large numbers of Skoda cars. Car dealers themselves such as Daewoo now locate themselves alongside the B&Qs, Tescos and Dixons on out-of-town retail parks. Not surprisingly, old loyalties, insofar as they ever existed, change. Competitively, no prisoners are taken.

Customer loyalty is not a black and white science, however, if a science at all. In some cases customers tend to be loyal even when their loyalty is not really earned, based on any objective criteria. Conversely, other customers exhibit low loyalty when companies apparently achieve total satisfaction. In other words, customers are simply different.

Differences in demographic status and transaction history are easy enough to take into account, of course, but are patently not enough to crack the loyalty issue. Even transaction data doesn't tell the 'mind' story. A run of high value purchases doesn't explain a sudden switch to a competitor, for example. That's where detailed psychographic information about the customer (not just broad personality type) and a mind to mind relationship are needed. A so-called loyal-type customer acts differently in response to different stimuli (communication, service standards, interactivity) compared to a so-called non-loyal-type customer. Loyalty is not genetic. It's just that every customer is different and will act and react differently. The key to loyalty lies in the customer's mind.

Having said that, the key marketing objective is not to understand the customer's loyalty, but to understand the *customer*. Specifically, to understand his or her preferences, attitudes, fears and desires, perception of pleasure and perception of pain. That's a tall order. But paradoxically, fairly long-in-the-tooth NLP methodology about thinking types is readily accessible and has been for years. How to elicit live mind data has been simply ignored by marketing, in its unending love affair with mass markets and faceless customer stereotypes. In fact, it's an even taller order to keep customers content in face of all the competition if you don't know what makes them tick.

MATCHING

According to the important principle of matching, each of us is attracted to someone of similar experience or thinking characteristics – including sensory preference and brain (right–left) dominance. That brings quick rapport and relationships. And this applies as much between seller or supplier and customer or client as between work colleagues or social acquaintances. A sort of mind to mind law applies where there is 'likeness'. This universal human feature is too important to be left out of your marketing strategy. The more areas of 'perceived likeness' you can identify and incorporate in your marketing communications, the better will be your relationship. Ideally, a brand should be matched to a market segment sharing the same characteristics. The soft drink Tango, for example, appeals to the young and zany, so it has a mind to mind affinity. Similarly, Volvo cars appeal (or used to) to more conservative drivers.

The insurance company AIG Landmark avoids standard call centre telescripts and tries to match appropriately selected and trained staff to different customer groups. This is no more than a token attempt at 'relationship matching' but nonetheless reflects a genuine desire to cultivate customer relationships. As well as an attempt at customer matching, it is an example of the sadly declining 'human face' approach to marketing and customer service.

Note that the Meta Programs we met in the last chapter are discrete thinking characteristics. You will usually find that people fall into one category or other, however marginally, just as we tend to be right- or left-brain biased, or show some degree of sensory preference. Situations change things, of course, but only in the sense that a situation might make a peace-loving person angry from time to time. A person's *habitual* behaviour, based on established mental Meta Programs, is more robust. Once you have identified a recurrent Meta Program, the next stage of adjusting your language and message becomes almost routine in comparison.

THE ECONOMICS OF CUSTOMER LOYALTY

This is a simple matter of economics. Although loyalty happens in the mind, it translates into cash and bottom-line benefits, both in the short and long term.

Customer retention

It is several times more expensive to gain a new customer than to keep an existing one. More than two-thirds of companies put 'customer retention' as their main problem. Most have introduced CRM initiatives to address this. Positively, about a half say the results on this score have been good, and about 10 per cent describe them as excellent. In many cases they used special software to assist the CRM process. Customer retention is not the only issue, however. In the long run, basic performance, flexibility, and the ability to rise to the competition will separate the 'excellent' companies. The question must arise as to whether companies have the basic skills to change their culture and organization to the level of customer friendliness demanded.

Earning loyalty

Loyalty cannot be bought with heavy, *ad hoc* promotion. It has to be earned through real experience over a period of time. Another research finding – again no surprise to seasoned customer-centred enterprises – is the detrimental effect of 'broken promises'. Give them half a chance and customers will soon tell you where you are going wrong – enquiry handling – response times – service – information management – poor measurement systems – poor basic marketing, and so on. This doesn't begin to cover the external threats a supplier has to cope with, such as fierce competition and the global reach of the Internet. Moreover, however efficient you become, it's a movable feast, as customers' expectations continuously increase. They might tell you something different each time you ask them – further reason to establish ongoing, interactive communication with your customers.

The pressure is on for companies to reduce costs but still add value for the customer, and in consequence for the shareholders. Fortunately there is no conflict between a low cost base with shareholder growth on the one hand and a lifetime customer loyalty strategy on the other. Here are some more economic reasons for majoring on customer loyalty:

- A loyal customer not only generates 'retention cost' advantages, but also tends to be a more frequent and higher value purchaser. In other words, is more profitable.
- A loyal customer often acts as a powerful advocate for the company or product. This makes for even lower costs, especially when compared with conventional advertising and promotion, and yet greater profitability. Word-of-mouth referral is more effective, whatever the promotion spend.
- Loyal customers are essential for building strong product and corporate brands. The power of branding is no less in a one to one relationship and is the main factor in generating customer trust and loyalty.
- Loyalty is not so vulnerable to competition as price and product features, being based on subjective, 'invisible' criteria, which are hard to measure, let alone emulate. It therefore makes sense to put more effort and creativity into building loyalty.

Brand loyalty is the jewel in the relationship-marketing crown. Companies who recognize this invest in it a great deal of strategic marketing effort. John Pepper of Procter & Gamble is quoted on the first page of a recent annual report as saying that 'Brand loyalty builds market leadership'. Other corporate leaders have alluded to this. And the proliferation of CRM software supports the present crucial status of customer loyalty.

COMMODITIZATION

As quality and features become standardized, consumers differentiate less and less between brands. Hence the 'commoditization' of many products within a category and the growth of own-label products. As far as *product* loyalty is concerned, only the world brands command real loyalty, and even they have to work very hard to keep it. So, to build customer loyalty you need to build product brands, or you will run the risk of your products being perceived as commodities, differentiated only by price, and commanding no loyalty. As always, the crux of marketing success lies in the customer's mind.

LOYALTY STRATEGIES

The big question, then, is how do we go about building customer loyalty? The answer is by building strong relationships with individual customers, based on how they perceive you and your products. This doesn't require rocket science. Many readers will no doubt recognize an immediate link with the corner shop of yesteryear. The owner-shopkeeper sold most of the goods that local families required, knew all of his or her customers by name, their background, temperament and purchasing habits, and gave them a truly personal service.

Zane's cycles in Connecticut has built up a large, loyal customer base. It recognizes all of its customers. By allowing customers to return items without a receipt if there is a database record, the retailer ensures that nearly all transactions are captured. The information helps marketing promotions. Items less than a dollar are given free, and customers remember and talk about such small touches. The principles of loyalty building are simple. Any astute business can adopt a customer-first approach. The biggest change required is usually in attitude and taking a longer-term view.

The companies that have replaced corner shops with mega retail outlets have begun to realize the value of getting to know and befriend the individual customer. Increasingly, they attempt to recreate this lost heritage with customer loyalty strategies.

THE ONE TO ONE RED CARPET

Millions of households are part of frequent shopper card programmes through which they receive checkpoint discounts and other benefits. In exchange, suppliers hold some of the most intimate details of customers' lives, such as grocery and other household purchases, from hygiene products to junk food. Few companies, however, are making any real use of the wealth of personal information at their disposal. 'Data mining' companies are now pushing beefed-up loyalty programmes aimed at the top end of customers. They are targeted with recipes, free merchandise, opinion surveys, alerts about products and special offers, and all manner of goodies designed to reward loyalty. It's one to one red carpet treatment. However, you've got to do this right. Each household has on average 3.2 cards. So, it seems that somebody's frequent shopper is somebody else's also.

Loyalty benefits take many forms. British Airways Gold members can be notified of delays to flights they are booked on. But loyalty rewards are not confined to the best customers. Special service can attract as well as retain customers. Sonera, a Finnish mobile telephone operator, makes the same information available as standard to all its mobile customers via a simple text message.

Similarly, the carrier UPS in some countries allows all of its customers to receive a text mobile message for every scan of their package, some being scanned as many as 10 times between pick-up and delivery. Such a service is already available globally on the Internet, as it is from other carriers. Gold-card-type services will soon become the norm as the customer relationship becomes paramount.

SWITCHERS AND TOP LOYALS

A Nielson survey showed that only 10 per cent of an average grocery chain's customers could be considered 'top loyals' – heavy spenders who are loyal to the chain. Another 20 per cent, called 'top switchers', are also heavy spenders, but tend to spread their purchases over several chains. It seems that frequent shopper cards are more to do with measuring loyalty than creating it. In other words, loyalty comes not just from having information, however valuable, but also in the way it is used to promote further loyalty. Relationship management is a dynamic process requiring creativity and a permanently customer-centred perspective. Given the widespread use of frequency shopper cards, this offers competitive advantage to suppliers who understand:

- the potential of customer loyalty;
- the need for investment, and what customers value as incentives;
- individual customer profitability and lifetime value;
- the need to project a supplier 'mind' and personality.

ONLINE PRODUCT REGISTRATION

Registration of product purchases offers an important opportunity to gain valuable customer information. The customer has already committed to a purchase, and usually a warranty or other incentive is enough to obtain a few personal details. But it is not an easy task and increasingly special software is needed to help the process. Companies like Hewlett-Packard find it hard to get customers to register purchases, with registration sometimes as low as 5 per cent. They hired an online registration firm to provide an automatic link once a customer installs any HP software. Thirty seconds after registration the customer receives a personalized e-mail to the effect: 'Thank you for your printer purchase. Did you know you could add a tray for legal sized paper? Click here to connect to the Web page or to print out a coupon redeemable at a local HP dealer.' As customer interaction increases, HP uses 'drip irrigation' questioning (one or two simple questions at a time rather than lengthy questionnaires) to build a 'learning relationship'. Customer registration rates more than tripled, registration-related costs plummeted by nearly 90 per cent and implementation costs came down 65 per cent. According to the press release HP are now working with the registration vendor to send out automatic reminders for ink cartridges – an obvious way to keep loyal customers and get repeat (in this case high margin) business.

RELATIONSHIP-BUILDING PROMOTIONS

Historically, special promotions have not enjoyed a good reputation. They have sometimes been blamed for reducing value in the minds of customers, being merely tactical and of short-term benefit only. Generally, they have not been used for relationship building but have tended to be product rather than customer based. However, if correctly targeted and used in a more strategic way to get customers to stay with the company and its brands over time, they can be extremely effective. The important thing is to integrate promotions with a long-term relationship-building strategy rather than use them as a short-term revenue-producing tactic. That means interaction, and, probably, rewarding your best customers in some way, as they produce the lion's share of profit.

A relationship-building promotion might be geared to increasing the range and quality of information about your customers, an investment in the mutual loyalty relationship, rather than to boost current profits. Under one network incentives programme, members earn cash by filling out surveys, reading ads, trying out a product or service and buying from affiliated suppliers. E-mails can be tailored based on past take-up of incentives. A homeowners' association will pay you $5 (cash, product, or paid to your favourite charity) if you sign up for 30-day trial membership. Yet another e-business offers 600 Air Miles to customers who spend $50 or more. Registration means information, which can be translated into customer relationships. So trading, or rewarding registration and membership, like product registration, will increasingly be seen as a sound loyalty investment.

SATISFACTION AND LOYALTY

Most companies profess to measure customer satisfaction, and the rest plan to do so. Unfortunately, satisfaction is a lagging indicator. It can change before you have realized it, and well before you have got round to correcting it. Nor is satisfaction a predictor of future loyalty. You can 'satisfy' a customer with a generous bonus offer or coupon but you can lose him or her in an instant if another supplier appears to be more generous. Brand awareness is a far more robust indicator, and heavily correlated to loyalty, but few companies address this factor seriously at the individual customer level.

THE FULL RELATIONSHIP CIRCLE

We seem to have come full circle. Old-fashioned, corner shop marketing is making another entrance, but in ways that are relevant to the modern customer, and on a grand scale. By applying 'corner shop ' principles, but using technology that the corner shop never had, even the largest companies can build up loyalty. So the mutual benefits of relationship marketing are not subject to the limits of one person's memory and ingenuity. Mass customization, in particular, has shown the feasibility of adding a personal touch to a large customer population.

The corner shop has never gone away, of course. Alex, who has a small tailor's shop in Kuala Lumpur, keeps all his customers' measurements and clothing preferences on a small computer. He sends them notes to remind them to visit him on their next trip, and will work overnight if necessary to complete a suit order for a foreign visitor who has to leave the next day for another business destination, carrying out fittings and final delivery at the customer's hotel. Alex's little business is unique in its unforgettable service and remarkable mutual loyalty.

Relationship marketing relies on good products and services. But larger companies are finding other opportunities to tie the customer into a long-lasting relationship, using monetary and non-monetary rewards. Alex's transition into the information era was simple and painless – he added to his 'memory' but didn't need to change his successful strategy. Large, mass production companies, on the other hand, however sophisticated their systems, usually have a lot to relearn. As streetwise customers are increasingly demanding of personal attention, some may not survive the change.

Relationship marketing focuses on the lifetime value of customers. Customer loyalty is the big prize, and of the utmost survival importance. To be able to retain customers, and create loyalty, companies must continuously add *perceived value* to the relationship. True loyalty results, not just in repeat purchases, but also advocacy and brand association. A loyal customer will be an ambassador for your company. He or she is a blue chip investment in your future.

MASS CUSTOMIZATION

Getcustom.com is a new one-stop shop Web site for every conceivable type of customizable product. It includes about 150 manufacturer/partners. It helps customers customize everything from sporting goods and clothing to gourmet foods and other gifts. The software is based on standard modular-type product features that can be combined in various ways and used in personal tailoring. The learning relationship grows stronger over time. Say you want to customize a mountain bike. You will watch a customized model of your bike change onscreen as you 'build' by specifying the options. A customized watch can be created in five steps, giving the customer access to more than 500,000 combinations. You can save all your product configurations in your shopping basket to make shopping easier in the future.

Manufacturers use the information to evolve their products. For instance, a bicycle manufacturer may be spending three times longer designing wheels than handlebars, and learn that handlebars are more important to the customer. Product development is thus prioritized according to customers' needs and preferences in true customer-first fashion. The supplier can also add more options as they get to know what customers want. It has been found that customers who purchase customized goods are seven to eight times more likely to return to a site than to those who don't have the option. It seems there is also a lot of word-of-mouth referral from this sort of enterprise.

Another example of mass customization is a new technology that will remember customer clothing preferences. Radio frequency identification (RFID) tags, or microchips, will soon be able to transmit and store personal laundry information – name and billing information, washing and ironing instructions, etc. The idea is to be able to send a family's load of dirty laundry to an automated plant that will wash each piece and sort the load according to family member preferences, returned folded and hung to the family locker.

The need for customization is well accepted and most firms say they are doing something along these lines, including bringing customers into the new product decision process.

INTELLIGENT TYRES

According to Josh Stailey, a senior consultant at the Peppers and Rogers Group, Pirelli is applying mass customization to the tyre business. The production process, currently in prototype, uses software-automated robots for everything from basic construction to vulcanization and labelling. It produces one tyre every three minutes, with production time down from six days to 77 minutes, and has cut production costs by 25 per cent. This means that the tyres you specify on your new vehicle can be part of the original order rather than handled by the dealer. This benefits tyre retailers also, who can slash inventories, relying on Pirelli's just-in-time ordering system and production facilities. Even the tyres themselves will incorporate microchip-based sensors to diagnose their own condition (pressure, wear, temperature) and 'report' back to the vehicle or dealer. It seems that some products will outsmart marketers in 'intelligence'.

CUSTOMIZED ROSES AND RADIO

A flower shop calculated that 20 per cent of its business came from two-thirds of the customers – close to the old, universal '80–20' ratio. They set out to design a business plan aimed at satisfying their Most Valued Customers (MVCs), using proprietary software. Buying habits are captured at order entry, and this data is enhanced by asking questions on the phone or reviewing responses to direct mail, and monitoring aspects of customers' purchasing behaviour. They then customized their products and services, for example ordering a uniquely coloured rose from a particular farm, or providing special packaging if requested. Traditional advertising is no longer used as new customers are added daily through word-of-mouth referral. Not surprisingly, business has boomed and – more to the point – an enormous loyalty has been built up which, if they continue to innovate and put the customer first, should stand the test of time. Some mass customization is not so 'mass', but the principle remains. Customers rather than suppliers' interests come first, and production and marketing methods have somehow to make this possible.

New software technology allows radio stations broadcasting live on the Web to delete local ads and simultaneously replace them with ads based on each listener's profile. These are based on the increasingly effective 'drip irrigation' principle of getting a little information at a time. This is an unusual example of combining an obviously mass communication medium (radio) with real one to one customization. The technological change to Web-based radio made this possible. I have found no record of marketers having spotted this opportunity before the technology happened to emerge.

ONLINE CUSTOMIZATION

How do you know what potential customers want if you don't know who they are? Customizing Web content to first-time site visitors has presented an obvious CRM problem. Greatcoffee.com has gone a long way to overcoming this problem using online marketing provider Angara. They can now serve up personalized content without asking a single question. For instance, you will see a page based on your anonymous demographic profile (annual income, address, age). It works through a system of online data suppliers, getting access to more than 20 million anonymous profiles of users around the world. The data suppliers buy data from large firms such as Dell, stripping it of any personally identifiable information and selling it on to Greatcoffee.com. Another e-targeting service combines offline consumer data with online interests and behaviour. As visitors log on to an Angara client site (like Greatcoffee.com) they are redirected to their targeting engine, which immediately matches them with their corresponding demographic profiles. Once identified, Angara sends specific content back such as a home page with a promotion based on their location.

A *localized* response goes part way to customization. For instance, Californians might be welcomed with 'Drink our coffee, win free San Francisco Giants tickets'. All this happens in less than half a second. International shoppers will be greeted with 'Welcome international shopper – we ship to Germany'. That answers a top question of international shoppers, 'do you ship to so-and-so country?' and differentiates them from the mass US market. Personalized content can be even more effective on a first visit than over a period as a profile has been built up – the site visitor is pleasantly surprised at the intelligence displayed.

CUSTOMER PROFITABILITY

It pays to have a long-term relationship with your customers. One company calculated that a 5 per cent increase in customer retention added 60 per cent to company profit by the fifth year. Similar results have been reported of up to 85 per cent profit increase. Another study found that a decrease in customer defection rates of 5 per cent can increase profits by 25 per cent. Paradoxically, 60 to 80 per cent of defecting customers described themselves as either 'satisfied' or 'very satisfied'. This result may say more about the validity of questionnaires, whether of the 'how much do you love me?' or 'rant and rave' kind, than the irrationality of customers. It is well known that customers don't do what they say they do, did or will do. That's the whole point of mind to mind marketing.

It has been found that long-term relationships lead to a lower 'relationship cost' for the customer as well as the supplier. The 'relationship cost theory', propounded by Gronroos, is based on the distinction between 'transaction costs' and 'quality costs'. The customer who does not have to switch suppliers avoids transaction costs, and suppliers save quality costs. Buyer and seller benefit alike, so the relationship makes financial as well as marketing sense.

LVC

Research has shown the economic impact of long-term customer relationships on profitability, at corporate as well as customer level. Some companies now routinely calculate the lifetime value of a customer (LVC) (mostly using proprietary software), and focus on share of customer rather than market share. One large company, for example, encourages its salespeople to consider the value of one transaction with one customer, and what that value or worth might be if the customer repeats that transaction once a month, say, for 10 or even 20 years. This puts the relationship, even with the average customer, in a completely new perspective, and suggests a serious need for a strategy to achieve it.

Cadillac calculated the lifetime value of its top customers as $332,000. But that doesn't tell the real loyalty story. Pizza Hut calculates its customers are worth $38,000 in bottom-line lifetime value. Lifetime value is not just the value of purchases, but also the indirect result of referrals that you inevitably get from loyal customers.

Cadillac buyers are just a tiny part of the market, of course, but that is not the whole story. 'Anticipatory consumption' refers to the products customers intend to buy that they believe to be associated with an aspired-to lifestyle. Customers don't just act out different lifestyles, but they want to be associated with certain lifestyles. And if it's not a Cadillac it might be the next model up from their present car, a house in a better neighbourhood, or designer clothing. Few people want to be stuck where they are for life. This tells us what they will buy next, which cannot be deduced from what they bought last week. It's in their minds.

CUSTOMER MEASUREMENT

We have already seen the importance of customer measures such as turnover, frequency, profitability and loyalty. Unfortunately these basic measures are not being generally obtained. Most companies are in the dark, both about which customers they should concentrate on and what are the direct results of their marketing initiatives. Without systems to log this information even the best relationship strategy can be a drain on profits, and no better than untargeted mass advertising. Probably less than half of companies (who practise CRM) have customer measurement processes in place, although at the time of writing many are planning to do so. The most widely used criterion for customer value is sales value – a blunt weapon at best, if cost and marginal value are ignored.

GROWABILITY

As customer relationship systems proliferate, customer valuation is becoming more sophisticated. A bank undertook a statistical analysis of its customers, developing and defining the prototype for an algorithm to model their lifetime values. Part of this included a 'client potential' model that measured the 'growability' of certain customers. The bank also analysed customers' vulnerability to attrition and flagged the most vulnerable in advance of departure in order to take focused, preventive action.

A lot of valuable information emerged. For instance, customers owning small farms and previously classified as unprofitable were allocated to lower cost delivery channels. However, it transpired that many wealthy customers operated small farms as hobbies. This led to linking personal and commercial banking so that all information about a customer was captured. Common sense, of course, but it only becomes apparent if you treat each customer as an individual, rather than segmenting the overall market, on whatever basis.

Another finding was that customers with a (monthly) flat fee service tend to stay loyal about three years longer than those on a per service transaction basis (such as per ATM withdrawal). With this information, the bank successfully moved more than 60 per cent of its customers on to the flat fee tariff. They also actively suggest the right package in the interests of the customer, acting as an independent consultant. In the long run, looking after the interests of customers is very much in the interest of the bank or any other business. Rather than strategically 'unloading' unprofitable customers (the usual CRM policy), they opted to change the way they operate, reduce costs, or stop selling the product. In other words, they followed the principle that even the worst customer is always right.

DEVELOPING BRAND EQUITY

Companies have come to realize that relationships with customers develop 'equity' and contribute profit in their own right. Although not classified as a 'book' asset, customer loyalty adds real value to the business. The equity is the equivalent of the goodwill generated by the corner shopkeeper through his extensive, up to date customer knowledge. The more you can add value to the customer relationship – however difficult the day to day process is to measure – then the greater will be that 'equity' and the profit it yields.

Loyalty can be considered a part of brand equity, long since considered a balance sheet asset – at least by marketers, if not accountants. But the realization that it can be addressed and achieved as a separate entity, and in conjunction with a one to one customer–supplier relationship, is fairly new. By adding value to the overall worth of a brand or company, it can be a powerful leverage in mergers and acquisitions – a true test of its value in hard financial terms.

B2B LOYALTY

B2B (business to business) commerce is growing fast. So-called B2B exchanges are all the rage. Examples are verticalNet, ventro, CommerceOne, and industry-sponsored exchanges like GM/Ford, Daimler/Chrysler and Sears/Carrefour. One to one 'functionality' is not the most notable feature of these, although the steel industry's e-STEEL and MetalSite attempt integration with customer processes.

LoopNet, a multi-billion online commercial real estate marketplace, has launched MarketNow, a new B2B tool. Brokers can now send electronic brochures of their properties to prospects that match their buying and leasing requirements. Prospects register their requirements in another system called LoopLeads, giving permission to receive brochures on properties that match their preferences. Brokers pay a nominal fee to use the services. Brokers submit property listings to the system and immediately know how many matches they have. Instantaneous, permission-based, highly targeted electronic brochures are a big change from the imperfect markets of the past.

As well as following the one to one trend, such industry-wide information systems have revolutionized, or even created – as with the steel industry – the marketplace. Brokers are recording massive savings, as well as higher turnover, when comparing costs with traditional mass marketing campaigns. B2B systems have hardly begun to exploit the possibilities of one to one relationships, and the successes to date only highlight the potential.

WHICH CUSTOMERS DO WE WANT?

Relationship marketing does not imply that every customer is of equal value. Just as products vary in their quality and profit margin, some customers are 'more equal' than others. That raises the questions: 'which customers do we want?' and just as important, 'which customers do we not want?' In every company there is invariably a group of customers who represent a drain on profits, as well as a test of nerves. The main CRM criterion, as we have seen, is loyalty, which translates into customer profitability.

A relationship marketing strategy sensibly does not target every customer. The notion of the high value customer (HVC) is important. Effort is directed towards discovering who are the profitable customers, and who are not. There is now the technology to provide this information with relative ease, and give more precision to the old 20/80 rule, valuable though it may be in giving approximations.

Profitability per customer is a major issue, yet in many companies it is still an unknown factor. The sorts of questions you need to ask are:

- Who are our high value customers?
- Who are potential high value customers?
- What is the relationship between frequency of purchase and profitability?
- What are the opportunities to extend the purchase portfolio of these customers?
- Who are our low value customers?
- How can we get them to become mid- to high-value customers?
- How can we entice all the customers we want to stay with us, and buy more from us?
- Which customers can we best do without?

Looking at your customer base in this way can sometimes provide astonishing insights. UK grocery retailer Tesco, for example, found that the bottom 25 per cent of customers represented only 2 per cent of sales – literally more bother than they were worth. However, the top 5 per cent represented 20 per cent of sales. They also found that the top 100 customers were worth the same as the bottom 4,000. Tesco now measures valuable customers by frequency of purchase and value of spend. Only customer-by-customer information will reveal this important financial dimension. Customer profitability can now be calculated according to sophisticated algorithms, and can increasingly be accommodated by proprietary software and subcontract services. That is just as well, as it is an important part of customer relationship strategy.

INTERACTIVITY

Interactivity is a key factor in successful customer understanding, and is implicit in the mind to mind marketing approach. Promotion is an example, in the form of interactive advertising such as via cable television. But interactivity embraces the entire seller–customer communication process. For example, you can check your Amazon account, read and offer reviews, and check the status of your last order, as well as search for a title or author you have heard about or browse a favourite subject.

Interactivity can also help to give a database extra meaning and value. Just as in a personal relationship, the mutual exchange of information is an important part of any relationship-building programme. It implies mutual privilege, confidence and a common purpose. The more a customer 'invests' by way of divulging information, and the more customized the product or service, the more committed and loyal they will become.

Interaction is a natural phenomenon on which marketers can build. The tendency is for customers to want to ratify, or show reason for, the purchase decision in the first place. Hence, not just self-fulfilling repeat purchases, but a relationship in which customers are ready to give more and more information about how they think.

INTERACTIVE ADVERTISING

Interactive advertising happens in the promotional part of customer communication. It is a major area of interest as it builds on conventional, mass advertising that has been a major, big-spending function of marketing. As two-way communication becomes more technologically feasible and available, interactive advertising extends the scope of relationship marketing. It involves asking people to respond, take some direct action, and experience the relationship with a company or product. This may be to give or get information, have a chat, create awareness, project an image, give feedback about a product or service, or whatever. The important factor is involvement – not for the sake of it, but for some mutual benefit. Implicitly, at least, to 'exchange value' and develop an ongoing relationship.

In RM mode, interactive advertising should, at minimum, gain useful information, about customers and what they perceive about the product. Typically, customers will be rewarded in some way. Any communication, and especially when interactive, is an opportunity to learn about the customer directly – their likes, dislikes, perceptions and aspirations. At the same time, through the interaction you communicate to them (whether intentionally or not) the special characteristics of your product, service or company.

Technology has made customer interactivity a realistic marketing feature. For example, cable TV services can send multiple versions of commercials and receive feedback via an 'applause/boo' remote button. The seller–customer relationship is not just interactive, but instant, and in real time. Customers may soon be spoilt for any other kind of buying experience so competitors will have little choice but to go one to one.

INTERACTIVE INFORMATION

More traditional market research methods have also used interactivity. One such case was the major success British Airways enjoyed with their 'World's Biggest Offer' campaign. Its purpose was to revive flagging sales following the Gulf war and create a valuable customer database. Five million responses in 10 days furnished BA with details of entrants and what they wanted from the travel experience. The campaign was an unqualified success, all achieved through direct response advertising.

Smarterkids.com is an online store specializing in educational books, games, toys and software for children. They build a relationship by getting parents to key in a Kid Profile after they log on to the MySmarterKids page, disclosing their children's grades, learning goals and learning style. The site makes personalized product recommendations as the child progresses through his or her education. Each product has more than 250 attributes that are matched against the detailed profile. Parents can also chat online with a customer representative, or request an immediate telephone callback. They then keep in touch by customized e-mails with promotional pieces and newsletters. The results speak for themselves. Repeat custom is on the increase quarter to quarter. Revenue from repeat custom doubled between 1999 and 2000. And an outside survey found that when asked whether it is likely or highly likely they will make another purchase, 87 per cent answered yes.

Realhome.com offers a free, mini-course that guides the customer through the different steps to owning a home. Members can post questions and get replies from experts. It can mail information reports on a neighbourhood you are considering moving to – schools, transport, environment etc. This is an example of a genuine two-way flow of useful information – an example of perceived value.

How do you know what customers perceive as quality/value? Ask them. That includes their value *weighting* – how they rank features, services and such. Not only do most customers expect a lot, but also each customer ranks his or her 'value' differently. That is what 21st-century market research is all about. The questions you ask and how you ask them – the syntax, channels (e-mail, telephone etc), incentives and rewards, technology, interactivity, etc – are an ongoing learning experience that can be perfected, but only over time. The important thing is to know where your key marketing skills lie, what you have to do best to succeed, and how you weight what is important.

MULTI-CHANNEL INTERACTIVITY

Interaction is one of the keys to building a relationship. The important thing is to exploit all available channels: the Internet, telephone, mail, e-mail, sales force, point of sale, etc. So an important element of CRM software is 'channel integration'. Customers don't like to give the same information twice, and some prefer one channel to another. Given the increasing scope of online channels, most Internet sites are not marketing effectively. In particular, e-retailers have not developed the opportunities for two-way traffic, and the giving of information 'value' as well as the taking of cash. This illustrates that efficient communication channels don't necessarily mean a customer relationship. Nor does technology create customer loyalty. Wasting the interaction opportunities of powerful, flexible media like e-mail and the World Wide Web is an indictment of e-marketers.

Here are the results of one survey in 1999:

- Only 16 per cent of e-commerce sites sent a follow-up marketing offer to customers who had purchased from the site in the past 30 days. Of these, only two were personalized.
- Forty-seven per cent did not ask customers if they would like more information on related products and services.
- Many sites turn over 60 per cent of customers over a six-week period. Many are competing mainly on price and are not building customer loyalty.
- Only 4 per cent of sites used personalization in follow-up marketing.
- Less than half of customers receiving a follow-up offer rated it as 'appealing', based on products they had purchased recently.
- Repeat buyers did not receive special attention. Only 25 per cent of the sites recognized customers as repeat buyers when they responded to a follow-on offer.
- Fewer than 5 per cent of the sites allowed customers to request reminders when it was time to buy again.
- Forty per cent of e-mail questions went unanswered, including sites that promised a reply within two days.
- Forty-three per cent of sites did not offer customers Web-based self-service to check the status of their orders.

DATABASE TECHNOLOGY

Relationship marketing is a continuous process that involves getting to know individual customers and them getting to know you. The more you know about individual customers, and the better the content and quality of your information, the easier it will be to create the relationship. Similarly, although rarely understood by sellers, the more the customer 'knows' *you* – your past record, reliability, honesty, care, interest, idiosyncrasies, uniqueness – the more committed they will be to the relationship in which they have invested in good faith. Meaningful information is the vital factor. Both the volume and accessibility of data means that database marketing is now a major field of activity in its own right.

STRATEGIC DATABASE MARKETING

Strategic database marketing involves:

- identifying specific customers or prospects;
- communicating with them;
- capturing meaningful information;
- using that information to further build the relationship.

Companies claim that with database marketing they can track 50 million customers individually, and at a reasonable cost. Techniques are now so sophisticated that marketers can get to know all their customers on a one to one, 'quasi-corner-shop' basis. However, the growth of direct marketing and the reawakening of customer relationships have left most companies lagging behind in terms of database technology. They don't have the in-company skills, and specialized external software support is expensive and in short supply. The use of direct marketing as part of an overall CRM strategy is far from widespread, and understood by relatively few well-known companies, such as American Express, BT, Barclaycard and British Airways.

INTELLIGENT DATABASES

Database marketing in the 21st century will provide more and more information about the customer. Apart from the usual demographic data, companies can now monitor, in real time, who has purchased their products and those of competitors. They can in turn cross-refer all this to psychographic data to provide detailed pictures of how individuals and families live, and how they perceive you and your products. Much of this data has been around in one form or another for a long time. But the new, powerful database technology allows better data capture, analysis and interpretation, with ever-reducing costs.

An effective data-gathering system requires that you can handle both the type and volume of information required of relationship marketing. The process – stemming lifetime horizons – may not be cost effective in the short term. Information alone is not enough anyway. Database marketing, applied to long-term customer relationships, concentrates on the *meaning* of the information. The *meaning* enables you to serve your customers better and enhance the relationship.

Already companies are segmenting customers based on personality types, as well as demographic characteristics. The next stage is to gather psychographic data on actual customers at an increasingly personal level, along with individual buying or transaction information. 'Intelligent' databases will enable relationship marketers to move another huge step towards predicting consumer behaviour, maintaining powerful 'relationship dialogues' and fostering two-way loyalty. This involves a 'meeting of minds', the basis of successful, mind to mind marketing.

Market research has had to keep pace with the need for more meaningful customer databases. For instance, in-store market research attempts to find what people do rather than what they say they do. By communicating with customers at the place and time of actual purchase there is a better chance of getting the answer to 'why' questions. Whether in the store or the pantry, the closer you can get to the point of decision, the better.

TWO DATABASE TECHNOLOGIES

Two main technologies underlie one to one marketing: 1) rules-based matching creates user profiles based on their preferences and information requests; 2) collaborative filtering, which we met earlier, sorts previously created profiles into 'affinity groups' in the hope of inferring what products a customer might be inclined to buy.

In effect, customers can be made aware of what they want before they became aware of it, based on the experience of many other buyers with similar interests. For instance, if a large group of customers show interest in three main financial services, another customer who has purchased one of them will be offered the other two. This experience further contributes to the collaborative filter pool, and the data becomes increasingly refined. Clearly, such intelligent promotion – even if not perfect – will be many times more effective than shotgun promotions.

A personalized communication adds further to the effectiveness of the promotion. In financial services, rules-based matching will flag high-balance account customers with investment products – where to get a better return on their deposits. Interactive incentives such as a 'financial planning personal calculator' (a decision tree process) will increase two-way information flow by virtue of the perceived customer benefit. For instance, a customer can quickly calculate how much they would have to save each month to buy a certain level of pension annuity, or a retirement lump sum.

Such volunteered information might take considerable time and money to obtain through traditional questionnaire techniques, possibly annoying customers in the process. Rules-based matching can also track Web pages visited, e-mail content, and search words and match them with relevant product information, coupons, offers etc. Junk mail is not so useless when you are interested in the junk. Hikers or mountaineers, for instance, can't get too much information on their special interest, poring over advertisements for technical equipment that others would consider spam. Known sci-fi or horror readers will always be interested in the latest titles from their favourite authors, and new suggestions with good referrals. As user profiles are progressively refined, Web site 'click through' rates will increase, and consequently sales volume and loyalty.

At a simpler level, rules-based matching would go something like: 'if user is male and in the following age group in the following zip codes, show him the following content'. Any data gathering has to start somewhere, and basic demographic data is easily obtained.

READING CUSTOMERS' MINDS

'Recommendation software' is used by online auction sites. Based on an individual's viewing and bidding history the software engine will score and recommend other items targeted to the individual's specific preferences. It all happens in real time. Recommendation software is not confined to auctions, so this is another tool for serious one to one online businesses. This is an example of 'collaborative filtering' proprietary software. An online bookstore will ask site visitors to give ratings to books they have read. Those ratings are then compared with other people's ratings. Whenever a person returns to the site titles will be recommended based on the purchases of people with similar tastes. The more ratings recorded, the more accurate and useful the system.

The software can take it further, and measure the customer interface in other ways. For instance, it will know if you linger a bit longer on a particular book review, indicating a greater interest (unless the telephone rang just as you were about to read it). In other words, it will flag what you do (without you knowing it) rather than what you say. People lie anyway. (Who gives their correct age, occupation and salary when filling out a compulsory registration form? Who knows?) In a crude sense, collaborative filtering systems read the customer's mind.

Reading minds has a sinister connotation for some customers. So as databases become more intelligent, privacy will no doubt remain an issue for a while. However, it all boils down to whether the extra value the customer receives – in customization, information, speed of service, familiarity, etc – is worth their divulging personal information. This also is a matter of culture and habit. Now that plastic money is a way of life, credit card operators know where we dined out last week and how much tip we left, but we probably don't lose any sleep over it. It depends on what the information is used for. If it is used to give a better service, most customers will jump at the trade-off.

Top football team Glasgow Rangers introduced a CRM project that offered value to club members. By combining existing databases and simplifying phone numbers, answered call volumes rose nearly 500 per cent – from 2,500 to 12,000 per week – and first call resolution soared to 60 per cent from 5 per cent. The club can now pin down cross-selling opportunities and a loyalty scheme has paved the way for a future reduction in ticket costs for individual fans. When the end customer benefits it's a good sign you are doing something right.

MULTI-SUPPLIER DATA WAREHOUSING

Buy a loaf of bread from one of the supermarkets using the appropriate software, and you will be sharing important relationship information worth far more than a loaf of bread. The shop gets a snapshot of the transaction, including the time of day, how it was paid for, and whether you bought milk or butter also. Apart from the one to one significance of this instant data, the shopping habits of some 150 million shoppers in more than 11,000 supermarkets are available for whatever marketing use they can be put to. For instance, how many cans of a certain cat food were bought between 2 and 3 o'clock on Thursday – say after a national TV shot. Or, better still, following a 'stealth campaign' in which promotion is carried out without the knowledge of competitors. This allows the sort of measurement previously confined to direct marketing.

Again, multi-supplier data warehousing has its one to one applications. We can now know customer behaviour across brands and stores – important information in any analysis of loyalty. One customer might be offered a coupon to stay loyal, and another who has switched to a competitive brand given a free sample as a loyalty incentive. Three people in the same supermarket checkout will get different, customized offers. The result? In the short term, higher coupon retention rates, increased per item sales value, frequency of purchase and so on. In the longer term, greater loyalty to the brand or company showing the special interest.

One proprietary system links to a database of purchase data from 55,000 households to track buying in any outlets. Combined with specific loyal customer data by retail output, they now have a powerful tool for predicting customer loyalty. These tools can track what products loyal customers may be buying elsewhere because a particular outlet does not stock them. This is an important factor, as out of about a million or so possible grocery items the typical store sells only about 30,000. Knowing what items to stock, in what quantities, flavours, etc, makes it easier for customers to be loyal. One retailer found from this programme that loyal customers were going down the street to buy a particular brand of food, which they did not stock. That's a minor bit of information, but it hides the fact that the store lost the money that would have been spent on other items also at one shopping visit. A 'reward' for good customers is having what they want available.

NEURAL NETWORKS

Online neural networks may take collaborative filtering to new degrees of customer understanding. The customer becomes what he or she views or clicks, right down to the level of individual words. Individual words – such as 'pension' and 'garden' – are turned into neighbouring 'vectors'. Every bit of data received moves some vectors closer and others further away. Browsing 'interest' or 'dividend', for instance, would move you closer to a finance vector. User profiles are thus constantly refined. Over time, aberrations (such as interest or dividend used in another, non-financial context) lose their effect and personal interest weightings are established.

These systems are fast and relatively cheap information providers. They can also make logical connections between vectors that humans would miss. They will always do the odd stupid thing, of course. But as AI (artificial intelligence) advances, customers' preferences will be monitored with uncanny accuracy. As it happens, we can get to know the customer's mind without fancy algorithms – such as by asking them nicely and making it worth their while. But neural network technology promises even further surprises along the one to one marketing route.

DIRECT MARKETING

Direct marketing combines database management with one or more media to achieve a 'transaction' or another type of customer response. Whilst it is intended to be personal, modern consumers have learnt to spot 'personalized' messages, and treat direct marketing promotions as junk mail. This is a function of the crude level of data (mainly demographic) and the under-use of data that is to hand. Simple data can be made valuable when analysed for RM purposes. In particular, it underlines the failure to understand the customer at the level of the mind.

Direct marketing is more expensive than ordinary advertising in terms of customer contact, but can be very effective in profit-per-customer terms. It has the special advantage of immediate measurement of response rates. Nowadays, in addition to conventional advertising (such as through newspapers, television commercials and direct mail catalogues), direct marketing may involve the World Wide Web, e-mail, loyalty and club cards, telesales, and interactive cable television. Increasingly these channels involve a one to one customer relationship. Direct marketing has already been proven to be effective, and has seen high growth as compared with conventional, indirect distribution through wholesalers and retailers.

Direct marketing does not usually mean face to face communication, of course. Telemarketing is probably the nearest it gets to personal selling. On the contrary, it tends to work on a large-scale, physically remote basis, as in the case of mail order or online selling. However, this need not preclude a relationship. Just as in the case of e-mail correspondence, the successor to pen-letters, an 'intimate' and lasting relationship can be formed.

Even without any truly one to one relationship, direct marketing forms a sound basis for relationship marketing. At best middle agents block communication, and more likely prevent any mind to mind relationship between the end supplier and customer. The main aim of direct marketing is to bring customers more directly in touch with the company and its products. A mind to mind customer strategy uses this direct customer access more effectively and over a longer time-scale.

Relationship marketing is the corporate response to a multitude of shifting consumer attitudes, which culminate in programmes designed to capture and keep the individual customer. It need not be a desperate response, and should not be used as a short-term fix to meet profit demands. But it is a compelling response that has become a vital component of marketing strategy. The key to relationship marketing is knowing your customers and their value, and involving them in what your company is doing and how it does it. Customers are as ready as suppliers to form a relationship in which there are mutual benefits. But this will not happen by accident. Nor will it come cheap. At minimum, the strategy demands one to one communication and a new attitude on the part of suppliers towards the customer. More than likely, it will require the sort of technology now being used for online one to one, interactive relationships.

MATCHING BRAND TO CUSTOMERS

Tango appeals to the young and zany. The Nike faithful seek after authenticity. Orange represents the globalized loner and Microsoft the technologically anxious. These personalities ring true in the new century.

Relationship marketing has sinister overtones. We allow ourselves to be watched, listened to and measured. Our every behaviour is clocked into a database that is potentially available to the world and beyond our control. Not many years ago we would have recoiled at the idea. But, along with security cameras that help to keep down crime, we have come to accept such an assault on our freedom and privacy. In fact we like it. It's good to be recognized, even if companies need the help of clever computers to do it. It's convenient not to have to give the same information over and over again. And we certainly welcome any freebies, such as Air Miles or a free dessert, and other benefits that come from being a special customer.

Companies need to communicate by dialogue rather than mono-logue. It is a two-way communication. Like everyday communication between people in a more personal relationship, this can sometimes be painful as well as joyful. It involves honesty and trust. But the growth of any relationship, and the loyalty it creates, depends on mutual understanding and two-way feedback. Relationship marketing is well established in putting the customer first and building individual rela-tionships, and is growing rapidly. It is an almost essential precursor for the mind to mind approach that is described further in the following chapters.

5

Appealing to both brains

A high-tech headset is on the market that allows advertisers, television programmers and Web site designers literally to read consumers' minds. It records brain waves, to see which messages are actually sinking in. Although the technology is simplistic and not too effective in terms of the mind information that a mind to mind marketing strategy could use, it is an important breakthrough and perhaps a sign of what is to come. Up to now we have had to depend on what people say or, far more recently, what they do (such as buy and consume products). Now we can probe into how they think. It's hard to mask your emotions when they are measured from the inside of your cortex. Sometimes these thoughts are unconscious, of course, although they inevitably will affect behaviour.

The device could be useful in a more conventional focus group setting. Subjects might be able to explain, for instance, why they reacted to a certain point in the advertisement as shown by the readout – a form of biofeedback. Technology of this sort, if you can get customers to use it, is a very direct route to general mind data such as what excites or bores the customer. However, the system might save us from a few questionnaires, and as we become more familiar with the technology the occasional EEG may be the lesser of two evils.

The criterion is probably whether customers can envisage real benefits in return for their cooperation. The EEG-based technology was developed by NASA to monitor astronauts' alertness levels. The headset reads the subject's brainwaves five times a second as the person interacts with the advertising or other medium. The readout allows the researcher to identify exactly which parts of the content excite the viewer and which have little or no effect. Marketers are not so interested in what part of the brain lights up, but they do want to know when something happens in the customer's mind in response to their ingenious promotional messages.

THE BATTLE FOR TWO MINDS

Positioning, or how your customer perceives you, has been referred to as the 'battle for the mind'. In seeking to understand the mind of the customer this is, however, too simplistic. It ignores to a great extent the bicameral, or two-sided, aspects of the brain, and how people make their purchase decisions. In reality, the battle is for *two minds.* Companies are now beginning to take this fact into account in developing strategic positions for themselves and their products.

The power of emotion has been under-rated in efforts to capture customers and keep them. We now know that our emotions play a part in every aspect of our lives, including what we think are logical decisions. It happens all the time, although we usually associate emotion with extreme experiences, and strong memories. Rather than being the vestige of ancient survival traits, different emotions comprise complex neural 'firings' in many parts of the brain – the newer as well as older parts. Apart from some important work on disgust and fear, we know very little about the neurology of emotion. To the extent that it happens in the neo-cortex, or upper brain, emotion is more associated with the right than the left side.

So far the dual-brain approach, combining logic and feelings, has cropped up in a limited way in advertising copy. This is mainly when describing product benefits in a more emotionally appealing way. Everybody has a two-sided brain, of course, and to different degrees we respond to both a logical and emotional appeal. Clearly this can be done better with more knowledge about how each side processes thoughts, and know-how as to the kind of messages that will appeal and how to communicate them.

Addressing both sides of the brain has obvious advantages in conventional, mass promotion. Brain dominance, however, or the tendency to use the right or left side of the brain disproportionately, has even more potential as a basis for communication with individual customers, on a one to one basis.

This chapter explores this important feature of the way we think. I explain why it may be necessary to adopt right-brain strategies in addition to, and sometimes to the exclusion of, left-brain strategies. Using this approach you can gain not just 'share of mind' but also 'share of heart', appealing to what we colloquially refer to as 'heart and mind'. This is a simple example of the mind to mind marketing paradigm and a good one to start with.

APPEALING TO HEART AND MIND

Brain dominance is truly a 'macro' thinking characteristic. It acts at a higher level, or beyond (hence 'meta' programme) specific behavioural strategies such as drinking tea or catching a bus. Loosely speaking, it reflects half of the brain. Specifically, left-brain characteristics are associated with the left cortex (ie the outer brain, next to the skull, above your left hand) and right-brain ones with the right cortex (exactly opposite). But certain intuitive characteristics are associated with the lower and mid-brain as well as with the newer right cortex.

You are probably familiar with this major thinking characteristic, which is loosely categorized as the logical versus intuitive, heart versus mind or rational versus instinctive distinction. It doesn't matter which physical sides we refer to, although for the record the left side of the brain is usually associated with logical, rational, sequential, conscious thinking. And the right side is usually associated with instinct, intuition, feelings and creativity. Furthermore, the distinction lies in the different ways in which each side *operates*, rather than the *function* it performs best, such as language, maths or art.

The right–left distinction

For instance, the left brain operates in a logical, sequential way that lends itself to language and maths functions. Unlike the holistic right brain, it is concerned with parts, specifics and detail. But such a mode of operation also applies to some aspects of art and music, which are usually better known as right-brain functions. Thus, paradoxically, mathematical and scientific insights and discoveries may be associated with the creative right brain, while the structures and principles of art and music are at home in the left brain. The distinction is between:

- *Left brain*: those aspects of thinking that can be operated in symbols (such as numbers and words), perhaps with structures, understood consciously, and logically or rationally explainable, and amenable to parts rather than holistic. It solves things one rational, incremental, understandable step at a time. An analogy with this side of the brain is the electronic computer.
- *Right brain*: those aspects that comprise feelings, intuition, emotion, insights and spiritual awareness, and operate at a less conscious mental level, in parallel rather than in ABC- or 123-type sequence, addressing whole issues rather than parts. It tends to jump to conclusions without seemingly essential intermediate steps, the logic of which is only discovered by tracing backwards. It associates with sense, such as vision, feelings, movement and musical sounds, rather than sensibility. It seems to be more body-related than cerebral, more feeling than thinking, more heart than mind. The brain analogy in this case is more of a boiling cauldron of soup or tropical forest than a neat, hardwired computer or telephone exchange.

This distinction applies to functions and behaviour universally. Thus there are both left- and right-brain aspects to sport, problem solving, poetry and prose, interpersonal communication, cosmology and so on. These are completely different ways of thinking, or 'representing' the world. Bicameral (two parts, as in a bicameral 'two house' parliament) thinking is analogous to using two completely different operating software systems – say Unix and Windows – with otherwise standard computer hardware.

A marketing opportunity

This major thinking characteristic presents a marketing opportunity when bias or brain dominance exists. It applies to mass marketing, because it is a universal human factor and lends itself to impressively large population types, or (psychographic) market segments. It applies even more to relationship or one to one marketing. That is, as well as being a macro human attribute, it is also a major aspect of an individual customer's way of thinking, and a basis for his or her motivation and buying behaviour. It is *one* of the mind factors that, together, make each person absolutely unique.

Brain dominance simply means that there is a bias towards left-brain or right-brain processing. For example, most managers and professional people (eastern as well as western) tend to be left-brain dominant. (This is also linked with right-handedness, although there is not an exact correlation.) This should be no surprise, as our education systems, and indeed institutions (including large companies and public service organizations), have the same bias. These 'left brain thinkers', moreover, managers and educationalists included, *perpetuate* the dominance, as the organizations they run mirror their rational, structured approach.

Aristotelian logic – a classic example of left-brain thinking – offers a fine pedigree for rational thinking which has tended to permeate western culture, governments and institutions. It is no less surprising that people such as artists and musicians, or those who for whatever reason have been spared left-brain conditioning, are more likely to display a right-brain dominance and will follow their feelings rather than bow to logic or institutional norms.

Two people

As compared with some of the thinking characteristics I discuss in the following chapters, the right-brain/left-brain distinction is special in at least one respect. It relates to the main physical construction of the brain, which comprises two, close to symmetrical, and more or less identical, hemispheres. If it were not for the busy freeway (the corpus callosum) linking each side, comprising some 200 million fibres (like a bundle of fibre optic cable), we would indeed think and act as two people. Research carried out in the 1960s by joint Nobel prize-winner Roger Sperry and others confirmed this in remarkable ways when the corpus callosum was physically severed in famous 'split-brain' experiments. So this particular thinking classification is not so much a psychological model of human perception as the physiological fact of a dual brain. My book *The Right Brain Manager* (Piatkus) goes further into this aspect of the mind, including the above split-brain experiments. For present purposes, brain dominance or 'hemispherical polarization' is a key indicator of human behaviour.

From customer brain dominance information it is possible to frame your message in a direct (literally), meaningful way. Rather than appeal to logic and feelings, as in conventional one to many promotion, you can appeal to *either* logic *or* intuition and feelings.

ADDRESSING BOTH SIDES OF THE BRAIN

How does this mental distinction apply to the marketing concept, which, you will recall, involves not just reaching customers but selling to enough of them to make a profit? Clearly, if your appeal is to logic and you direct it to a right-brain-dominant customer it will tend to be rejected. One advertisement referred to the 'bootlogical choice'. It was for walking boots using the 'Bootlogic system', so there was no mistaking which side of the brain it was aimed at. Directed to a strongly left-brain customer, that tack could get an extraordinary response. However, a lot of right-brain thinkers might reject the same message, and walkers are not known to be brain-skewed either way.

This starkly illustrates the lament of marketing managers that half their advertising budget is wasted (it doesn't reach, or at least have an effect on, the intended audience) but they don't know which half. By the same token, the brain dominance distinction allows for vital customer-by-customer segmentation, thus reducing wholesale wastage of promotional messages.

A Marks & Spencer advert for personal loans ran 'You might find that life's little pleasures become a lot more affordable'. In this case, imagined right-brain indulgences (little pleasures) could slip through the logic of the left brain (affordability) and address the bigger 'market' that two rather than one brain represents. Even the subtlest messages can get to the unconscious mind without the risk of counterproductive rejection by the conscious, logical left brain. This illustrates the use of right-brain/left-brain characteristics in conventional mass marketing.

An appeal to the right brain alone might run: 'Can you see yourself… just imagine . . . go on, spoil yourself', stirring the emotion. However, left-brain logic is powerful, and would probably make you 'see sense' just before you signed the cheque. Although emotionally motivated, you were not offered a 'justifier' – a logical reason for the purchase. A simple justifier like 'you've earned it' or 'it's great value for money' might keep the left brain satisfied while you draw the cheque.

A strongly intuitive (right-brain dominant) person may not respond to rational arguments. In fact, he or she may actually resent the dominance of reason and having to conform or be 'sensible'. They place importance on their feelings and intuition, and behave accordingly. Price, for instance, means little if a person *feels* strongly enough about what they want to buy.

MISMATCHED MESSAGES

What will a logical, left-brain communication do for customer relationships if mismatched? A mismatched message – either way – may mean, not just a lost sale, but also a lost customer. And if you want to develop long-term relationships, what do customers think of a company that is so unlike themselves that it seems to 'speak another language'? That's the way people 'think' about someone who communicates with them in an unfamiliar, alien way.

On the other hand, if your message is based on spontaneous feelings, what effect will it have on left-brain-dominant people? You say 'Trust your feelings, you don't need to have a reason'. They say to themselves (literally, as a sort of inner dialogue) 'that's simply illogical. There has got to be a reason. What I do has to make sense. That's nonsense'. So the message – however powerful the rhetoric – is rejected. Moreover, what do people think about an organization that talks such nonsense? This, of course, is where communicating at the level of the individual mind can build relationships. Sense and nonsense are in the mind of the thinker.

High odds

Misdirected or non-directed messages in mass promotion result in wasted advertising expenditure and lower sales. In one to one marketing, both the opportunities and liabilities are multiplied. The odds are high. You are dealing with real customers and they can fall out with you like a friend you thought was loyal. Conversely, a special, appreciated deed will be remembered for a long time and will cover a multitude of marketing sins.

We saw earlier that right-brain motivation is little affected by product *features* or maybe even the benefits you describe – unless they stir the emotions. Nor do right-brain spenders stick to lists and plans. One study found that the average shopper spends 21 minutes buying groceries and covers just 23 per cent of the store. People with shopping lists don't necessarily keep to them. List makers are just as liable to make spontaneous purchases as are others. Sixty per cent of super-market purchases are unplanned.

Similarly, other elements in the marketing mix, such as price, may have little effect when the right mental hot button is pressed. What matters is simply the way your message is perceived by the customers by virtue of a right- or left-brain inclination. They will make all the necessary justifications, or 'picture' the benefits themselves. You just have to speak in the 'brain language' that your customer will understand. By not relying on price positioning, you need not walk the competitive, me-too treadmill. Your particular knowledge about a particular customer will give you a unique competitive edge, which will be reinforced as their loyalty increases over time.

THE BRAIN DOMINANCE SPECTRUM

So far we have considered customers with a marked 'hemispherical polarization', or brain dominance, one way or the other. However, we need to communicate to a whole spectrum of customers, some of whom may show little bias either way, and some of whom seem to be more or less 'balanced' in the way they use their dual brain. However, in terms of one to one marketing, even a slight dominance either way would suggest a more directed message. This is simple common sense. For example, a directed message is better based on a scale of earnings – a different message for a different level of earnings – rather than an amorphous 'neither rich nor poor' customer segment. In the same way a 'mind-customized' message, being better directed, will get a better response. Indeed, brain preference information may be far more valuable than other continuums such as age or earnings. And brain preference across a spectrum is more valuable than either/or, right-brain/left-brain data.

As we have already seen, the one to one aim is for 'share of customer' rather than market share. Thus, even a marginal improvement in the effectiveness of your communication will have a *compounding* effect over time. This will bring big dividends, potentially over a lifetime. This incremental edge in customer intelligence becomes even greater if (unlike in the demographic distinctions) you can identify psychographic characteristics, or segments, your competitors are unaware of, or have not used for marketing purposes. Anyone can get hold of postal code and earnings data. A portfolio of brain preference, say on a scale of 1 to 10, will provide a useful overall view of a single customer. Not as unique as a fingerprint, but personal and relevant.

Figure 5.1 The brain dominance spectrum

Better still, you can make better *use* of your customer information by communicating in new, creative ways. That is, you can do more with a little bit of knowledge. Either way, your aim is to understand your customers better *over time* and to communicate in a language they can easily understand.

In the case of so-called balanced or 'bicameral' thinkers a different strategy is called for: address *both* sides of the brain. Appeal to heart *as well as* mind. This of course is what advertisers have done since we became aware of the importance of the right–left brain distinction. But they were addressing the populous centre of the right-brain/left-brain continuum of *all* potential customers, so they missed out on people with a dominance either way.

The same two-sided approach will work with one to one communication where you have psychographically identified the customer as bicameral (two-sided in the sense of *using* both sides) or, in other words, neutral (not having a bias either way). One slogan cleverly ran 'Seriously Jaguar. Instinctively TVR'. The human brain is designed bicamerally to be serious and logical and *at the same time* instinctive and imaginative. There is no contradiction in this – except as seen by a 'left-brain' thinker who cannot cope with anomaly – it's just the way we are made.

SHOTGUN OR RIFLE MARKETING

This shotgun rather than rifle strategy applies itself to the majority of customers falling in the Gaussian probability curve of brain polarization. It's a numbers game, and only in the case of the small minority who display a marked dominance one way or the other might a combined (heart and mind) message be ineffective. This is the price to pay for mass promotion. You can turn people off as easily as you can motivate them. Once you get to know your customer's thinking profile, you will be able to purpose-direct your message. It is then no longer a 'numbers game', however big the number of real customers. Every customer is special, and worth getting to know.

Using the shotgun approach, advertisers often get away with simply listing the logical reasons for buying as well as appealing to the emotions. They appeal to both heart and mind, but give the left brain plenty of reasons (justifiers) why it is 'sensible' and 'rational' to buy. For instance, a simple dual message might be: 'There are three good reasons why you should invest in so and so (which you list, of course), but doesn't it feel right anyway?'

Perception of choice

The key is to create a perception of choice (a basic human hot button), in the hope that one choice will appeal. 'Go on, treat yourself, you deserve it' might be just as powerful. People usually agree that they 'deserve' a treat. Indeed, given the right, logical *suggestion*, customers will think of far more reasons why they deserve a treat than the seller ever can. It is more important to create the words and mind pictures that will trigger the customer's mind, than to spell out the message.

We are all, in fact, two-sided thinkers, to some degree. So, for the great majority of customers, provided the dual message is well communicated, *both* perspectives have a chance of 'registering' and the chances of success are increased. An appeal to both sides of the brain does not just apply to customers without a strong dominance either way – we all use both sides of our brain. So this is the obvious one to one communication strategy when you don't know. The point here is that there are benefits to be got by understanding the way people – all people – think, even without adapting a relationship marketing strategy. In other words, getting to know customers as sensory, dual-brain thinkers will help under any marketing paradigm.

Having said this, the biggest winnings are from long-term customer loyalty, and that requires a one to one strategy. This is the trend of marketing in any event. So the competition may well dictate a more sophisticated approach than simply hoping that one message sticks. That may be bad for the under-performing supplier, but good for the customer.

USING YOUR BRAINS

How you use this Meta Program in your marketing message will depend on whether you have or want to have a one to one strategy, as well as the nature of your business, resources and other factors that we will consider as we go on. But either way, by designing your message to appeal, not just to the whole brain, but also to the *individual* brain, you will relate better to your customers and sell more. You are beginning to think of marketing as a mind to mind process.

Think about how your product and service benefits can best be communicated using these two very different thinking approaches. Are there solid, logical reasons why people should buy your products rather than competitors'? Find people in the company with a definite brain bias (you can use the questionnaire in this chapter or the mini one in Appendix C). Find out which of the two approaches appeals to them, and what turns them off. It is one thing to understand you are addressing two different brains, but it is quite another thing to create the messages that appeal to them.

Advertising and promotion activities exist to create 'positions' for companies' products and services in the minds of consumers. Unless they can establish a firm position in people's minds they have no chance of being successful, such is the state of competition today, with a proliferation of products and services in every category. In conventional promotion you need to exploit brain processing to the full, and I describe some specific left-brain and right-brain strategies in the next sections. In one to one communication you will be able to refine your message and avoid the customary waste that advertising involves.

LEFT-BRAIN POSITIONING STRATEGIES

The left-brain approach is used a lot in advertising. Market research often determines this approach because surveys are understandably addressed to the conscious mind (associated with the left brain), and constructed using logical questions. People tend to give socially acceptable responses to semi-formal questionnaires, and even the feelings they express will have been 'filtered' to sound 'sensible'.

JUSTIFIERS

Typically, statistics, product features and benefits are marshalled to 'prove' a product's superiority. Facts and figures (or what purport to be facts and figures) have an important place, and form part of a left-brain positioning strategy. People seek justification for whatever they do, especially spending money. They are happier if what they do is based on hard facts. In a left-brain positioning strategy you *provide* the consumer with buying rationale, *suggesting* preferably a choice of 'justifiers'.

A justifier may be more important than your main product offering. Most people want all sorts of things, including your products, but that doesn't mean they buy them. The marketing job is to make it easy for them to justify spending the money and translating a want into a purchase. Good marketing helps them to answer the question 'Why should I buy it?' or, better still, 'Why should I buy it now?'. Rationalization can come in many forms – price reductions, convenience, special offers and promotions, highlighted features and so on. The aim is to get your message to the 'top of your customer's mind'.

'Justifiers' may or may not be 'true', but they must be *perceived* to be true. A washing powder, for example, may not wash whiter than white but if the consumer believes it will, then the argument is won. Perception, as we have seen already, is the key to product and supplier positioning. And perception happens in the mind.

Justifiers can work in two ways: they provide the necessary justification to buy; and they provide justification after a purchase. The latter is often required in the case of impulse buying after the impulsive emotion wears off. Impulse buyers will justify their action in different ways:

- 'Honestly, I really needed this new dress.'
- 'Well, it was on special offer, so it was worth it.'
- 'A bargain like this won't come round again.'

These may have to be extended and revised after the event – when, perhaps, the product didn't do exactly what you thought it would but you are not ready to admit (even to yourself) to having made a poor decision. Amazingly, our naturally creative brain will make any number of ingenious excuses (logical reasons) for behaviour. Paradoxically, it may call upon right-brain inventiveness to support left-brain rationality, just as families, whatever the normal enmity, close ranks when in difficulty.

Advertising and promotion strategies have on the whole taken the traditional approach of appealing to the left brain. Various strategies use this positioning approach, which I will describe now:

- features and attributes;
- benefits received;
- usage, occasion or time of use;
- price and value.

FEATURES AND ATTRIBUTES

The car manufacturer Volvo has for many years adopted a position mainly based on the attribute of safety. So successful has this been that

Volvo 'owns' the safety dimension in consumer minds. It will appeal to balanced, rational, perhaps conservative buyers – in short, to the stereotypical Volvo buyer. Ask people what the safest car is, and most will reply 'Volvo'. This is a good left-brain justifier. For many others, however, the safety feature may be seen as negative, and will not have a positive appeal to the heart.

Fast-moving consumer goods often rely on attributes or features. 'Brand X washing powder washes biologically whiter', 'Brand Y toothpaste with fortified fluoride gives you clinically cleaner teeth' are typical of this approach. Categories crowded with products make for highly competitive and costly marketing, as it is hard to convince consumers of the superiority of a particular brand. Plenty of attributes mean plenty of logical reasons to buy, whatever the emotional appeal, if any, of the message. So this is a sound left-brain positioning strategy. But this strategy is wide open to competition. Features often change fast as new technology is adopted, and can usually be copied, or leapfrogged by competitors.

BENEFITS RECEIVED

Benefit-related positioning is favoured more in orthodox selling and is regarded as being more effective than attribute or feature-related positioning. As most customers buy for benefits, whether or not articulated, it gets closer to customer perception. That is, it better reflects what the customer thinks and feels. Benefits (unlike features such as fluoride or electrostatic suspension) are pleasurable or advantageous in some way. They appeal to emotion more than features and are more customer- than product-oriented. For instance, what will whiter teeth or cleaner clothes do for you? A new partner? A better job? However, depending on the benefit, it may provide a logical reason to buy and thus appeal to the left brain.

However, multiple benefits can diffuse focus in the customer's mind (we just picture one thing at a time, and do our own enhancements) and leave uncertainty about the real reason to buy. So whether selling features or benefits, the customer wants a simple, clear message.

A better approach for some companies is to combine the two approaches, describing a feature or attribute that leads to a benefit. Features or attributes are presented more successfully this way, as part of a two-brain communication. For example, side-impact protection in cars (feature) means less likelihood of serious injury in an accident (benefit), many of which involve not head-on but side-on collisions. In this case the feature, especially if backed by facts and figures, will appeal to the left brain in all of us, and to the left-brain-dominant person in particular. By making the safety feature a 'benefit', for instance linking it with family safety (caring for your children), it has emotional appeal, and is more amenable to a right-brain message. But insofar as caring for your children is a justifier – a reason – it has logical appeal as well. The important thing is to get the message, whether about features or benefits, in the right 'brain language', appealing (in conventional advertising or to bicameral individual customers) to both sides of the brain.

USAGE, OCCASION OR TIME OF USE

Positioning by usage, occasion or time of use has also traditionally been left-brain-oriented. For example, having a cup of a nutritious hot drink *before you go to bed* – the 'goodnight cup' – establishes a disciplined as well as sensible appeal. Rubbing a child's chest with Vick before bed has a similar effect as part of an ordered routine.

Products can also be positioned by versatility, if they possess a variety of uses, perhaps linked to occasions. For instance, a certain type of food (such as potato crisps) could be used as a mid-morning snack, as part of a meal, as part of an aperitif selection, or even as a sandwich filling. Even if in practice you don't use the product in those ways, each nevertheless forms a buying justifier. Overall it spells good value, so it has 'sensible', left-brain appeal. Once a product becomes part of a habit, a person will unconsciously justify it (along with the habit itself). However the person might (consciously) respond in a researcher's questionnaire, you have built in loyalty that is hard for a competitor to dislodge. The customer may not even be aware of his or her habitual acceptance of the product.

PRICE AND VALUE

Positioning on price and value for money usually relies on low production and distribution costs, such as those enjoyed by fast food suppliers such as McDonald's and KFC, or mass-produced electronic products. Volume sales are needed, as the price-sensitive decision to buy may well be a left-brain, logical, analytical process – 'I would prefer that one, but this one is better value'. Notice that the unit price itself may not be critical, but rather the value for money perceived, other indirect factors (such as savings on other kinds of purchases), and a longer-term perspective.

Performance-based positioning can also link an attribute to price and value, as in the case of a 'longest-lasting battery'. The performance feature gives the perception of good value for money even when the price of the battery is higher than the competition. Long life justifies the purchase: you pay more in the short term, but they last a lot longer so it is perceived to be a 'wise' decision – whether quantified or verified or not.

Price/value positioning certainly has its appeal, especially to lower income groups and in developing economies, where thrift is a laudable mindset in itself. This becomes a problem for the big brands, as low price copies begin to flood the market and pirating becomes endemic.

As with any aspect of a product or service, price and value can be emphasized in either a left-brain or right-brain way, which is where you can apply some marketing creativity. On the one hand the rationale of low price, and on the other hand the wider, long-term aspects of value when intangible quality or convenience benefits as well as tangible features are considered. A perceived bargain, for example, can have an emotional appeal out of all proportion to the actual money saved, or the logic of the purchase. That is, the 'bargain' – the product's 'position' in the mind of the buyer – provides the justifier. In some cases people will justify buying a once for all bargain even if they don't need the product! Price and value have traditionally been communicated in a left-brain way, so those companies who can add emotional, right-brain appeal without increasing the cost base can gain a competitive edge.

These traditional left-brain approaches have been used extensively. They have tended to be more successful in times when product categories were less crowded, people in general had more identifiable and tangible needs and wants, and the customer had not begun to be king in the way that Levitt predicted. In a mind to mind approach, it is only a part of (half) the story.

RIGHT-BRAIN STRATEGIES IN A LEFT-BRAIN WORLD

Successful advertising happens when the consumer is influenced to buy the product or service. If we consider what goes on in a consumer's mind in making purchase decisions, there are two important elements. First, the person must have a logical or rational reason to buy what is being offered. Second, he or she must be motivated actually to buy it. So if you want to influence the buying decision you have to appeal to both the left and right sides of the brain.

Traditional left-brain advertising can easily adapt to right-brain appeal by stirring up emotion and providing added motivation to buy: 'It's only half the price and the sale ends tomorrow – I'd better rush out and get it before it's too late.'

Urgency adds emotion. In fact research seems to confirm that most consumer decisions are based on emotion rather than logic. So, whatever the explicit factors in the purchase decision, unconscious, right-brain operations are inevitably at work.

EMOTION MARKETING POWER

Emotions are not easy to understand – even our own, let alone those of unknown customers. We do not understand why people do things – what moves them to act in certain ways. This is an important factor when dealing here with the part of the brain that is most associated with the unconscious mind. Ask people why they do what they do (especially a habit) and they often do not know or cannot articulate it. In other cases they will give a rational reason *in hindsight* as justification, even though no such logic was used in their behaviour, such as a purchase. Clearly there is a strong link between emotion and motivation to buy, or do anything.

Emotion sells. Although people often don't realize it, their hearts often overrule their heads when making the decision to buy something. Companies are now beginning to realize just how powerful the pull of emotion, in its various forms, can be in marketing, and the inclusion of emotional strategies in advertising is a growing trend. Marketers have known the importance of emotion for many years, but the increasing knowledge of the way in which the right brain works is giving rise to more sophisticated advertising weaponry.

None of this is to suggest that rational, left-brain strategies be thrown away. In fact they add a vital element even to emotional ideas, because 'both' brains are involved in the purchasing decision. The fact that the brains are joined means, in any event, that we cannot isolate the way in which the final 'mind' decision is made. As we said earlier, we all use both sides of the brain – we simply have, in some cases, a bias.

GAINING A SHARE OF 'HEART'

So how can we trigger and capture emotion, or gain a share of 'heart'? Let's start with a list of ways in which people can be switched on to the emotional side of their personality:

- experiencing a thrill of excitement;
- experiencing a thrill of anticipation;
- reference to a strongly held value or belief;
- association with a particular cause;
- association with a certain event in time;
- a state of anxiety;
- a state of hope;
- a moment of discovery;
- an appeal to the senses;
- a feeling of belonging;
- a feeling of happiness;
- experiencing something entirely new;
- a love of competing;
- the satisfaction of winning;
- a feeling of sadness or loss;
- a feeling of fear.

The list is far from comprehensive but it illustrates the scope for emotional appeal. Each of these, when triggered, can, for a short time at least, overpower all the rationality we are conditioned to employ. Usually the more pleasant triggers work best. But negative feelings can also be used to advantage in persuading the customer to buy. Pain as well as pleasure can cause the motivation, and different customers have a different tendency. The emotional motivation does not only create a purchase decision, but takes the customer right through the buying action, from perception of a need to post-purchase justification.

COMMON RIGHT-BRAIN STRATEGIES

Some common forms of right-brain positioning strategies are:

- sensory;
- aspiration;
- cause;
- belonging;
- family.

SENSORY

Fashion and cosmetics goods are good examples of how companies appeal to the senses. The Body Shop, for instance, uses colour to endorse its 'cause positioning' strategy with dark green façades to all its outlets, symbolizing the green of the environment. This recognition factor is important when people are looking to find the company in a busy shopping mall. 'Aroma marketing' is now also more widely used. As a supplier you can buy virtually any smell you want to help sell a product or service (downloading smells from the Internet via a gizmo on your PC will surely come).

So, for instance, a quality car sales outlet can be made to smell of leather. A supermarket will welcome you with the smell of freshly baked bread. If you are selling your house, have some fresh coffee percolating away when potential buyers visit. If you are a travel agent you can let your customers browse through catalogues to the scent of tropical flowers. Although sight and hearing are by far the major senses in everyday communication, the senses of smell and taste can have a strong emotional appeal, sometimes invoking memories going back to childhood.

Some companies link product taste to segments and positioning. Light beers, for instance, appeal more to women than men. According to research, using what is known as perceptual mapping, this product is positioned far away from the strong, outdoors type of person more attracted to stronger brews. Consequently, advertising is directed at the lady drinker, the macho male, the outdoor type, or whoever.

The use of colour has been successful for other companies, such as Marlboro, who use bold red and white packaging to symbolize strength and independence, the core personality characteristics of its brand. Symbols and logos, of course, are used by every company to attract customers visually to recognize its presence. A strong, powerful brand symbol can immediately give rise to several associations in the minds of consumers. The secret is to appeal to the senses.

We shall see in more detail the importance of sensory appeal in Chapter 6, especially the main three modalities – seeing, hearing and feeling. Sound, in the form of loved or hated 'muzak' that confronts us in every department store or supermarket, is a well-known example of auditory communication. Large, realistic pictures of double burgers bombard us visually in the fast food outlet.

Sensory appeal is a fundamental rule in influencing the perception of customers. This is primarily a right-brain phenomenon, and positioning should be part of a well-thought-out two-brain strategy.

ASPIRATION

Our buying doesn't just reflect what or who we are, but what or who we would like to be. Companies use aspirational positioning in many ways but the two common ones are: status and prestige (usually via monetary achievement); and competitive self-development (non-monetary achievement).

Both rely on the need for self-expression. Rolex watches are probably one of the most famous examples of status, prestige-driven positioning. Other companies reaping the rewards of this strategy include Mercedes, Rolls Royce, BMW and others. Concorde fits the bill when it comes to air travel. Consumers who can afford brands such as these can demonstrate their financial worth and find a vehicle for self-expression. The self-expression may not be recognized and admitted, as this is a particular feature of unconscious right-brain thinking. But this makes it all the more powerful when mind marketing. The unconscious appeal is not subjected to left-brain argument, as are more tangible factors, such as price and reliability.

Clearly, one customer will have greater aspirations than another and be more 'mobile', both between products and companies, who need to match their aspirations. This further underlines the need for a mind to mind understanding. Aspiration is just another aspect of the way we think.

CAUSE

Companies using cause-related positioning such as Avon, Benetton, Body Shop and others target customer groups who they believe will subscribe to the philosophy or ideals they advocate. In the case of Avon it is women's issues. In the case of Benetton, racial and social equality. Body Shop appeals to 'green' sentiments and the environment. Such appeal to deeper beliefs and values, as well as feelings, also requires a right-brain approach. A sense of what is right or wrong, for instance, can overpower the strongest reasoning, and dictate buying or any other behaviour. Although more associated with charitable, non-profit organizations, so-called cause marketing has been found to be a profitable strategy and an example of appealing to the customer's mind.

BELONGING

All human beings have a need to belong and this too is associated more with the right than the left brain. We do not set out to fulfil the need logically, or even knowingly. More likely, we don't even recognize or admit such a basic feeling. Often this manifests itself in positioning strategies that relate club-like belonging to other needs. Private banking membership, and other forms of exclusive customer recognition, can appeal to this group identity. Car owner clubs, such as Jaguar and Morgan, and Harley Davidson in the case of motorbikes, have used this belonging factor as a major marketing strategy. This reveals a far more holistic aspect of the customer than, say, price awareness, and is ripe for a holistic, right-brain message.

FAMILY

One of the strongest emotional positioning strategies concerns a person's family or relatives. Life insurance companies ask people how their families will fare if something happens to them, and offer parents 'peace of mind'. Educational products, including very expensive encyclopaedias, appeal to family responsibility, and the guilt that may accompany it. Who doesn't want to be a better parent (husband, wife and so on)? Other companies appeal to family interests, saying or implying 'Only the best' for your family. Maternal and paternal emotions are powerful marketing hot buttons, and illustrate the scope for the two-brain approach.

DETERMINING RIGHT–LEFT BRAIN PREFERENCE

You may find it useful to assess your own current mode of thinking. The following is based on a questionnaire used at management seminars. It should give you an idea of whether you tend more towards the left or right side of your brain. Just answer the questions quickly and instinctively. Don't think about scoring until you have finished, and don't worry about whether an answer seems good or bad. There are no goods and bads or rights and wrongs.

Tick just one letter – the one that fits you the nearest, unless the question asks otherwise.

1. In a problem-solving situation, do you:

    a. Take a walk and mull solutions over, then discuss them? ☐
    b. Think about and write down all alternatives, arrange them according to priorities and then pick the best? ☐
    c. Recall past experiences that were successful and implement them? ☐
    d. Wait to see if the situation will right itself? ☐

2. Day-dreaming is:

    a. A waste of time ☐
    b. Amusing and relaxing. ☐
    c. A real help in problem-solving and creative thinking. ☐
    d. A viable tool for planning my future. ☐

3. Glance quickly at this picture.

    Was the face smiling?

    a. Yes. ☐
    b. No. ☐

4. Concerning hunches:

    a. I frequently have strong ones and follow them. ☐
    b. I have strong hunches but don't place much faith in them. ☐
    c. I occasionally have hunches but don't place much faith in them. ☐
    d. I would not rely on hunches to help me make important decisions. ☐

5. In thinking about your day to day activities, which is most typical of your 'style'?

   a. I make a list of all the things I need to do, people to see. □
   b. I picture the places I will go and people I will see. □
   c. I just let it happen. □
   d. I plan the day's schedule, working out appropriate times for each item or activity. □

6. Do you usually have a place for everything, a system for doing things, and an ability to organize information and materials?

   a. Yes. □
   b. No. □

7. Do you like to move your furniture, or change the decor of your home or office frequently?

   a. Yes. □
   b. No. □

8. Please tick the activities you enjoy:

Swimming	□	Travel	□
Tennis	□	Cycling	□
Golf	□	Collecting	□
Camping/Hiking	□	Writing	□
Skiing	□	Chess	□
Fishing	□	Bridge	□
Singing	□	Roulette	□
Gardening	□	Charades	□
Playing an instrument	□	Dancing	□
Home improvements	□	Walking	□
Sewing	□	Running	□
Reading	□	Hugging	□
Arts/Crafts	□	Kissing	□
Cooking	□	Touching	□
Photography	□	Chatting	□
Doing nothing	□	Debating	□

9. Do you learn athletics and dancing better by:

   a. Imitating, or getting the feel of the music? □
   b. Learning the sequence and repeating it mentally? □

10. When playing a sport or performing in public, do you often perform better than your training and natural abilities warrant?

    a. Yes. ☐
    b. No. ☐

11. Do you express yourself well verbally?

    a. Yes. ☐
    b. No. ☐

12. Are you goal-oriented?

    a. Yes. ☐
    b. No. ☐

13. When you want to remember directions, a name or a news item, do you:

    a. Visualize the information? ☐
    b. Write notes? ☐
    c. Verbalize it (repeat it to yourself or out loud)? ☐
    d. Associate it with previous information? ☐

14. Do you remember faces easily?

    a. Yes. ☐
    b. No. ☐

15. When you use language, do you:

    a. Make up words? ☐
    b. Devise rhymes and incorporate metaphors? ☐
    c. Choose exact, precise terms? ☐

16. In a conversation, are you more comfortable being:

    a. The listener? ☐
    b. The talker? ☐

17. When you are asked to speak off the cuff at a meeting, do you:

    a. Make a quick outline? ☐
    b. Just start talking? ☐

    c. Shift the focus to someone else or say as little as possible? ☐
    d. Speak slowly and carefully? ☐

18.   In an argument, do you tend to:

    a. Talk until your point is made? ☐
    b. Find an authority to support your point? ☐
    c. Just become withdrawn? ☐
    d. Push the chair or table, bang the table, talk louder – shout? ☐

19.   Can you tell fairly accurately how much time has passed without looking at your watch?

    a. Yes. ☐
    b. No. ☐

20.   Do you prefer social events that are:

    a. Planned in advance? ☐
    b. Spontaneous? ☐

21.   In preparing yourself for a new or difficult task, do you:

    a. Visualize yourself accomplishing it effectively? ☐
    b. Recall past successes in similar situations? ☐
    c. Prepare extensive data relating to the task? ☐

22.   Do you prefer working:

    a. Alone? ☐
    b. In a group? ☐

23.   When it comes to 'bending the rules' or altering company policy, do you feel that:

    a. Rules and policy are to be followed? ☐
    b. Progress comes through challenging the structure? ☐
    c. Rules are made to be broken? ☐

24.   At school did you prefer:

    a. Algebra? ☐
    b. Geometry? ☐

25. Which of these handwriting positions most closely resembles yours?

    a. Normal right-hand position. ☐
    b. Hooked right-hand position (fingers pointing towards your chest). ☐
    c. Normal left-hand position. ☐
    d. Hooked left-hand position (fingers pointing towards your chest). ☐

26. When taking notes, do you print:

    a. Never? ☐
    b. Frequently? ☐

27. Do you use gestures to:

    a. Emphasize a point? ☐
    b. Express your feelings? ☐

28. Do you instinctively feel an issue is right or correct, or do you decide on the basis of information?

    a. Feel. ☐
    b. Decide. ☐

29. Do you enjoy taking risks?

    a. Yes. ☐
    b. No. ☐

30. After attending a musical, can you:

    a. Hum many parts of the score? ☐
    b. Recall many of the lyrics? ☐

31. Please hold a pencil perpendicularly to the ground at arm's length, centred in your line of vision and lined up with a frame, board or door. Holding that position, close your left eye. Did the pencil appear to move?

    a. Yes. ☐
    b. No. ☐

32. Sit in a relaxed position and clasp your hands comfortably in your lap. Which thumb is on top?

   a. Left. ☐
   b. Right. ☐
   c. Parallel. ☐

33. Tick the statements you feel are true about you:

   I can extract meaning from contracts, instruction manuals and legal documents. ☐
   I prefer to work from diagrams and plans. ☐
   I strongly visualize the characters, setting and plot of novels. ☐
   I prefer friends to phone in advance of their visits. ☐
   I dislike chatting on the phone. ☐
   I find it satisfying to plan and arrange the details of a trip. ☐
   I postpone making telephone calls. ☐
   I can easily find words in a dictionary and names in a telephone directory. ☐
   I love puns. ☐
   I take lots of notes at meetings and lectures. ☐
   I freeze when I have to operate mechanical things under stress. ☐
   Ideas frequently come to me out of nowhere. ☐

34. I have:

   a. Frequent mood changes. ☐
   b. Almost no mood changes. ☐

35. I am:

   a. Not very conscious of body language; I prefer to listen to what people say. ☐
   b. Good at interpreting body language. ☐
   c. Good at understanding what people say and the body language they use. ☐

SCORING

Circle the scores for each of your answers.

1.

    a) 7   b) 1   c) 3   d) 9

2.

    a) 1   b) 5   c) 7   d) 9

3.

    a) 3   b) 7

4.

    a) 9   b) 7   c) 3   d) 1

5.

    a) 1   b) 7   c) 9   d) 3

6.

    a) 1   b) 9

7.

    a) 9   b) 1

8.

Swimming	9	Travel	5
Tennis	4	Cycling	8
Golf	4	Collecting	1
Camping/Hiking	7	Writing	2
Skiing	7	Chess	2
Fishing	8	Bridge	2
Singing	3	Roulette	7
Gardening	5	Charades	5

Playing an instrument	4	Dancing	7
Home improvements	3	Walking	8
Sewing	3	Running	8
Reading	3	Hugging	9
Arts/Crafts	5	Kissing	9
Cooking	5	Touching	9
Photography	3	Chatting	4
Doing nothing	9	Debating	2

9.

   a) 9   b) 1

10.

   a) 9   b) 1

11.

   a) 1   b) 7

12.

   a) 1   b) 9

13.

   a) 9   b) 1   c) 3   d) 5

14.

   a) 7   b) 1

15.

   a) 9   b) 5   c) 1

16.

   a) 6   b) 3

17.

    a) 1   b) 6   c) 9   d) 4

18.

    a) 3   b) 1   c) 7   d) 9

19.

    a) 1   b) 9

20.

    a) 1   b) 9

21.

    a) 9   b) 5   c) 1

22.

    a) 3   b) 7

23.

    a) 1   b) 5   c) 9

24.

    a) 1   b) 9

25.

    a) 1   b) 7   c) 9   d) 3

26.

    a) 1   b) 9

27.

    a) 2   b) 8

28.

    a) 9   b) 1

29.

  a) 7   b) 3

30.

  a) 9   b) 1

31.

  a) 8   b) 2

32.

  a) 1   b) 9   c) 3

33.

Contracts	1		Postpone	7
Diagrams	7		Find words	1
Visualize	9		Puns	3
Advance	2		Notes	1
Chatting	3		Freeze	3
Plan trip	1		Nowhere	9

34.

  a) 9   b) 1

35.

  a) 1   b) 7   c) 5

Now add up the number of points you have scored and divide the total by the number of questions you have answered. (This latter number will vary, since questions 8 and 33 have a large number of parts.) If your points total 300 in 40 answers, for example, your final score would be 7.5, revealing a definite tendency towards right-brain thinking.

```
1            3            5            7            9
Left ——————————————————————————————————— Right
```

6

Making sense of communication

The next major thinking type concerns which senses your customer prefers to use: visual, auditory, kinaesthetic (touch, feeling). For present purposes I will not include taste and smell, as these are not significant in everyday human communication, and have their own special place in marketing. The idea of a 'visual person' or a 'feelings person' is quite common, and often we identify close friends and colleagues in this way. NLP refers to these main senses as 'representational' systems or 'modalities'.

SENSORY PREFERENCE

We use all our senses all the time, of course. So the significance of this 'thinking' category (which we will lump together loosely with Meta Programs) is where there is a *preference*, just as with a right- or left-brain bias. This is immediately obvious when we observe people in different jobs requiring an intensive use of one sense or another. For example, an artist or architect will need to have visual acuity, being able to 'picture' things in his or her mind. Similarly a person concerned with music or a profession involving careful listening probably displays an auditory awareness greater than other people.

But our preference may not be confined to the sorts of jobs or hobbies we have, although we do develop sensory skills with practice. And nor is it confined to *external* representations – that is, using the senses to process external realities. An architect, for example, will need to picture a building or design internally before it ever becomes a successful physical project. Similarly a musical composer will typically be able to create compositions in his or her mind. So, although we usually have a preference, or indeed a pecking order of preference for the way we use our senses, this may not be directly related to how or to what degree we use each sense in representing the material world. It also includes how we use our memory and imagination.

Nor is our preference necessarily related to brain dominance, covered in the previous chapter. Sometimes, however, visual skills are associated with the right side of the brain. Similarly, auditory skills, especially when linked to language, may sometimes be associated with the left side.

Although there may not be a genetic explanation for sensory preference, a preference may remain quite constant over many years. So, like brain dominance, it seems like a fixed aspect of our personality. Sensory preference can and does change, at least in the long term. And just as with physical skills, sensory skills can be improved by practice, hence the obvious link with a person's work and hobbies. Fortunately, for the purpose of classifying customers, we can rely on sensory preference as a reasonably stable characteristic – more so, as it happens, than most demographic data such as address and income, which customer databases usually comprise.

How significant, then, is sensory preference as a customer thinking attribute? In simple terms, the sense we are 'at home' with is akin to the first language we speak. It seems comfortable and natural. Conversely, a sense we are not 'at home' with may have the same effect on us as a known but not-so-familiar language. In practice we don't usually 'think' about our sensory preference, even if we know it. But we stick habitually to the sense or couple of senses we prefer for most thought 'processing'. Nor are we usually aware that other people may think in different sensory language. It doesn't occur to us. So we sometimes find that we cannot relate to certain people in the way that we can to others. By identifying and using the customer's preferred representational system we begin in effect to speak their language and create rapport. We communicate better, which is what marketing is all about.

SENSORY LANGUAGE

The language comparison is more than analogy. We actually adjust our language to reflect which sense we use most. Thus a visual person will tend to use expressions such as 'I get the picture' or 'That's clearer now' or 'I can see what you mean'. An auditory person will use expressions such as 'I hear what you say' or 'that sounds fine'. And a kinaesthetic or feelings person will use kinaesthetic language such as 'that feels right', or 'let's get to grips with this'. These so-called sensory predicates occur frequently both in spoken and written language. These will increasingly form part of mind to mind communication, and provide a valid 'passive' indication of sensory preference. For instance, examining what a person writes will reveal a bias from the words and phrases used. I have included a more comprehensive list of sensory predicates as Appendix A.

There are other indicators of sensory preference, including voice pitch, speed and tone; posture and breathing; and of particular interest, eye movements. Some of these indicators are more applicable in face to face communication, although the techniques are not used widely in face to face selling. In some cases they require advanced skills to elicit them. I have tried, as far as possible, to select and adapt those aspects of NLP that can readily apply to mainstream marketing.

Once you start to consider sensory preference there are lots of common-sense improvements you can make to a marketing communication. Visual imagery, for instance, has little effect on a person with a strong auditory preference. They want sounds, and typically enjoy the human voice spoken in musical, resonant tones. Strongly kinaesthetic people, on the other hand, will want to actually handle the product or somehow experience the service in a physical or tactile way before being convinced. And even when the medium does not permit this, such as a television or magazine advert, using kinaesthetic language or *predicates* will go some way towards 'speaking their language'.

If you want to know what part of your advertising budget is wasted, mismatching sensory messages is a prime suspect. As far as some of your customers are concerned, you may as well communicate in a foreign language. Conversely, 'matching' sensory preference offers a consistent hot button to motivate your customers.

THE SENSORY HOT BUTTON

An understanding of these Meta Programs will help in forming a relationship marketing strategy. In particular, how they are best 'matched' in any communication, so that each customer is treated differently. Pressing the sensory hot button of an individual can make an extraordinary difference to a communication. The use of sensory preference in person to person communication is well established in the form of NLP techniques. Its potential application to one to one marketing is obvious, although little applied in practice. There is, however, a compromise strategy for mass marketing: make your communication *multi*-sensory. Offer a variety of sensory representations and language – pictures, sounds and feelings. This is equivalent to giving a message that appeals to both the logical and intuitive sides of the brain.

The idea of sensory communication is not confined to addressing individual sensory preference. Multi-sensory communication has applications in mass marketing. As it happens, we know that the visual modality is the most used in everyday communication, followed by auditory, then feelings. So you can *weight* your advertising and use of sensory language to reflect this distribution, in an advertisement or other promotion. In the case of mass marketing, a multi-sensory message will optimize your communication to reflect the three main senses. As we saw earlier, the other two senses, smell and taste, are used little in ordinary communication.

Seeing red

We 'see' examples of the visual modality in the way colour affects our behaviour. 'Seeing red' is more than a figure of speech, for instance. When our ancestors 'saw red' it was probably blood, which meant it was time to run. But whatever the scientific basis for the effect of colours, it has long been known that they affect customers' perceptions of products. A package can evoke an expensive, luxury product or a cheap tacky substitute, just by changing its colour. Studies show that perhaps 60 per cent of a first impression of a product or display comes from colour.

A detergent was once tested for three different colours of specks added – red, blue and yellow. Consumers reported that the yellow flecks didn't get clothes clean enough, and claimed that the red specks actually damaged clothes. Only the blue specks were singled out as getting clothes cleaner. In fact the colours made no difference one way or the other in cleaning ability. It was simply the perception of consumers based on the psychological effect of colours. To reinforce the point, the detergent in question was manufactured with blue specks and proved to be a top seller for many years. Another popular detergent is bright white, suggesting cleanliness, but with bold orange added to the packaging, denoting power and strength.

These are examples of how we can influence customers' perceptions, and how colours have a fairly universal impact. However, the importance of visual stimuli generally varies from person to person, depending not just on their sensory preference, but also on personal associations, perhaps from childhood, of a particular colour.

Individual preference doesn't lend itself to the mass advertising and packaging successes I have just referred to, of course. But it opens up all sorts of possibilities for communicating one to one with customers at the most powerful mind level. For dubious, left-brained marketers who take a cynical approach to psychological factors in customers, the US Supreme Court has deemed colour such a potent brand indicator that a particular shade alone can serve as a legally defensive trademark. What value, for instance, are Golden Arches to fast food marketing?

But major benefits will only apply in a one to one situation. Imagine how people of different preference respond to standard selling pitches. A visual person in the car showroom will say to him- or herself, 'Why doesn't the salesperson stop talking and show me – I want to *see* for myself.' A kinaesthetic person will put the visually attractive, glossy brochures to one side, and even get impatient at looking at the actual car, just waiting to sit in the driver's seat and *feel* it for him- or herself. Conversely, an auditory person is inclined to say 'Just tell me the facts, I'm listening.' We all tend to hit it off naturally with certain salespeople and not with others, although rarely do we analyse why. One of the biggest reasons for lack of rapport or 'chemistry' between people, in any situation, is sensory mismatch.

SENSORY SYNERGY

The fact that it happens unconsciously (usually in the case of both parties, including the professional seller) means that a mismatched communication is not corrected. In practice this may mean that a customer is lost for ever. It might also explain situations where a loyal customer defects for no reason. Where a sensory match occurs by default (which statistically it will, of course) the salesperson's self-esteem is restored, but their complacency may be strengthened. They don't know why the sale went like a dream so they don't learn from the experience. Next time it doesn't happen that way because the next customer prefers a different sensory language. That is a hard way to market when hot buttons are there for the pressing. Remarkably strong relationships can be created through 'sensory synergy', even with a mediocre service and product level. That's because the 'likeness' and familiar language affect the customer's perception disproportionately.

What applies to face to face selling applies to some extent in conventional direct marketing, of course. Whatever the medium, we can only communicate through basic sensory organs. Obviously, some media are more appropriate to one sense than to others, such as telephone in the case of an auditory person, or video in the case of a visual person. But the current wide choice of media makes it possible to address individual sensory preferences and thus multiply the impact of a communication.

COMMUNICATING WITH THE UNCONSCIOUS MIND

We don't use these sensory predicates consciously. Similarly, we do not consciously 'represent' things in the outside world, like a country walk or a staff meeting, in a particular sense. It just happens. In conversation, we usually think about the meaning we want to get across or the person we are addressing rather than the precise language we use, or body language such as hand gestures to depict what we are 'seeing' mentally. Similarly, when we remember or imagine something, we are not usually aware of which modalities we use, or often even the expressions or predicates we use in describing our thoughts. It is no surprise to linguists, therefore, that our sensory language is usually a disarmingly true indicator of sensory use and preference. In terms of market research, we can probably get a more reliable indication of a customer through sensory preference than from the highly conscious, but not always truthful, answers to typical customer survey questionnaires.

IDENTIFYING AND USING SENSORY PREFERENCE

This brings us to two major practical issues. First, how to identify your customer's sensory preference. And second, how best to use this information to maximize your marketing communications and build up a long-term relationship.

So far I have distinguished between mass marketing and relationship or one to one marketing when describing the application of these Meta Programs. The same distinction applies when addressing these practical questions. When selling to a mass market you will not be able to identify the preference of individual prospective customers. In this case, however, you can use the known distribution of sensory use as I suggested earlier, weighting your messages accordingly. And you can in any case use strongly sensory language rather than vague generalities (which is simply better communication). That is, although you cannot identify individual customer preference, you can *improve* your mass communication by using a multi-sensory message, just as you can by using a dual-brain approach.

SENSORY PREDICATES

Even neutral sensory words such as 'just imagine', 'think about' and 'consider' will elicit a sensory response, whatever a customer's preference. 'Imagine' will mean to each customer whatever they do when they imagine – see, hear or feel. Advertising copywriters get to know the effect of different words through long hit-and-miss experience, but rarely base it on this NLP sensory model. Sensory predicates will add to this impact. But again, in competitive marketing, it is preferable to know what you are doing and why.

One advertisement, to which I have added my own comments in parentheses, chose the multi-sensory approach:

> it may sound too good to be true (a familiar figure of speech will bypass conscious objection better than a less familiar, sensory-specific term)… until you have run your eyes (perhaps a contradiction in terms, but running appeals to the kinaesthetic, movement sense)… over its sensual lines (although seemingly 'neutral', sensual may have kinaesthetic overtones, and 'lines' visual ones) and felt for yourself (some more kinaesthetic) its captivating personality (personalizing the product to create a 'quasi-human' relationship) you'll simply never know how much fun…' (emotion and the childlike right brain)…

Mass marketing cannot capitalize on the hot button of individual sensory preference because it doesn't deal in real people. In the case of direct marketing no such limits apply. Various simple questionnaires have been designed to determine sensory preference and these are far less complex than many standard questionnaires designed to get, say, reactions to a product or service. On reflection this should be no surprise. People are usually more interested in themselves (including their preferences and personality characteristics) than anything else – including your company and products. In this book I can do no more than offer specimen data-gathering instruments. However, once the importance of these Meta Programs is grasped, you will be able to design your data-gathering methods and instruments to match, not just the different characteristics I am describing, but the nature of your business and customers.

REWARDING INFORMATION

You may need to offer some reward to get this basic customer data. A restaurant proprietor, for example, might obtain questionnaire information while the client is in the restaurant in exchange for a free dessert, glass of wine or half the price of the next meal. The main rule is to keep questionnaires simple, brief and as far as possible enjoyable. By obtaining data on one major thinking characteristic at a time, this is quite feasible. The relationship value of this information is so high that you can afford to get it in increments, and to invest time and money in the process. Your prize is *lifetime share of customer* rather than market share, and any investment has to be judged on that time-scale. In practice, the cost of data gathering for relationship marketing can be less than the abortive advertising expense on mismatched promotions.

As it happens, usually a very small inducement is needed to get people to give information about how they think and feel about something. Most people are secretly flattered. It depends on how you present and couch the questions. The restaurant ideas can be adapted to any service-type business where you meet the client personally, such as professional practice, a manned car wash, hairdressing, hotels, health care, and such. And you need little further adaptation when dealing remotely but directly, as in the case of mail order direct marketing. Once again, an inducement will probably be needed, but this will repay itself many times over. The cost is almost bound to be less than the promotion costs wasted by speaking the wrong language.

IDENTIFYING YOUR PREFERENCE

The simplest exercises will give a good indication of sensory preference. In my book *NLP: The new art and science of getting what you want* (Piatkus), I used the following sort of exercise. Each had to be scored between 1 and 9 (9 means 'I can imagine this as if in real life'; 1 means 'I just can't imagine this in my head'; 2–8, somewhere in between).

Visual

1. Visualize a friend or acquaintance with long hair.
2. Recall the face of a teacher from when you were at school.
3. Visualize the stripes on a tiger.
4. See the colour of the front door where you live or work.
5. See a favourite entertainer on your TV screen wearing a top hat.
6. Visualize the largest book in your house.

Auditory

1. Hear a favourite tune.
2. Listen to church bells ringing in the distance.
3. Which of your friends has the quietest voice? Hear it.
4. Hear a car engine starting on a cold morning.
5. Imagine hearing the voice of a childhood friend.
6. Listen to the sound your voice makes under water.

Kinaesthetic

1. Feel your left hand in very cold water.
2. Hold a smooth, glass paperweight in both hands.
3. Stroke a cat or dog.
4. Put on a pair of wet socks.
5. Imagine jumping off a four-foot-high wall.
6. Roll a car wheel down the road.

Work out your average score for each of the three modalities (divide by six) and you will see whether you have a preference. The more sensory questions of this sort you ask yourself (and you can think of obvious ones yourself) the more accurate will be the resulting preference.

Typically, one modality will score higher than the other two, or sometimes two are about the same with the third scoring lower. You may have a fairly even score across all three, but the average score is still significant. Some people have a very strong internal representation (high scores) while others find it hard to see, hear or feel things internally (low scores).

THE COST OF MISMATCHING

The benefits of communicating in the right thinking style are not immediately obvious. Bear in mind, for instance, that the effect of sensory mismatch may not be neutral. Mismatches are not just ignored. People can actually be annoyed if your message does not make sense to them, so they will in future keep clear of you. And a dissatisfied customer, even without objective reasons, will pass on their experience far more than a satisfied customer. It is socially acceptable to complain about poor service. So you don't just get nothing from your advertising or promotional investment but you risk losing customers into the bargain.

A magazine advertisement, included in the fairly short copy 'you won't believe your eyes... the table above is a real eye-opener... keeps an eye on costs... visible cost savings' and so on. Addressed to a strong visualizer in a one to one communication the effect could have been magical. But in a mass advertisement it was destined to turn off a very large percentage of the readers. Note that although vision is the prime sense we use in communication, and visual processing takes up a large chunk of the brain, this is not necessarily reflected in the proportion of people for whom it is the *preferred* sense – for instance, an auditory-dominant person.

Another advertiser used the auditory sense in a similar way: 'are you all ears?... you may have heard... if you would like to hear more...' and so on. No other sensory communication was used. Once again, in a one to one targeted message this could have ignited an auditory customer's neural systems and produced remarkable results. But it would be wasted or counterproductive on a non-auditory person. Strongly sensory advertising messages do not necessarily indicate sophistication on the part of copywriters. The customer – even a representative or modal customer – may never have got into the equation. Sensory language may simply reflect the unconscious preference of the copy-writer.

DIRECT MARKETING APPLICATIONS

These examples illustrate how direct marketing can benefit if basic customer preferences are first identified. Direct marketing offers unlimited potential for purpose-designed communication based on sensory preference. So a mind to mind strategy fits well with the trend towards direct, database marketing, using ever-cheaper computer resources. It is a simple matter to personalize mail shots by name or other simple demographic data and very little additional effort is needed to take account of other personal factors such as sensory preference.

Imagine the increased hit rate by addressing a letter in a person's mother tongue rather than their second or third language. That is the sort of difference you can expect by carefully couching your message in specific sensory terms to match a person's preference.

People who have used these techniques in business or in motivating sports people cite extraordinary communication improvements as if by magic. In fact there is no magic about speaking a person's language to get your message across; it is common sense. And we can now apply the principle to sensory preference. According to the NLP model, this is the prime language of thought and experience.

The results of sensory matching can seem remarkable. This is because we all have our own sensory preference and cannot appreciate what it is like to think differently. We have no direct experience of the other person's thinking world or 'map' and how they 'represent' things through the senses. So we assume people think like we do. It all happens unconsciously in any case. In my experience in training and consulting, people were not even aware that they used repeated sensory predicates in their everyday speech such as 'that sounds OK' in the case of an auditory person, even though their work colleagues confirmed that such was the case. Similarly, non-visual people who insisted that they *did* use common expressions such as 'I see what you mean' in fact did nothing of the sort. They *thought* they did. Video recordings of these training sessions disarmingly reveal these unconscious habits linked to thinking style.

ELICITING SENSORY PREFERENCE

Here are the sorts of simple questions that will elicit a sensory preference.

What do you prefer? The:

- smooth cool taste?
- metallic colour range?
- crackling sound?
- crumbling texture?
- beautiful visual lines?
- snap, crackle and pop?
- silky feeling when you touch it?
- roar of the engine?
- hi-fi sound system?

- smell of the leather?
- new colour choice?
- glassy smooth finish?
- feel of the sun and sand on your body?
- sound of the birds and gentle waves?

If you can apply these sorts of sensory stimuli to specific products, so much the better. But they nonetheless will quickly indicate sensory preference. You may have noticed that sensory appeal can apply to services as well as products. It concerns customer perception rather than objective, tangible features. It is the special language of human experience, and the key to understanding and communicating with your customers.

7

How customers decide

We have met two important Meta Programs: brain dominance and sensory preference. In this chapter we shall consider another main category of Meta Program, which has been called the Life Content model. I will then address another important mind programme that affects decision making, known as Convincer strategy. In the next chapter I will cover a few more common Meta Programs, so that you have plenty of choice in gathering and analysing one to one customer data.

The Life Content model is about how people express and go about achieving their goals and desires. This includes buying and deciding about products and services. The model comprises five 'Life Content' categories which are characteristic of how people think about what they want – their 'outcomes':

- getting or having;
- doing;
- knowing;

- relating;
- being.

For example:

- to *get* or *have* a new car;
- to *do* a course of study;
- to learn or find out about something (knowing);

- to gain respect or admiration of others (relating);
- to *be* happy, independent or secure.

These are dispositions or tendencies towards achieving different kinds of goals. They help to express our different aspirations and what is important to us. As with the Meta Programs you have already met, we usually have a preference, or order of preference, for these Life Content characteristics. All your customers have a Life Content profile, and this offers another way to communicate with them as individuals.

THE LIFE CONTENT MODEL

First I will describe each category, and the type of people for whom it applies. You will probably recall people you know who typify each of them.

GETTING OR HAVING

These people are concerned with possession – getting things, owning, and having material evidence of their attainments. For such people, being happy means *having* certain things. If they concern themselves with doing things they will be very concerned about their kit, such as skiing equipment, the best tools, the right car if they are travelling, the best books if they are learning. They may also take account of possessions, including perhaps car, house and clothes, that they think will help their relationships. If they gain a qualification, they will be concerned about getting a certificate as material evidence of their success. This characteristic is not necessarily acquisitiveness, or materialism, but reflects the need for tangible evidence of attainment – 'having something to show for it'.

It can be important in the case of invisible services like hotels or insurance where the customer does not have anything tangible following the sale. Even token physical, souvenir-type products or documents with a valuable 'feel' can fill this gap. The 'free' gift also helps to fill this need. But conversely, such material gestures may be completely wasted on a non-getting person.

DOING

These people are activists. They have to have a go. They must experience things for themselves. They are the first to volunteer in a training session or get up on the dance floor and will try out new experiences such as holidays or hobbies and interests given half a chance. As customers they may enjoy bartering and the shopping 'experience' almost as much as owning the goods. For them, learning is by experience. So, for such a person, having possessions is often about what those possessions enable you to do. Similarly, relationships are often about sharing experiences and activities – doing things together. And being happy and fulfilled means living life to the full and packing in as many new experiences as possible. These people don't waste time reading the instruction book. They will just start fiddling with the knobs and see what happens. They are just as likely to want to *do* in the buying process – scratching out numbers, transferring stickers, joining the sale queue – any active or inter*active* process.

KNOWING

These people will spend a long time getting information, such as before making a purchase. They will read up all the magazine reports and statistics, get comparative information, then will pore over the instruction manual to know all they can about a gadget or activity. Sometimes their pleasure comprises just the knowledge. For example, they may learn all about a foreign country, its history and culture without ever travelling there. Or they might know about all the latest computer technology without committing to a purchase, or using their knowledge practically. When undertaking a course of study, for instance, they will be more interested in the knowledge they are acquiring rather than in the 'piece of paper' they receive at the end, or the social aspects of the course. They are happy to know for knowing's sake. They will typically see knowledge as a route to achievement and important in reaching their goals, insofar as the knowledge is not a goal in itself. In this case, and contrary to marketing wisdom, product 'facts and figures' features (as distinct from benefits) may be of 'perceived value' to the customer who needs to know.

RELATING

These people will adopt any disposition provided that others are aware of it and respect or admire them for it. 'What will so-and-so think?' is their bottom-line question. They need to keep up with the Jones's. Their actions and possessions will depend on what a partner, close friends and colleagues or 'people' will think. This might be to impress, gain respect, and show love and support – whatever. The common denominator is relationships; these are *people people*. Money, to them – or indeed knowledge and possessions – is valued for the friendships it can buy and the relationships it can secure. House, mod cons and the tangible trappings of success are valued for the relationships they will create and enhance. Similarly, knowledge, for them, means being able to communicate intelligently, gain respect and admiration, and enter a desired social or business circle.

BEING

These people aim straight for the ultimate feeling of happiness, contentment, fulfilment, security and identity – of *being* what they want to be. They will adopt the other Life Content modes, but as an interim stepping stone to achieve their *being* desire. They are concerned with who they are as unique individuals, their identity. They are interested in the present more than the past or the future. Such a person is often content when surrounded by nature rather than relying on man-made possessions. Nor do they need to travel the world as they can usually find pleasure in their immediate surroundings and in the moment. Often they will discount the value of possessions and knowledge for knowledge's sake, and may not even depend upon relationships to guarantee their happiness. When they do aspire to other Life Content elements they will often describe what they are doing as a means to an end, rather than, as is the case with the other categories, as being the outcome itself.

IDENTIFYING A LIFE CONTENT PROFILE

How can we identify these? In some cases the person acts stereotypically – the materialistic getter, the activist doer, the knowledge 'nerd', and the 'being' person who lives for the moment. In other cases it is not so obvious without listening and gaining the right sort of information, just as sensory predicates indicate sensory preference

You can use the following exercise to prove the validity of the model and also identify your own Life Content profile. It will then be easy to apply it in various marketing ways. First list down all your goals, wants, wishes, desires, hopes, dreams, resolutions and so on – short-term or long-term, realistic or far-fetched. Do this quickly and instinctively but in complete, short statements that express just what you want in your own words and the emotion behind it.

Your list might look like this:

- I want to try free fall parachuting.
- I should really get to know the filing system.
- I would like to speak Spanish.
- I wish I were half a stone lighter.
- I need a new dishwasher.
- I wish John would telephone more often.
- I would like to be financially independent.
- I would like to visit Rome.
- I want to understand how the Internet works.
- I'd like to exercise more.

Although each of these may not use the actual Life Content words they will usually fit into the categories. The next step is to allocate each of them to one of the five categories. You can do this however long your list is. The language usually gives clues. For instance, to visit Rome is about doing something – knowing all about it is not enough. When losing weight, doing exercises is of course *doing*, whereas wanting to be thin is the *being* category. Finding out about diets and the effect of exercise may well imply a knowledge desire, and in many cases losing weight is all to do with a relationship. Understanding how the Internet works is about knowing. 'I would like to try surfing the Internet' probably indicates a *doing* disposition. Similarly, wanting to speak Spanish may be more than wanting to understand or *know* Spanish. If you expanded the goal it may refer, for instance, to being able to speak the language on holiday or with a Spanish friend – a particular goal other than just knowing a language. So the nuances of expression are important in the same way as are sensory predicates.

Even if border line, try to place each of your outcomes in one of these categories. If unsure, try expanding the outcome statement a little, by adding *because*, or *so that*. The extra description of your outcome will give further clues as to the Life Content category. For example: I'd like to exercise more *so that* I will feel good in myself suggests *being*. I'd like to exercise more *so that* I can take up tennis seriously suggests *doing*.

Count up the number of outcomes in each of the Life Content categories. Then, quite simply, the *weighting* of Life Content types in your list will indicate your Life Content disposition, as well as the pecking order of importance – most to least categories. So the longer the list the more representative will be the profile. And the more instinctively you express your goals, the truer will it reflect your personal Life Content profile.

PUTTING THINGS IN ORDER

In fact the model goes a lot deeper than this. In the same way that in practice we are all multi-sensory, we all tend to display perhaps three or more of these Life Content categories. How did your list turn out? But more than this, we tend to keep to the same order or syntax in a whole range of goal setting or decision making.

For example:

- One person may need to know something *before* they do something, and *then* they are happy (the order is therefore: knowing, doing, being).
- Another person will need to get something *before* they achieve their relationship goals *then* they will be content (getting/having, relating, being).
- Another person may have to try something out first *after which* they learn more about the subject or activity (doing, knowing).
- Another person may put their getting at the end – 'I will only make a lot of money *if* I learn so and so, do so and so (say gaining experience or doing a course of study) and sort out my relationships' (knowing, doing, relating, getting).

This is not so much the order of importance, which you identified in the above exercise, but the actual sequence of the outcomes – like the combination number to open a safe. Remarkably, the sequence, once established, is usually consistent and reliable. Thus, for instance, it will apply to very different sorts of outcomes and purchases, from choosing a partner to buying a holiday or car. As customer relationship data, it is invaluable.

This sequence reveals itself in all sorts of aspects of our lives. In effect it reflects our 'comfort zone of experience'. Or, just like sensory preference or brain dominance, *how we think* at a meta level. Of course we know no other way to think and rarely imagine that other people's dispositions are quite different, both in the weighting of their Life Content and also in the sequence in which they apply.

This is further explained in *NLP: The new art and science of getting what you want* (Piatkus). For our purposes, having identified the preference of a customer, you can use this information to communicate any product or service more effectively, and to build a better customer relationship.

MARKETING APPLICATIONS

Once you are familiar with this model you will easily be able to translate it into marketing communication messages that make sense to your potential customers. For example:

- 'You can do...'
- 'You can know...'
- 'You can have...'
- 'Imagine what you friends will say...' (relating)
- 'You can be...'

DIRECT MARKETING

Just like the sensory predicates you have met, these are hot-button words and concepts because they reflect the thinking disposition of the person. So the model has particular application in face to face selling and direct marketing where you are dealing with an individual customer. Each will appeal to the person who prefers that particular Life Content characteristic. Conversely, using the wrong characteristic will seem foreign and may have a counterproductive effect.

For example, stressing possessions to a person who, as a basic thinking style or Meta Program, does not value them, will not lift the seller in his or her esteem. Nor will suggesting further deliberation and more information to a person who just wants to 'get on with it'. The same sort of mismatch might apply between any of the categories. Having said this, just as we use all our senses even though we have a preference, or in any event a pecking order, in the same way most people will relate to some or all of the Life Content characteristics, but in an order of importance.

Thus, if you are selling encyclopaedias, you can turn on potential customers according to their preferred Life Content profile:

- the beautiful lifetime possession they have – the physical product;
- the untold knowledge they will acquire;
- the thrill of working their way through a topic and activity exploring the reference system (doing);
- impressing work colleagues or sharing their purchase with the children;
- being a better parent, being more knowledgeable, and so on.

You can design a promotion to match exactly the syntax, or order, of a person's Life Content profile, not just their dominant tendency. In this way you can market an otherwise generic product in ways that reflect the unique disposition of the individual. Your message will connect with their personality and values. You thus add a new, intangible benefit (knowing, being, doing etc) to the actual product or service. This may well augment the Total Product we met earlier, in the mind of the customer.

SELLING SENSORY BENEFITS

Selling benefits is standard marketing wisdom. Instead of 'here's what I'm trying to sell you', the message is 'here's how much better your life will be'. By reflecting how customers represent their outcomes (what they want) in their *senses* you will focus always on benefits rather than product or service features. You can create a personal 'benefit' in every product and service if you mirror the customer's Life Content profile. Life Content is a dependable personality characteristic that strongly influences buying behaviour as well as long-term relationships and loyalty. It illustrates the importance of mind to mind marketing. For example, a doing person will relate to a doing personality company.

In a direct marketing context it takes little imagination to personalize the message according to Life Content, but you can probably quadruple response to a promotion. Simply repeat the sort of phrases above that indicate Life Content. The biggest effect, however, is the long-term relationship built up with clients whose 'language' you always seem to speak. They interpret your message in terms of your company's personality and corporate attributes as well as perceiving specific product benefits. So as well as creating loyalty to a product you create loyalty to your organization. Your customers interpret your behaviour as being wise, right, thoughtful, etc. Each new product or service message then gets a better response.

SELLING IN SEQUENCE

In particular, the *sequence* of Life Content can enhance relationships. This is unique qualitative information about your customers, rather like their DNA profile. Or, like the number sequence on a combination lock. Get it right and the treasures inside are all yours. We usually stick to our Life Content characteristics over a long period, so it will work again and again in your customer relationships. Identifying a customer Life Content sequence will present a far greater challenge than a simple preference. But the investment value is obvious when viewed in terms of lifetime share of customer.

MASS MARKETING

You can apply Life Content information to mass marketing, just as with the previous categories of Meta Program (brain dominance and sensory preference), by using the 'shotgun' approach. Most of us approach our goals in more than one of these ways, so we are quite amenable to combined messages – '*Do* this and you will *get* this and *be* happy.' Indeed, getting the syntax, or sequence, right is more powerful than adopting an absolute preference. As with language, the syntax of thought – including priorities, comparisons and trade-offs – is important in decision making. In mass marketing you can only use a modal syntax, of course, in which case you will use very common profiles such as: *do* and you will *get* and you will then *be*.

Often 'being' is the final element in the sequence. So, just as the fact that we use the visual mode most, you can use this with advantage as a feature of human nature rather than a specific customer characteristic. This will become apparent as you apply the model to yourself and observe it in others.

Simply by relating to these different dispositions you can communicate better. To market effectively we need to know how people tick.

First as human beings: I said earlier that in many basic respects we act in the same way. So there is plenty of mileage in understanding the basic model. Second, you need to know how your individual customers tick. The application in a one to one context, however, gives results many times greater.

CONVINCER STRATEGY

For every behaviour we carry out we have a strategy. This is the mental programme we consistently follow to achieve what we set out to get. For instance, we each have a strategy for making decisions, being motivated, being bored, spelling words, frying an egg or any other behaviour we carry out. The convincer strategy concerns how we become convinced to make a decision, such as what to buy.

CONVINCER TYPES

Convincer strategies might be described as buying or decision-making personalities. Here are the four convincer 'types':

Automatic

This sort of person, on seeing a product or hearing about it, needs little convincing before committing themselves to a purchase. The process seems to be automatic. A marketer's and salesperson's dream.

Number of times

Here, the number of times the person runs through their decision strategy determines how they will be convinced to make a purchase. Some people, for instance, need to compare lots of products, holiday destinations, different suppliers, and try on clothes and such before making the decision. In this case the major difference between individual customers using this style of thinking will be, in effect, the number of times they need to be convinced or convince themselves.

This supports what top salespeople know – the importance of persistence. One final reminder might get the important order. A good salesperson will usually recognize which convincer strategy a customer falls into, and will adopt an appropriate strategy. More than likely he or she will not be conscious of the decision process, and just works on what seems right. This decision characteristic is easily measurable online. It should not require rocket science to check on how many times a site visitor clicks through a topic, aborts a buying trolley and so on. It needs little more thought to automate repeated customized promotions to this sort of decision maker.

Consistent

These people take it to the extreme. They want to check on everything available, and gain all the necessary information before being finally satisfied. Enormous selling effort and patience is required to convince them. A marketer or salesperson's nightmare.

Period of time

The people in this convincer category need plenty of time. They will frequently spend days, and possibly weeks, deciding on a purchase. But again, in this case, the only difference between individual customers in the category is the amount of time they need.

Convincer strategy is an invaluable indicator of how your customer will behave. The strategy, it seems, is consistent between all kinds of decision, and all kinds of product and service purchases. So it is another key to the thinking language of the customers on whom you depend. Some salespeople can fit their customers or clients easily into these groupings. In other cases they might miss the signals and lose a sale or a customer. For instance, there is little point in pressing for an immediate decision from the person who needs time. You might lose a person for good. Similarly, some people may have to be exposed to a range of products before ever they make a decision. You can be almost certain that they will not choose the first couple of products shown. So your marketing and sales strategy, in a one to one customer relationship, can reflect this individual preference.

As with sensory predicates, you can plan your language and message to reflect each convincer style. For instance, 'take your time, sir' or 'let me show you some of the other styles we have in stock'. In direct marketing, the type and number of mail shots will reflect the customer's strategy.

RECOGNIZING CONVINCER TYPES

Simple questions will elicit this information, which will then become confirmed by actual selling and transaction information. In the case of online business, software can identify the convincer strategies of site visitors. For instance, a person who circumnavigates the site several times, returning repeatedly to a product or information, is a 'number of times' decider. It doesn't mean they will not buy, just that they need to repeat the information process a number of times.

Another person may visit a site several times over a period, clearly interested in a certain product or product range, without committing to a purchase. It would be short-sighted policy to write off such a potential customer. Once you identify their convincer strategy, you can customize either Web pages (as with Yahoo, Line One etc) or the sequence of hypertext links accordingly.

Similar considerations apply when time is a factor. In this case a site visitor might turn up after several weeks and make an immediate purchase. The period of time, for careful weighing of the pros and cons, and the built-in period for allowing a change of mind, is all the person needs before making a commitment. It follows that when identifying Meta Programs is based on site visits and purchase transactions, you will need time to identify a 'period of time' customer. Patience, or, more specifically, a long-term view, is an important mind to mind message to learn. But once you accept the principle of lifetime share of customer, the time spent in obtaining this valuable information will present no dilemma. It will also give you a competitive advantage over suppliers working to a shorter time horizon, or not concerned how their customers actually think.

By the same reckoning it would be unnecessary to incorporate repeats and a period of time into the communication in the case of an automatic buyer. They might get annoyed at diversions, and what makes sense for another customer might be counterproductive. An automatic buyer just wants price and ordering information and no hassle or delay. Similarly, a consistent convincer type would not be immediately linked to a shopping trolley, but would be invited to make comparisons, get further information, and perhaps see reviews from other customers.

Meta Programs may be at the Life Content level, or they may apply to a narrower range of behaviour such as the convincer strategy, which might relate to decision making and buying. Together, and with the programmes you will meet in the next chapter, these Meta Programs open the mind of your customer at several levels and reveal a disarmingly true perspective on their behaviour.

8

Keys to the customer's mind

The Meta Programs you have met so far are universal and generic and lend themselves to better mass marketing as well as individual customer communication. The right–left brain distinction reflects actual neurophysiological characteristics – the physical halves of the brain. Sensory preference involves, at least partly, the physical input mechanisms of the senses. The Life Content Meta Programs are equally universal, and you will find that any customer need or want can be classified in this simple way. But these Life Content biases are not so much associated with any brain or sensory physiology, as with the *neurology* of all these physiological systems – what happens in the cortex of the brain that produces a person's unique understanding. Mind to mind segmentation can thus be based on physiologic, sensory or cognitive features – any aspect of the customer's mind.

A customer's 'experience' comprises externally and internally generated sensory representations over a lifetime. By structuring experience into discrete Meta Programs, we can start to understand individual customers and use the information for better marketing.

If you are new to segmenting in this way, or indeed new to relationship marketing, you have more than enough to think about in the few Meta Programs I have already described. But Meta Programs cover a far wider range of ways of thinking than these. For example, we can add typical attitudes such as optimism and pessimism, or introversion and extroversion. These are the sorts of personality dimensions described by psychologist Karl Jung, which appear in several profiles such as the Myers Briggs Type Indicator. As well as these better-known Meta Programs we can add values and personality characteristics such as:

- acting independently – being your own person;
- enjoying trying out new experiences – a pioneer;
- being easy going – 'live and let live';
- being tolerant;
- being outspoken and an independent thinker;
- being respectful;
- being careful and conservative;
- being intense and of strong opinions;
- seeing the 'big picture';
- seeing the detail;
- not giving offence;
- being a follower rather than a leader.

As we move down a sort of hierarchy of thinking programs, generic, universal characteristics become more unique to a certain type of person. Right- or left-brain dominance, for instance, embraces a large part of the whole population. An auditory sensory preference embraces a smaller proportion, being based on one of five senses yet more prevalent than touch and smell in communication, but less prevalent than the visual sense. Similarly, a far smaller part of the population will value the idea of being first, trying new things and ideas, or being pioneering and adventurous, for example. Yet there is little doubt that these well-known characteristics will form a big enough segment of the population to represent a viable market segment. Each may be of greater value, for instance, than income category, age or where a customer lives, the sort of demographic classification that is presently used.

But even if the psychographic category does not seem large enough for mass marketing, no such dilemma exists in the case of one to one marketing. In this case we need to respond to individual rather than modal characteristics. There is no need to treat the characteristics as market segments. They are simply the non-standard customer information the corner shopkeeper possessed about his or her customers before supermarkets took over.

In this chapter we will consider some of these other Meta Programs. These offer further examples of the way that you can understand and identify different customer thinking styles. Each can give you a marketing edge in terms of long-term relationships and customer loyalty.

INTERNAL–EXTERNAL REFERENCE

You will have noticed how some people seem to depend upon outside recognition for their motivation and pleasure. If they do a good job they expect someone to recognize and acknowledge it. Indeed, their measure of success may well depend upon such recognition. If silence or neutrality follows their behaviour, they may construe it as a failure. Recognition, for them, however, may not mean material reward. Often all they need is a simple acknowledgement or psychological 'stroking' – perhaps a 'well done' or 'thank you'. The important distinction is that their success or achievement reference is external to them. They measure themselves against other people, or standards other than their own intrinsic ones.

Similarly you have probably come across people who don't need this sort of recognition. It is enough for them if they consider a job well done. They measure against their own standards whatever those standards are and are not continually looking for the praises of others. They are not concerned with the proverbial Jones's. If someone does not value an action or behaviour that they intrinsically value they will typically consider that as the other person's problem. So they can happily work on their own on long tasks, without regular feedback. As customers, what they buy need not require approval of others. They set and adhere to their own values.

Each customer is motivated differently, and falls somewhere along this spectrum of internal–external reference, one according to the implicit hope of receiving praise and recognition, the other in the implicit pleasure in a job they feel they have done well. Others lie somewhere in between.

It is not difficult, once you realize this important difference in Meta Program, to decide how to motivate each respective kind of person. 'So-and-so will be very impressed if you get this done on time' will not do much for an internal reference person who does not value so-and-so's praise. Similarly, an external reference person is the last person you should entrust with a succession of tasks for which they have to use their initiative and carry on from one to the next without measurement, feedback or recognition. In fact, such a person does not know *how* to measure internally, so cannot motivate themselves to take other than a routine job through to a successful conclusion. They need someone to 'hold their hand'. However, the distinction is not to do with ability or intelligence. Rather, it concerns how each person is motivated differently to achieve an outcome or make a decision. Each will perform as well as the other given that one is 'stroked' and the other is left free to get on with the job in their own way.

ELICITING INTERNAL–EXTERNAL CHARACTERISTICS

Meta Programs do not operate in a vacuum, but in relation to some aspect of our lives, behaviour or values. Thus, they are best elicited, not as abstract personality traits, but as examples of what we would do or think in certain real-life situations that we can easily imagine. The same applied to eliciting values, which we covered in Chapter 2. Any responses a person gives to questions of interest will not just help to identify their values, but will also help to identify their Meta Programs.

For instance, valuing and respecting other people, and being mindful of their opinions and feelings, will suggest an externally rather than internally focused person. Similarly, values concerning 'independence', 'leadership', 'single-mindedness' and a 'sense of purpose' probably indicate an internally motivated person. Because we each run a number of Meta Programs, any such response will give insight into those programmes. That is, into how we think. This is useful data in a mind to mind relationship strategy. Through ongoing interactive information gathering, we can identify an individual's profile of mental strategies. This will be strengthened and refined over time, as information is incrementally obtained.

THE MARKETING MESSAGE

An internal or external bias, as with any Meta Program, readily translates into a marketing or sales message. External 'references' or yardsticks, to measure success or achievement against, apply also to making decisions, including buying decisions. Some people need outside support for their decisions and buying behaviour. This may come from people, or from logic and reasons that will stand up to scrutiny in the eyes of the world – that is, externally. Others happily make their own decisions, on whatever basis, and have no problem in internally justifying them. They don't even need reasons, as such, as they see themselves as only answerable to themselves.

You may notice from these examples that the 'external reference' person is similar to the 'relating' disposition in the Life Content model. Similar communication rules indeed apply to them, but there are distinct differences.

In some cases an introverted, non-relating person, although not bothered about working on their own, nevertheless demands some external reference. They might appreciate a simple written 'thank you', or some formalized system of appraisal and recognition that does not involve too much people contact. Their external recognition may amount to salary level, treated as an objective measure of their career success. A Life Content 'having/getting' person will want some tangible evidence, while a 'being' person will be glad to *be* well organized, a good secretary, or whatever.

Conversely, an extroverted person, although enjoying working with people, may not depend on them for the value they place on a task or project. However much they enjoy being with people, their basic self-esteem and positive motivation keep them succeeding from task to task. In other words, relating, as a Life Content characteristic, does not necessarily equate with the need for external recognition.

When it comes to buying, an introvert may not require family and social acquaintances to support their buying decision, and may not even communicate it to them. But he or she may nevertheless want the approval of a mentor or other outside figure of respect or authority. That is, an external reference that does not involve people intercourse and close relationships.

Introversion–extraversion is just one of many Meta Program dimensions, of course, and other programmes may throw light on, or verify, a programme such as internal or external reference.

Once you know which style your customer tends towards, it will be easy to frame a marketing message. The marketing power lies in the information, and the understanding of the customer you gain from it, rather than in technical advertising know-how. It is possible to go through magazine or other advertisements and quickly categorize them into either internal or external reference, neutral – that aspect of the market audience is not addressed at all – or messages that address both tendencies. As it happens, addressing both tendencies, as a deliberate policy, is very rare (as compared, for instance, with appealing to both left and right brain as we have seen), even though mass advertisers have no idea of the bias of their market audience. Advertisers mostly appeal to externally rather than internally referenced people, hence the recourse to big-name references and multiple endorsements. This perhaps reflects a tendency dominant in advertising executives themselves.

Examples of either tendency will suggest how you can communicate with an individual customer on a one to one basis. This will multiply the impact of the message, of course. But, just as there are good and bad ads that get very different hit rates, in the same way you will get a better response with a better, more creative message. In other words, it depends on how you use the information you have, and how well you match the customer's mind.

You will notice that these and other Meta Programs overlap. When applied in a one to one marketing approach, the more specifically you can target your customer, the better you will match them with your message. And you have the advantage of synergy in that several over-lapping programmes are taken into account.

RISK TAKER/CONSERVATIVE

In the earlier short list I referred briefly to the independent, pioneering, adventurous person. This Meta Program category is usually referred to as a 'risk taker' as against the more timid or conservative person. A simple close comparison is leader/follower, not necessarily in terms of leading people, but rather leading or following in ideas, decisions and action.

You have no doubt met the person who is attracted to any kind of novelty – a new product, new system, gadgets, a new holiday location or whatever – even new partners. They don't shrink from the unknown. They like the inherent risks in being a pioneer, and thrive on the buzz of constant uncertainty and change. They are baffled by people who take their holidays at the same place year after year, just as they cannot envisage ever buying the same model of car a second time, however reliable it has been.

You can just as easily picture the opposite, cautious personality, always aiming for least risk and tending to follow the masses for 'safety in numbers'. They will tend to test things before commitment, wanting references, accreditation, a pedigree, continuity and consistency – anything but risk and the unfamiliar. 'It's our fifth Nissan', or 'we are off to the holiday cottage again this year' is the sort of comment you expect to hear. Such people can be very loyal to major brands once they have created a buying habit, so they respond well to properly directed marketing messages. But they are not guinea pigs. Don't push an innovative product on to them.

AN EXAMPLE

Keeping to the earlier encyclopaedia example so that you can make comparisons with the other Meta Programs, the same generic product (a set of books) can be marketed and thus perceived in very different ways.

On the one hand you could emphasize the:

- novel aspects of the product;
- new technology incorporated;
- different style and layout;
- all-new, easy to use index;

and any other 'first' you can think of.

'Be the first in your neighbourhood to experience this all-new series.' 'Take a parent's lead in giving your children all the wealth of the information age.' And so on.

Conversely, the encyclopaedia:

- is the 'real thing';
- uses the 1790 centenary cover design;
- is just as important a part of a home as it has been over generations;
- is tried and tested;
- is always dependable;
- is 'original';
- has been the market leader for 100 years.

'So, why take risks?' And so on.

SELLING PERCEPTIONS OF BENEFIT

We have seen that products and services are sold on perceptions. And perceptions are simply whatever is in the eye (or, literally, the mind) of the beholder (customer). This raises the question of what constitutes a benefit, and what doesn't. Dependability is not necessarily a benefit to a person who doesn't want to be seen as conservative and cautious. Yet it is certainly perceived as a benefit by a 'dependable' sort of person. Even a basic understanding of these different ways of thinking will enable you to adopt a mind to mind approach, and to identify and communicate real benefits. The risk taker/cautious distinction can be applied whether you are communicating a product function, features or benefits, or any invisible attributes of the Total Product that might appeal to such a person.

Untargeted advertising messages, however creative they seem, may be at odds with your customers' well-entrenched mindsets, or Meta Programs. Once you know how they 'tick', however, you can communicate perception or understanding that you know reflects their own mental language. You know it will 'make sense'.

In everyday life, once we know a person's disposition, say in terms of risk taking or conservatism, we instinctively allow for that disposition, whether in the case of a spouse, child or close work colleague. In this way, rather than relying on luck, or the heartaches of experience that relationships involve, we can consciously and optimally achieve our different outcomes. In other words, we take the other person into consideration in order to achieve our own ends. We know it works best that way. Moreover, the more we understand the person's mind – how they tick – the better we are at relating to them. The same mind to mind common sense applies in marketing, if we are to establish a long-term profitable relationship.

From a marketing viewpoint the real significance of this knowledge comes when we purposely identify and incorporate this knowledge as part of a customer relationship strategy. The sheer potential of using and developing psychographic segments starts to account for the increasing interest in relationship marketing, and the increasing redundancy of classical marketing models.

TOWARDS OR AWAY FROM

We all tend to move towards pleasure and away from pain, as a natural and basic human trait. Both tendencies act as motivators to behaviour. I refer of course to our *perception* of pleasure and pain. As the saying goes, 'One man's meat is another man's poison.' For present purposes, one man's pleasure is another man's pain. So this pleasure–pain human tendency is not confined to physical, sensory characteristics. We can as readily experience a positive or negative state of mind, or a pleasant or distasteful emotion. A person, or bank overdraft, can induce 'pain', and we can gain pleasure from doing a good job or solving a purely mental problem.

Like other 'hardwired' human characteristics, such as the will to survive, this is a trait we all share. It therefore differs in this respect from the preferences we have already considered (such as sensory preference) which, as individuals, we may not share, or at least experience only to different degrees. As such, pain–pleasure would not form a market 'segment'. In effect, we need the person's strategy, or programme, for experiencing pleasure and pain. What do they feel, do, say, think, etc that translates into pleasure and pain?

But there is another pleasure–pain distinction that does provide a basis both for market segmentation and individual customer profiling. Some people have more of a tendency to move towards pleasure than away from pain, while others have a tendency to move away from pain rather than towards pleasure. The distinction is important. One is more focused on the positive and where they are heading, while the other is focused on the negative and what they are trying to get away from. One, if you like, looks *forward* to the pleasure, the other looks *behind* to the pain. They both move away from pain and towards pleasure, but with a completely different focus. Psychologically they are headed, or at least facing, in different directions. Both are motivated, but not to the same extent.

It has been found that there is greater motivation in heading towards a goal than in avoiding an unwanted outcome. There are a few exceptions, such as in the discipline of a wartime environment when fear (of 'pain', however perceived) may be the predominant motivator. The other exception, important for our purposes, is the person who is strongly 'away from', motivated more by the fear of pain than by the anticipation of pleasure. They are (meta) programmed that way and speak the 'language' of pain avoidance. In their case, an 'away from' sales message, for instance, would have more impact than a 'towards' message.

This distinction has also been confirmed when applying well-known goal achievement criteria, such as SMART (usually Specific, Measurable, Achievable, Realistic, Timely – or similar model). It seems we have more chance of getting what we want than not getting what we don't want. Strangely, when asked what they want, many people respond in terms of what they don't want. These, of course, you will now recognize as 'away from' people.

In addressing the Life Content model in the previous chapter I suggested that you write a list of goals, desires and hopes as a basis for identifying the different ways you classify your outcomes according to that model. You can use the same list to illustrate this Meta Program. Just note whether the outcomes are towards or away from. This usually becomes clear as you restate your goal in different ways – that is, using different, but instinctive rather than carefully chosen, words to express your meaning.

POSITIVE OR NEGATIVE

Let me illustrate this further in terms of, say, career or job goals. If asked about their career intentions a person's response might be:

> Well, I've never wanted to be stuck in accounts, and I am not too keen on being in a large company. To be honest, I don't like working in a hierarchy with too many bosses and people checking on me. In any case I think I would like to get away from this district, my wife has never really settled. And, yes, I don't want to be tied to a fixed salary, or rigid office hours.

Note the *away from* bias in these responses. Alternatively, the reply might be something like:

> I want to get a section head job in the next couple of years. I am determined to start on my advanced certificate course in the summer. My aim then is to go self-employed as I enjoy working on my own and having flexibility. I will coincide this with moving to North Yorkshire.

The first person may have been no less career conscious or ambitious, but went about his outcome in a negative way, avoiding the possible pain rather than relishing the possible pleasure. In most situations a positive viewpoint is more effective in achievement, as generations of positive thinking will support. As we saw earlier when referring to wartime situations, the exception is in crisis or life and death situations where fear is a real survival mechanism. That's of little relevance to a normal buying–selling transaction. But for an individual person with an 'away from' bias, an 'away from' marketing strategy will be more effective.

The product *per se* does not change. But to communicate the Total Product we need to keep restating the message. So an insurance policy will, on the one hand, mean *avoiding* poverty, dependence, destitution; and on the other hand, *gaining* security, peace of mind, and bliss in the twilight years. As with other Meta Programs, a mismatched marketing message will have the effect of a foreign language, and will often be counterproductive to the intended sale, and certainly to any lasting relationship. You won't scare someone who doesn't know what 'scaring' means in this 'pain' context. Nor will you please or pacify a person who only thinks in terms of avoiding fear. But speak in a way they understand – towards or away from – and you have discovered yet another mind to mind hot button.

These are just examples, of course, and in practice most people will have a mixture of towards and away from outcomes, depending on the situation. But there is often a bias one way or the other, and this is what creates a distinct way of thinking or Meta Program. By identifying this bias in your customer, and communicating accordingly, you will establish a special relationship and gain a marketing edge.

MATCHER OR MISMATCHER

People sort out facts and information in different ways. For instance, some people sort in terms of what things have in common, while others notice differences and exceptions. On the one hand a person might notice a general tendency or trend, and on the other hand another person might easily notice exceptions, or the odd one out. One is a matcher, and the other is a mismatcher. The matcher tends to think in generalities or commonalities, whilst the mismatcher thinks in specifics and detail. One will conclude that the latest model of a car is more or less the same, in design specification and such. The other will quickly spot the two or three differences between them, apparently not aware that it is fundamentally the same car.

These thinking types are either–or, as with 'towards' and 'away from', and also form a continuum in terms of degree of bias. Once again, either way of thinking lends itself to a personalized marketing message – on the one hand emphasizing what is the same, and on the other hand emphasizing what is different. You will notice the comparison with the risk taker/conservative distinction. Most of these mental programmes overlap in some way. However, as we saw when comparing the external reference type with the 'relating' Life Content, they are not necessarily correlated in a significant way.

POSSIBILITY OR NECESSITY

Some people are motivated by what is necessary rather than by what is possible. They will tend to do things because they're obliged to, rather than because they positively want to. 'Necessity' types will often accept rule and authority figures whereas possibility types tend to act more independently. As with other mental programmes, each responds to the language of their style and to people or companies who seem to share their view of life. The language is simple: in the first case you *should* or *must*, and in the second case you *can*.

In advertising messages, the inference of authority can be strong. In other words, the importance of complying with a law, custom, more or authority figure. 'You need to do this straight away.'

You may see a link with the externally motivated person, the cautious, conservative person, and with the 'away from' personalities we met earlier. To communicate with a 'necessity' person, you don't, in fact, have to establish any real authority, or justify why something is necessary. They do the job for you. All you need to do is communicate in the appropriate language, using words such as should, must, obliged, necessary, ought, need to, required etc. That language 'makes sense' to the person, so will form an effective communication. Similarly, 'possibility', 'you can' language will appeal to the 'possibility' person.

PERSONALITY PROFILES

I referred in the introduction to the use of personality profiles as psychographic market segments. These are used increasingly for conventional market segmentation, typically in addition to basic demographic data. I referred to such classifications as 'swingers'. These are broad classifications established by market researchers to add a psychographic element to market segmentation. They are an obvious attempt to incorporate the customer's mind into the marketing process. However, these apply to modal rather than real customers. They are part of the search for perfect, representative customers who will reflect large populations of real customers. They may well be more valid as market segments, but they do not begin to help in a one to one situation. As we saw earlier, real customers bear little relationship to contrived stereotypes of the 2.4 children kind.

Indeed, nothing could make a customer less unique than being grouped with a few hundred million others who happen to fit the same broad psychographic characteristics.

Having said this, psychographic profiles are being used widely, and on balance have added a lot to market segmentation as far as mass marketing is concerned. They probably have more relevance to their constituent customers' buying habits than would be predicted by demographic data such as address and socio-economic ranking. But even in a mass marketing context, they present some insurmountable difficulties. At best, they are not standard in any way. The name labels themselves are many and varied, and their constituent characteristics even more so. This means that they cannot be used for competitive purposes. For instance, it would be impossible to determine which categories had been lost to a major competitor, unless that competitor happened to segment in the same way.

Basic demographic data such as postal code and income level, whatever their predictive validity, don't suffer from such a handicap. Validity is another main difficulty. Most of the psychographic profiles are not recognized outside the market research organizations that promote them and their enthusiastic clients.

No doubt many of the components of a personality profile are valid customer characteristics. Thus, if they were applied to individual customers, identified, and used for communication, they would no doubt result in some of the benefits of one to one marketing I have already outlined. However, as total personality profiles they can never fulfil a one to one function, any more than a complete modal demographic caricature (with 2.4 children, 1.2 cars and 2.6 bedrooms) has any probability of matching a real, unique person.

PROPRIETARY PROFILES

The Myers Briggs Type Indicator is a widely used personality test. It is based on the Jungian personality factors:

introvert   extravert

sensing   intuitive

thinking   feeling

judging   perceiving

This gives an overall personality profile according to a single question-naire so will not lend itself to incremental, flexible customer data gath-ering of the sort that a one to one relationship can usually elicit. Even if customers were inclined to complete the whole instrument, important dimensions such as sensory preference are missed. Moreover, *ad hoc* information gained about customers over a period could not be matched to a standardized, total personality profile. On the other hand one-off bits of information (such as gained from telephone complaints, for instance) can be easily slotted into a range of different Meta Programs.

The same applies to other profiles such as the PSI (Personal Style Inventory), the Reading Style Inventory, the Grasha-Reichmann Student Learning Style Scales, the LSI (Learning Style Indicator), the HBDI (Herrmann Brain Dominance Instrument), to name just a few. In any event, some of these are proprietary, licensed instruments and their use may not be economical in a commercial setting. Most important, however, the principle of mind to mind marketing means an ongoing relationship that the seller manages. The information needed, information-gathering methods and Meta Programs are decided, generated and maintained by the seller. The emphasis is on getting to know the customer better over a period rather than adhering to a particular brand of personality measurement. The purpose, of course, is to predict buying and loyalty behaviour rather than learning, lead-ership or any other personality characteristics.

LIFESTYLE CLUSTERING

Psychographic segmentation is big business within market research, and growing bigger. 'Lifestyle clustering' is one example. A research company will superimpose on your own (demographic) database related psychographic criteria based on several national sources, such as motor registrations, buying habits within postal districts, census data, etc. If you have a large database this will allow you to segment your catchment area according to similar profiles around the country, and thus predict purchasing behaviour. For instance, you could focus mail shots more accurately and vary the content based on a postal codes reflection of a lifestyle category. Along with the list you get a few lines of description of each lifestyle category. For a fee, you can get a much more detailed description of each cluster's customer predominant character-istics, education and occupation, with a short description of their lifestyle, media and product purchasing preferences.

If you don't have a database you can buy localized lists that will give you similar information. Or you can buy industry-specific lists, again based on national industry-related databases. 'Clustering' is based on averages, of course. So the larger your target population (or the more you can spend on a bigger list), the greater the chance of its mirroring large-scale, significant national statistics. Similarly, the greater the chance of correlation between demographic characteristics and lifestyle – 'lifestyle' in this context mainly meaning buying habits.

Lifestyle clustering is a good example of market research bending towards psychographic data. But it serves mass markets only, and does not attempt to serve one to one suppliers. Even less does it reflect the customer's – even a stereotypical, modal customer's – mind. Clusters totalling millions do not contain a single real person.

PROFILE PROFILES

How do personality profiles figure in the mind to mind marketing paradigm I have outlined? How do they fit the important trends of one to one customer relationships and mass customization of products and services? I will address these questions by examples of actual profiles.

VALS

VALs is one of the best-known psychographic profiles. It classifies all Americans into lifestyle categories within three main groups.

Principle oriented

Fulfilleds
These have little interest in image or prestige. They are above-average consumers of products for the home. They like educational and public affairs programming, and read widely and often.

Believers
These buy American, are slow to change habits and look for bargains. They watch TV more than average and read retirement, home and garden, and general interest magazines.

Status oriented

Achievers
Achievers are attached to premium products, but are a prime target for a variety of products. They are average TV watchers and read business, news and self-help publications.

Strivers
Typically image-conscious strivers have limited discretionary incomes, but carry credit balances. They spend on clothing and personal care products and prefer TV to reading.

Action oriented

Experiencers
This type follows fashion and spends much of their disposable income on socializing. They tend to buy on impulse, attend to advertising and listen to rock music.

Makers
Makers shop for comfort, durability and value. They are unimpressed by luxuries and buy the basics. They listen to radio, and read auto, home mechanics, fishing and outdoor magazines.

Strugglers
These are brand loyal, use coupons and watch out for sales. They trust advertising and watch TV often. They read tabloids and women's magazines.

Here are a few of the VALs 2 questionnaire statements I chose at random as examples:

- I am really interested in only a few things.
- I like to try new things.
- I like a lot of excitement in my life.
- I would like to understand more about how the universe works.

These are rated on the usual sort of scale:

mostly disagree   somewhat disagree   somewhat agree   mostly agree

Notice that the questions don't require mental gymnastics and are relatively unobtrusive to the average customer, who likes talking or writing about him- or herself anyway. Notice also that these implicit questions would have been equally applicable to some of the Meta Programs we have already covered. In other words, you don't need a proprietary batch of questions to rate a customer according to each main Meta Program. On the contrary. Little bits of information, whether answers to specific questions or gained in the course of the whole seller–buyer communication, will almost always slot into the range of psychographic information that will help to form a relationship database.

PAD

The PAD – Pleasure, Arousal, Dominance – temperament model is a well-known personality profile. This is based on wide research that identified three nearly independent dimensions of emotional states, all of which affect customers' buying habits as well as every other behaviour.

- The *pleasure–displeasure* dimension distinguishes positive versus negative emotional states. We have already discussed the importance of pleasure and pain as human motivators.
- *Arousal–non-arousal* refers to a combination of physical activity and mental alertness.
- *Dominance–submissiveness* is defined in terms of control versus lack of control.

Well-known personality traits and states of mind can be mapped on to this three-axis model. For instance:

- 'Angry' is a highly unpleasant, highly aroused, and moderately dominant emotional state.
- 'Sleepy' is a moderately pleasant, extremely unaroused, moderately submissive state.
- 'Bored' is typically highly unpleasant, highly unaroused, and moderately submissive.

Arousability measures the strength of a person's emotional reactions to either a positive or negative situation. Other psychographic labels based on the PAD model are:

Exuberant (+ P + A + D) vs Bored (– P – A – D)

Dependent (+ P + A – D) vs Disdainful (– P – A + D)

Relaxed (+ P – A + D) vs Anxious (– P + A – D)

Docile (+ P – A – D) vs Hostile (– P + A + D)

This scale has the advantage of ordinary language we understand, rather than 'baby-boomer' type folk labels. It is also better validated than most commercial market research classifications, being used in clinical and other experimental settings. However, emotional states, being relatively ephemeral, are far less valid than other more permanent personality traits of the sort we have discussed.

COLOUR

I referred in Chapter 6 to the importance of colour as part of a customer's sensory preference. As it happens, psychographic groups have been applied to colour also.

- *Colour Forward* shoppers are typically young and ethnic, or higher income, better-educated women over 45 who see themselves as fashion savvy.
- *Colour Prudents* comprise the mainstream of the population. By the time they accept a new colour, it has already passed from trendy to mass market.
- *Colour Loyals* resist colour changes. Millions of dollars of design work and store refurbishment can be wasted on them.

As with any psychographic classifications, these will bear little relation to demographic groupings. For instance, although income is a factor in one subgroup of Colour Forwards, it generally bears no relationship to a person's colour reactions. Nor does education and social background. Yet within the groups identified, buying behaviour can be strongly predicted. For example, three very different outlets – a French magazine, a US catalogue and an ice cream brand – all appealed to Colour Forward consumers. Incidentally, children are more visual than adults. In many cases the colour of a food is more important than its taste. Children also tend to like colours that repel their parents, so there is a generational element somewhere. We saw in Chapter 6 the extraordinary effect of colour on detergent promotion and packaging.

BENEFITS PROFILING

Earlier we discussed the importance of perceived benefits. These are
usually more appealing than product features, as was illustrated in the
Total Product Concept. So-called benefit segmentation is another
example of psychographic grouping. One benefits segmentation
profile comprises the:

- worriers;
- sociables;
- sensory segment;
- independent segment.

In this case the significance of the classification is in the way different
kinds of customers attribute different importance to different attributes
and benefits in the same product. For instance, a toothpaste can offer the
benefits of decay prevention and brightness of teeth, having the attributes
of, say, flavour, appearance and price. In this example, worriers and the
sensory segment went for decay prevention, flavour and appearance.
Sociables and independents went for brightness of teeth and price.

Other benefit segmentation studies have produced the:

- status seeker;
- swinger;
- conservative;
- rational person;
- inner directed person;
- hedonist.

There is little point in adding the descriptors. They turn out to be
similar to a dozen other commercial or private classifications. None is
sufficiently validated or standardized to be useful in any general way.
And when it comes to one to one marketing, no real customer will fit a
stereotype anyway, except by accident. The so-called average
consumer, upon which profiles are based, tells us more about the minds
of the originating market researchers than the minds of customers.

PC PROFILES

Dell computers used to define PC market segments according to where
computers were used, such as in the home, in small businesses and
such. It now looks at five segments based on the type of user:

- *techno-boomers*, or neophyte users with a priority on ease-of-use features;
- *techno to go* users with little patience for sales pitches, who simply want a computer in a box;
- *techno-teamers* who work as part of a network and need both the right hardware and software;
- *techno-critical* users whose work is in demanding environments where the best available equipment is essential;
- *techno-wizards* who are leading-edge users always focused on the newest features.

This illustrates that just by thinking a little deeper about the customer – who, in this case, is more than a place – you can market better. It also illustrates the shortcomings of mass segmentation. Techno-wizards may well be interested in the same product features, but, being individual people, they have different personalities and hot buttons, and may perceive benefits in a very different way.

The mind to mind marketing message is simply that any one of several personality factors might affect a techno-wizard's buying decision more than the factors that make him or her a techno-wizard. More generally, this sort of segmentation is still heavily product-related, rather than focused on the customer. That is always a sign that the mass marketing paradigm reigns.

9

The corporate mind

The corporate mind is the seller or supplier's mind. This is the other 'mind' in a mind to mind relationship. It is the subject of my book *Corporate Charisma* (Piatkus), which addresses what I call 'corporate personality'. That book showed how to create a corporate 'personality' and appeal to a chosen psychographic market segment, and the Meta Programs of individual customers described in the previous chapters. It shows also how a customer segment can be chosen to best reflect an existing corporate personality and culture. Mind to mind matching can multiply the effectiveness of your marketing message and give your company personality power.

PERSONALITY POWER

Customers' perceptions usually apply at a corporate as well as product level. You will recall from the mind to mind 'like' principle that they respond positively to organizations and people they deem to be like themselves. When establishing a corporate personality you can:

- Emulate the personality type of your chosen customer segments to 'be like them' – and thus create rapport and a quasi-personal relationship.

- Decide upon your own personality and attract customers to yourself using the one to one methods we have already met. As we have seen, an initial sale (winning customers) is not as important as the relationship you build over a period (keeping customers). Focusing on this fact will tend to attract 'like' customers, and thus foster a mind to mind relationship.
- Amend your personality with a view to making it more attractive and, with a view, more specifically, to attracting more customers than you lose.

CORPORATE PERSONALITY

Companies such as IBM, Marks & Spencer, British Airways and the Virgin group have heavily branded corporately, and created a 'personality' in addition to specific product brands. In some cases a very distinctive corporate image evolves. This may be linked with a charismatic leader such as Richard Branson of Virgin, a long-succeeded founder such as Fred Smith of Federal Express, or a strong internal culture, for instance. But it typically occurs without a positive, conscious corporate 'personality' strategy. Even mission and vision statements are a relatively new business phenomenon.

In fact, every organization has a personality in the eyes of customers or people who have heard about it in any way. If it hasn't, it might soon acquire one by default. As we have seen, these personalities simply match individual personalities, or the 'mind' of customers (see Figure 9.1). Appendix B shows the great variety of perceptions people have about companies and products.

A big enough individual personality, such as Fred Smith at Federal Express or Lord Sieff at Marks & Spencer, can have a dramatic effect both on the internal culture of the businesses and also on public perceptions. Leaders come and go, of course. Each new personality will not readily sit well in a handed-down culture, although a company culture can be hard to change. Customer perceptions change over time, and, as far as the seller company is concerned, usually by default. They are rarely managed and even more rarely managed as a one to one marketing strategy in the way I have described. In the same way, a corporate personality has to be managed strategically, over the long term. It is too important to leave to chance, or to the charisma of an ephemeral leader.

In some cases corporate personalities have been deliberately changed. In a retail environment this might be achieved by a complete

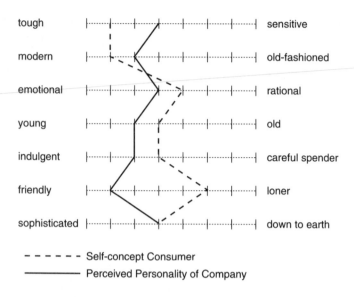

tough ┤- - - - - - - - - - - - - - - - - ├ sensitive

modern ┤- - - - - - - - - - - - - - - - - ├ old-fashioned

emotional ┤- - - - - - - - - - - - - - - - - ├ rational

young ┤- - - - - - - - - - - - - - - - - ├ old

indulgent ┤- - - - - - - - - - - - - - - - - ├ careful spender

friendly ┤- - - - - - - - - - - - - - - - - ├ loner

sophisticated ┤- - - - - - - - - - - - - - - - - ├ down to earth

– – – – – – Self-concept Consumer

———— Perceived Personality of Company

Figure 9.1 Perceived personality and self concept

redesign of storefronts and interiors, perhaps a new logo and promotional campaign, linked with PR and maybe a boardroom clearout. In an airline it might include new aeroplane livery. All this is sensory stuff that evokes a reaction from customers and the public at large. This might be for better or worse, depending on taste and customers' own personalities. If you like, a 'quasi-mind' is established to which customers can relate in as near as possible to a human sort of way.

The more emotion that is included, the greater the potential for a strong personality, but the greater the risk of losing customers if you get it wrong. The change of tail design, for instance, on the British Airways fleet caused much venom among many previously loyal fliers. The memorable change of ingredients in Coke caused no less than an outcry, even from the non-faithful, and unprecedented public emotion.

BEHIND THE CORPORATE IMAGE

It is possible positively and strategically to establish and manage a unique and truly corporate personality, to which every person in the company adheres. You can communicate a single, long-term message to customers. Corporate personality is the seller's human interface with the mind and heart of the customer. It requires a consistent image, or public face, and a true, long-term personality, or identity, to back it up. Corporate branding will communicate that personality, as a strong product brand communicates its intangible benefits.

Little attention was paid to this aspect of corporate personality in the days of mass marketing. Image campaigns have been all too common, and in the short term they can influence customer perceptions. But image is frequently a façade for a true personality that shrewd customers soon come to recognize in their various contacts with the company and its human representatives. They see through the corporate façade, if you like. In the end, it's what lies behind the public face that will determine a mind to mind relationship.

The seller's soul

As the customer himself or herself becomes more 'personified' as part of a one to one marketing process, the seller corporation will similarly have to bear its true 'soul'. In other words, what it is really like as a supplier, manufacturer, deliverer, promiser and so on. Faceless, impersonal institutions don't do well in the marketing league tables, however technically good their products or however superior their customer service. On the other hand, a human-type relationship can evoke loyalty and strong, human emotions. A company has to have its own *mind* behind any PR façade. Indeed, sooner or later, it has to *make up*, and sometimes *change*, its mind.

The marketing challenge is to create a supplier mind that understands and reflects the minds of its customers, and at the same time encapsulates the minds of its employees. Not every customer will relate to a given corporate personality, any more than two people will naturally hit it off. But those that do will be more loyal and profitable over a lifetime. We all have different personalities, and on the whole we get on together. The real problem occurs with a so-called split personality – a person who is 'two-faced', hypocritical and so on. In other words, people don't like incongruence between the personality displayed and the real person we come to know that lies behind. In the same way, a corporation can be forgiven for not fitting every type of customer, but not for living a lie.

Merging minds

Projecting a single personality is not an easy proposition, for the simple reason that a corporation comprises many individuals who each portray a different attitude and personality. They are as diverse and unique as their customers. There is no such thing as a corporate mind, of course – a company is just a legal entity. But there may be hundreds or thousands of *employees'* minds. That's where coherent corporate personality strategy and training become vital for mind to mind marketing to work.

Companies are becoming aware of the significance of top-level, consistent corporate branding. It is possible to identify and deliberately 'live out' the characteristics and culture you wish to communicate to staff, customers and the world. These characteristics are what, in a company's grass roots relationship with its customers, become the corporate 'mind' or 'heart'. Through a unifying vision, mission and values, these disparate minds within the seller organization can be synthesized into a consistent corporate culture and personality. And that, however it is treated on the balance sheet, is an invaluable asset to any business.

A CASE FOR CORPORATE PERSONALITY

There are several reasons why the seller needs to create a seller's 'mind' in the mind of the customer. In other words a corporate personality. I will outline these requirements in this section:

- creating perceived 'likeness';
- creating a true personality to differentiate you from the competition and avoid being labelled by default;
- attracting and keeping the best employees;
- creating pathways to the customer's mind to assist promotion and relationships.

CREATING PERCEIVED 'LIKENESS'

People like people more than things, or – worse – faceless organizations. They like a human touch. Otherwise they feel they cannot communicate their feelings, whether annoyance or pleasure. We tend to get frustrated at not being able to express ourselves, and this is often directed at a large, faceless organization.

People like, even more, people who are like them. Like attracts like. In particular, people associate with those who hold similar values and interests to themselves. A corporation, as well as a customer, can hold a value such as 'every individual is important and should always be given respect', and in this way they will establish like values with a like-minded customer. If likeness occurs in other ways – such as a perceived 'youthful', 'positive', 'outdoor type', company – so much the better. A more conservative person will relate more to a conservative supplier.

Creating 'perceived likeness' is part of a mind to mind strategy. By its nature, it involves both minds. In other words, there is little point in understanding your customer's mind if you are not ready to change your mind to meet them part way. Or there is no point in changing your corporate personality if it doesn't fit the sort of people to whom you are selling.

You can choose your own personality, culture, attitudes and mission. Companies are not born with a personality – they don't have genes. You can even choose to change your customer's mind by appropriate communication, and consistent behaviour that supports it. But it has to be a single mind to mind strategy. Neither mind – just like two ends of a piece of string – is more important than the other.

Mind to mind means matching. It's no use going for a conservative, older clientele if you are projecting a young, energetic, 'with it' image. If you have a well-established personality, you may be better choosing and grooming your customers to be like you rather than trying to change what you really are. Neither will happen automatically. Both approaches require knowledge and know-how, and a deliberate strategy. But the point about having a strategy is that you take control and manage your future rather than let it take control of you.

The aim is to align a customer's self-concept with their concept of you as a company. You will see from the hypothetical case in Figure 9.1 how these perceptions can be plotted. In this case they are reasonably well matched. A significant mismatch would signal the need for a specific strategy change programme.

CREATING A TRUE PERSONALITY

You can't fake true personality. As with individual customers, the seller's personality is a potentially unique feature of the business. Your competitors, for example, cannot begin to emulate a personality. By doing so they will be seen to be 'mimicking' and untrue to their own personality (which every organization has, knowingly or unknowingly). As we saw earlier, being two-faced, is the unpardonable corporate sin of hypocrisy.

Differentiating your personality

Companies now have wide access to information and technology. With increasing competition, it becomes more and more difficult for them to differentiate themselves and their products to create a competitive advantage. Personality offers a new opportunity that cannot be fully copied. Not only is there only one IBM or Marks & Spencer, but also there is only one so-and-so's small town grocery store, or any other business that has developed its own way of doing things and pattern of customer relationships. But opportunity also lies in the fact that so few companies are doing it in a strategic, effective way.

It's a mammoth task to position your business exactly in your customers' minds. One mistake on your part, one chat with a fellow customer, or some misunderstanding you will never be aware of, can lose you a hitherto loyal customer. The good news is that once you have created a true personality in the minds of your customers it will be hard to remove it. We are such creatures of habit, and reinforce our behaviour with more of the same, justifying it whether rationally or irrationally. In other words, a well-established personality will stand you in good stead, even in difficult times. It works just as with close friends who know each other well, and make allowances for each other's failings and idiosyncrasies.

A family is another useful mind to mind relationship analogy. Blood relationships are typically of the love–hate sort, like other intimate relationships. But when the going gets tough and you face a common enemy, a family closes ranks and displays an extraordinary mutual loyalty. What comes by blood relationship in the case of families has to be earned in the case of friends and colleagues, by rapport ('we really hit it off') and actual behaviour (deeds, not just words) over a period of time. That's the sort of mutual relationship that can develop between customers and suppliers.

Personality is an intangible asset that cannot be owned or emulated by competitors. The bottom line is that it's worth getting this right, and it makes sense to invest heavily in what is so crucial to your business.

Personality by default

You cannot not have a personality. This applies to companies as well as individuals. Even a bland person with 'no personality' is seen as just that. 'No personality' may mean an unattractive, insipid or weak personality. We are all perceived in some way or other, however unremarkable or nondescript. So you can't opt out, whether as an individual or a company. A retailer perceived to be old-fashioned and 'fuddy-duddy' rarely sets out to be seen in this light. On the contrary, they may see themselves as trendy and up-market, and seek to project such an image. The point is that every business has its traits, from the small-time store or trades person to the multinational giant. We 'own' a personality by default. This becomes apparent as you walk round a store, speak on the telephone to service staff, make a complaint and so on. Here are some ways in which corporate behaviour can influence how the customer perceives your 'mind' or personality:

Corporate behaviour	Possible perceived personality
Lots of promotions and discount campaigns	Unsophisticated, inferiority complex
Lots of advertising up-market	Extrovert, confident
Glossy advertising	Snobbish, rich
Premium pricing	Classy, sophisticated, somewhat aloof
Consistency of logos, lettering, design, written communications, etc	Reliable, trustworthy
Inconsistency of these	Changeable, shifty
Local sponsorships and community projects	Friendly, sensitive, caring
Mass, non-exclusive distribution	Roamer, 'Wherever I lay my hat...'
Exclusive, limited distribution	Concerned, principled
Promises not delivered	Cheat, untrustworthy
Good customer service	Caring
Poor customer service	Heartless

You can't hide your personality any more than a child becomes invisible by putting a blanket over his or her head. This offers an opportunity to even the smallest businesses. Small businesses can compete alongside the biggest on the Internet. All the world sees is a Web site, and the technology for doing a professional job is relatively cheap and widely available. But the opportunity lies in projecting a unique personality rather than in enjoying level playing fields with big timers. You don't have to do miracles to gain customers' loyalty. Market leaders can't do miracles anyway. You just have to come across as a trusted friend, and most people can do that if they put their minds to it and apply the Golden Rule: 'do unto others...'.

The chances are that if you do nothing about how you are perceived by customers you will come off worse than if you have a consistent strategy. That's a kind of Murphy's Law of business. Personality is not easy to achieve, but it is as controllable as product and service quality (they all involve people). You can do something about it. The first step is to understand its importance in marketing and business, the nature of the customer's mind and the corporation's quasi-mind, and the techniques for creating and managing a unique personality of your own.

Personality power: a national institution

Some of the most successful companies have grown on a 'personality'. Coke is one of the top brands in the world and its personality transcends national barriers and seems to get to the heart of its customers. Thus, an attempt to change the taste of the drink caused a massive reaction among faithful Coke drinkers. This was not so much a change of ingredients, as tampering with the very personality of Coke – a sort of family friend. In the US especially, the threat of a change touched emotions at a national level. It was a national institution rather than a soft, junk drink. It concerned values, memories and a valued way of life. Although Coke was acting on the best market research, research could not detect this important, unconscious personality dimension. From one perspective the change was a monumental corporate gaffe. Yet its personality saw the company through, and few enemies were created in the whole process. It is difficult to put a value on the amount of international PR that the new taste story generated. Sufficient to say that almost any level of investment could have been justified in creating such a robust personality in the place of an otherwise inanimate multinational group. When lifetime customer value comes first, market share will inevitably follow.

ATTRACTING THE BEST EMPLOYEES

An attractive corporate personality attracts employees as well as customers. In its early years IBM had almost cult status, and its employees were as recognizable as any logo as they proudly evangelized on behalf of their company. Competitors could spot an IBM salesperson at a distance – and before long so could customers. Such a strong culture results in low staff turnover, better morale and ultimately lower costs and higher profits. From a marketing point of view, it creates the important 'seller mind' in a mind to mind relationship.

Corporate personality is more than a name and an image. It is what lies behind the name and the public image. It can only be supported in the long run by actions. In other words, you have to walk the talk, do what you promise to do, and – most importantly – be consistent as between your different people, departments or functions.

The switch to knowledge-based, as compared with operational, processes is one example of the hurdle businesses face. Even getting salespeople to share information across the organization can present an insurmountable barrier. Staff attitudes as well as behaviour have to be retrained. Internal politics is another barrier. Who 'owns' the customer – customer service, marketing, sales people? Who is the relationship with? Companies that have already gone the re-engineering or similar route may have already adopted the multi-disciplinary culture essential for a single, seamless organizational focus on the customer. Others have a lot of relearning to do. Similarly, to change from an internally-focused perspective to an externally, customer-focused mindset requires a degree of change – at every level of the organization – that is not always understood in the excitement and rhetoric of the new customer era.

As well as the benefits of having a strong company identity, one to one strategies can equally apply between an employer and staff. Most firms give standard incentives to their staff such as stock options, salary rises etc. Some employees, however, value non-monetary benefits such as flexible time and personal control over their work. Not only are our needs and wants unique but they also change over time. So only a dynamic, one-to-one approach to compensation will give maximum mutual benefit, and loyalty.

PATHWAYS TO THE CUSTOMER'S MIND

The mind is multi-sensory and multi-channel. That means there are many ways in which you can influence the customer's mind. At the same time there are many ways in which you can relate to the customer by the way you establish your own corporate mind, or personality.

Some of these channels have been employed by advertisers and brand promoters for many years, so are quite familiar to us. However, as we have seen already, conventional marketing has usually been for boosting short-term sales, or (longer term) product brand awareness. It is rarely directed towards creating a corporate personality on the part of the supplier company, or of communicating with the mind of individual customers as a lifetime strategy. So enormous opportunities have been lost, especially when considering the large advertising budgets that have been ineffectively spent on mass marketing.

Promotional synergy

A well-established personality can enhance advertising and other promotion. Often an advertising campaign has short-term impact, and if it does not affect current sales it will be written off as expense. However, when advertising is consistent with personality, it can reinforce the personality and thus create long-term value in addition to any direct sales and market share. A personality theme gives rhyme and reason to what is often no more than hit-and-miss promotion.

As well as *ad hoc* sales promotion, personality can form part of any brand-building programme. Individual product brands that can be linked to a corporate brand – an overall identity or personality – will enjoy synergy for no extra cost or effort. For instance, the IBM corporate brand will support a product brand, such as a range of personal computers or a successful mainframe, while a successful product brand will enhance its parent company in the eyes of the customers. The inevitable synergy will mean a greater return on overall brand-building investment.

Personality branding

Positioning is about associations, so the general objective is to create the best associations with your company and products. As a simple example, KFC fast-fried chicken is strongly associated with Colonel Sanders, and thus with any associations he arouses. Thus, if the association is made strongly, and the Colonel is perceived positively (trusted, admired, etc), you will have created an important customer perception that will affect sales and loyalty. Even a fictional character, such as the Marlborough cowboy, will create a personality brand association. He is even depicted by an Asian actor in Asian commercials in order to get the right association.

Marks & Spencer has maintained its image for many years under leadership as different as Sir Richard Greenbury and Lord Sieff. The British Airways brand was probably affected by the reigns of Colin Marshal and Lord King, and less so by the dismissed scapegoat Bob Ayling.

There is no doubt about the effectiveness of big-name branding and sponsorship, as evidenced by the millions of pounds invested in sport and fashion advertising. This is simply the impact of *people* on the minds of customers, and it can play a very big part in mind to mind marketing. People can quickly arouse emotions, for better or worse. Get the right person, and you will create the right perception.

But it can work the wrong way, even when carefully choreographed. A change in the fortunes of a big star, or a moral fall from grace, can soon create counterproductive associations, as with the child abuse allegations against Michael Jackson. On balance, it is better to create and manage people associations than let them happen (as they will) by default. But you need to manage effectively, which is where a corporate personality strategy (the supplier end of the mind to mind relationship) comes into play.

Well-known people are not always deliberately used as brands as in the case of Colonel Sanders, Mr Kipling cakes and Remington's Victor ('I bought the company') Kiam. They just come as an association. For instance, Bill Gates just happens to own Microsoft and maybe does not intend to represent the brand, in the way that a Victor Kiam, or Richard Branson, the British owner of Virgin, does. But that doesn't stop the customer from making associations, and being influenced in their buying behaviour. So, depending on where Bill Gates lies in a customer's perception, Microsoft will be perceived accordingly. On the other hand, if Microsoft has a strong enough corporate brand image, this may supersede even a larger-than-life CEO or entrepreneur.

Non-people brand associations

Along with fictional characters you can add animals and children, such as cartoon character Peanuts, Tony the tiger and the Dulux sheep dog. All it needs is the ability to arouse human emotions, and the power of association.

Places also have emotional connotations for people. For instance, bottled water will typically be associated with some beautiful, fresh, pure mountain spring. An English village location will enhance a freshly baked bread brand. A twisting alpine road will provide a setting for a high performance car. On the other hand, the right place association might be a busy office or a great capital city of the world or a fictional place, whether Dickensian or sci-fi. A place can add realism both to a person already associated with a brand (as with Marlborough country, or Southern fried chicken) or the product or company itself.

Personality power in metaphors

Metaphors are ideal representations of otherwise meaningless entities like big companies. Part of the process of choosing a personality includes metaphors and analogies and this is covered in more depth in *Corporate Charisma* (Piatkus). Staff can ask the sorts of questions:

What if our company was a

- car;
- brand of clothing;
- an animal;
- book;
- character from a play;
- film star;
- place to live;
- movie;
- holiday destination;
- type of food; and so on.

There is often remarkable consistency between staff in the answers, which reinforces the idea of innate corporate identity. If there isn't a measure of consistency, the chances are that nor is there a common image among your customers. They have no personality with which to relate – no 'mind' with which they can communicate in a person to person way. So the metaphor exercise can be a good test of a current personality. It can be applied to staff, customers or potential customers who have heard of the company. Or it can be a discussion device for staff to come to agreement on an appropriate personality as a strategy is conceived.

The 'what if' exercise can be applied to competitors also. You can determine, for instance, where they score better than you, and how they have managed to evoke certain specific characteristics (a personality usually comprises a number of traits) that you would want to emulate. 'Reliability', for instance, may be based on the impression staff give, successful promotion and PR, a particular product that enforces that characteristic, or simply a track record of keeping promises. Competitor personality analysis is almost certain to suggest things to do and things not to do.

Mission and values

Often a company's personality is embodied in its mission, customer charter, values, written principles and suchlike. Intel, for instance, has six 'sigma' principles or values it wants to be known for: risk taking, quality, discipline, customer orientation, result orientation, and a 'great place to work'. Avon lists similar aims, but includes 'female' as a special characteristic.

However, a mission statement often boils down to just that – a statement in words – and does not reflect the culture or real identity of the firm. There is particularly the danger of too many characteristics. No individual is blessed with all the virtues, and companies (comprising the same imperfect species) will rarely aspire to them. A rather short list of traits is simple for customers to recognize and relate to. It also concentrates the mind of staff and is a more realistic proposition to maintain over whole lifetimes. The company mission is an ideal to aim for, and fulfils an important role as such, in giving overall, long-term direction ('this is where we're going'). A corporate personality should be created as part of the same strategic exercise, as should an image or culture exercise. Thus what the customer sees (the image) should reflect the true internal culture of the company ('how things are done round here'), its personality (real identity, values and attitudes), the 'person' behind the public persona that customers eventually get to know,) and the published mission statement or other written document.

CREATING A CORPORATE PERSONALITY

How do you create a personality for your company? It's a highly creative exercise and you can approach it in different ways. First you will have to determine your present personality. You learn that by asking – customers, members of the public, suppliers and staff. As we have already seen, you cannot *not* be perceived in a certain way (even if you are not noticed, or have no special traits, you may be seen as bland or boring) so it is as well to find out how you are perceived at the start. If you are happy with what you find, your likely strategy will be to enhance and communicate your personality.

You may not like what you find out, in which case your strategy will mean changes to your personality. Or you may take the chance to start from scratch and create a new one. A new personality strategy will also apply to a start-up business, of course. Indeed, a 'green field' situation, in which you have no history to take account of, is best all round. Not only can you communicate your identity from the start, but also you can choose the sort of customers who best match your chosen personality. That is a two-mind strategy before you win your first customer or promote your first product.

Having said that, the processes of creating and changing a personality are fairly standard, although you have a choice of approaches. You can take the well-known person, or metaphor, route that we met earlier in the chapter. Either way, it's a self-questioning process. Ask yourself, for instance, 'if this company were a person (or an animal, place etc) who or what would it be?' The objective is to humanize, personify, or animate the organization. In short, to make it *easy to imagine*. The trick is to associate the company with *sensory* characteristics – things you can see, hear, feel, and vividly imagine – and also with characteristics with human emotion, rather than abstractions.

PROBLEMS AND ASPIRATIONS

With those simple rules in mind, you then have another two basic choices. Ask yourself first, is your personality strategy to solve a present problem? For instance, relating to how you are now perceived, the vestige of previous years you want to throw off, shortcomings when compared with your competitors, and suchlike. The present problem of a past, or a company predecessor's past with which you are stuck.

This is a common approach, as staff are usually well aware of problems that need to be overcome. For instance, the need to be more friendly, responsive, faster, reliable and so on. Or maybe you are not communicating well, and thus not doing justice to what you do achieve. For instance, you may be able to demonstrate creativity in products and services but somehow the last thing your customers see you as is creative. That's a problem, especially if a creative personality would be an advantage in selling and building loyalty. So it's a valid basis for a personality makeover. As well as being seen to be creative, you may want to be perceived as a leader (in your industry, or socially), high tech, with intelligent staff, more trendy, more mature and conservative or whatever. It's your decision. Whatever you aspire to be, there are plenty of customers out there who will respond positively to a given set of personality traits.

Second, do you want your strategy to reflect what you *want* to be – your aspirations? This choice will depend on whether you are just starting up or continuing a long-standing business, as well as the degree to which you are happy with your present personality. You might opt for a combination. That is, a strategy that corrects what you want to change but replaces it with new characteristics you want to convey in the future.

OTHER PATHS TO PERSONALITY

You can identify your personality in other ways. As well as taking account of your problems and aspirations you can ask yourself specific questions that focus on the emotional or psychological side of your company and your people. For instance, what is it like to work here? What gives us particular pride in our work? What are we ashamed of? What motivates us? Are we loyal to the company? What motivates our loyalty, or disloyalty? What do we think about our customers? The nice ones, the difficult ones? How can we build better relationships with individual customers? What do we need to know about them in order to best fulfil this?

These questions will suggest the need to be, for instance, more caring, sincere, honest, environmentally aware and so on. That will help you to decide on a personality strategy, and whether to create or change it. These are the same sorts of questions that will help you communicate with individual customers, first on a one to one, then on a mind to mind basis.

Matching self-image

If your strategy is to best match your existing customers, part of the exercise is to determine how your customers see themselves. How do they live their lives? What is important to them? What are their main interests? What kind of people do they like to associate with? For instance, do they see themselves as trendy, carefree, home loving, adventurous, fashionable, intelligent and so on? This will not give the one to one data on which your relationship management will be based, of course. At the level of the mind each customer is unique. But by targeting customer groups in this way you will get a customer population as near as possible to your own corporate personality. In other words, establish maximum 'likeness'.

Dollar or disposition

Fortunately, there does not need to be the level of money investment usually associated with manufacturing upheaval. After all, the biggest changes that are likely to be needed are in attitude. However difficult it is to change minds, big spending does not solve it. Another plus is that a personality strategy can be carried out incrementally. For instance, you might identify the biggest problem insofar as how you are perceived, and work on that, or perhaps a short list. Whereas sales or market share promotion might not reach a critical threshold, and result in abortive expense, any communication that supports your personality will reinforce that personality. And it's a gradual, long-term process anyway, not aimed at short-term financial returns.

This incremental approach can be mirrored at the customer mind end. For instance, you can identify your best, say, 10 per cent of customers (by profitability) and apply interactive, mind to mind processes to them. This way, your 'mind strategies' (understanding and communicating your own corporate 'mind', and identifying and responding to your customer's mind) will not get out of kilter. An incremental policy, where such is possible, also has inherent, non-financial advantages. Not only will you learn as you do it, but measurable successes will give you the corporate muscle to extend the process further.

Management muscle

Even when introduced piecemeal or on a shoestring budget a personality strategy is too important not to demand top management backing. The chief executive, senior managers and all the staff need to be on board. It is not that any company-wide change should have top backing. It's because customers see the company through lots of windows – mainly people windows. This can be front-line staff involved in sales and after service, complaints handlers, your agents, consultants and suppliers, or the boss who appears on television. And the company's personality is no stronger than its weakest people link. Such company-wide support can only be marshalled from the top, or at least with their enthusiastic backing.

Technical product quality can go a long way to satisfying the customer, but it will not buy loyalty and enthusiasm. This comes through their perception of the attitude and true character of the company, as seen in its people – what it does rather than says. Courageous companies treat this as an opportunity. A unique personality, backed by attitude and performance, is a corporate asset that's hard to emulate and impossible to buy. You can't find it on a balance sheet even though it may represent a company's greatest value. It is the stuff of extraordinary mutual loyalty and is increasingly recognized as the foundation of any successful business.

Walking the talk

A strategy means nothing, and nor does a corporate personality, without equivalent, supporting behaviour. Success, in the end, depends on what you do, and how the customer perceives or interprets what you do. At one level you provide a product that works and give responsible service (check back to the Total Product Concept). At other levels this will embrace every communication (active or passive – you cannot not communicate) that allows the customer a glimpse of the 'mind' of the company. A corporate behaviour might result in a perceived personality different to what was intended.

Moreover, different customers will have their own perceptions. Each will have had different 'experiences' with the company and its products. Each customer will, in any event, filter them uniquely according to their own 'mind'. The latter, although on the face of it an impossible complication (the incomprehensible customer), is the opportunity to establish a one to one relationship. The marketing virtuosity is in 'coming across' to the customer as being 'like' (positively, 'my kind of company') while at the same time adhering to a consistent overall set of values – that is, a personality of your own.

This is not as Machiavellian a strategy as it may seem at first sight. In the end, a customer will believe whatever he or she wants to believe. Once you establish loyalty they will happily see black as white in order to sustain and justify (to themselves as well as others) that loyalty. Remember that brand loyalty is primarily a matter of emotion, not logic. So any apparent paradox in matching a single corporate entity (quasi-mind) with many customers (minds) is explained by no more than the physiological fact of a two-sided brain, each side doing its own thing.

Changing corporate personality is an important time in any company, and the scope and depth of the changes should not be under-estimated. It will be as far-reaching as any re-engineering or quality control project. Bearing your soul to customers is not without risk. But a greater risk faces the business that relies on luck or serendipity.

You will not get the benefit from understanding your customer's mind unless you use your own. First, you need to think about the customer's mind in a way that will outsmart your competitors and do a better, more professional long-term relationship job. Second, you need to establish a corporate (or supplier) 'mind' as an integral part of the relationship. You are *involved*, just like the corner shopkeeper was involved with his or her customers. You need to let the customer know that you can think and feel just as he or she does. That is the basis of an interactive, mutually beneficial, mind to mind, 21st century marketing relationship.

Appendix A

Sensory predicates

Auditory	Visual	Kinaesthetic
hear me out	an eye to	point out
sounds fine/ok/awful	with a view to	point the finger
listen to this	in view of	attract
listen in	see/look at it this way	strikes me
lend an ear	cast your eye	put... finger on
bend her ear	look at/into/out for	wrapped up
word in the ear	enlighten/throw light	speaks volumes
came to... ears	run/pass... eyes over	dig up
all ears	scan	(make an) impression
reach... ears	vision	tight (control, rein)
echo	shine, outshine	penetrate
prick up ears	clear/unclear, clarify	get a feel for
sound her out	reveal	empathize
(take) soundings	eye for detail	feel the pulse
amplify	mind's eye	tie up (loose ends)
(not a) murmur	on the lookout	feel your way
rattle(d)	eclipse	shake (up/out/off)

Auditory	Visual	Kinaesthetic
discuss	keep in sight/view/ perspective	lean/incline towards
call the tune	(have a) glance	at a stretch
(say it) out loud	shed/throw light	push (on/ahead/it/him/ her)
ring (a bell)	see to	pull it off
chime in	in the dark	pull together
make/don't make a noise	illuminate	get a /grip/hold/handle on
ask	notice	touch upon
(same, right) wavelength	see here	weigh/weight
tone (it down)	see how (it goes, works out, land lies)	take the plunge
voice an opinion	scope	stay in touch
harmony	review	touch base
call (on/for)	open… eyes to	push
(with a) bang/whimper	focus on/in focus	firm
report	perspective	feel/ing your way
comment	inspect	tangible
(not a) whisper	clear mind	step on it
speak up (for/against)	look/watch out for	impress/make impression
thunder	keep your eyes open	feel the need
tune in/out	blinding/ly	brush it off/have a brush
in tune	blind to	groping (eg in the dark)
rhyme (nor reason)	keep an eye on	run fingers over
in/out of sync	observe	(how she/he) feels
(not a) squeak	look to…	rub (dirt in)
sound off	reflect, reflection	stroke
(seemed to) click	point of view	heavy
take soundings	hindsight	throw/put (out a feeler)
resounding	retrospectively	tangible
unheard of	with regard	tackle
ear to the ground	dream up	grapple with
		sting (take the sting out of)

Visual	*Kinaesthetic*
overlook	put out a feeler
eyeball to eyeball	get wind of
(see/don't see) eye to eye	leap in the dark
spectacle/spectacular	contact
circumspect	feel pulse
see it (my/this way)	beat about
look at it (my/this way)	warmth, warm to
picture…	(go/be) soft
get the picture	hard (hearted/headed/ pushed/nosed)
big picture	not too hard on
keep/stop/start looking	rough with the smooth
	shake (off/out/up)
	cooled off
	cool it
	thrash it out
	tickle (fancy)
	itching (to go)
	sympathize with
	smooth out
	put my/your finger on
	poking (around/his nose in)
	bumped (into)
	feathers ruffled

Appendix B

Customers' perceptions of corporate personality

Able	Benevolent	Commendable
Accomplished	Big	Communicative
Accurate	Bold	Competent
Active	Brave	Concerned
Adaptable	Bright	Confident
Adventurous	Brilliant	Conservative
Aggressive	Calm	Consistent
Ambitious	Capable	Constructive
Amenable	Captivating	Cool
Approachable	Caring	Cooperative
Assertive	Charismatic	Courageous
Attentive	Charitable	Courteous
Attractive	Charming	Crazy
Balanced	Cheerful	Creative
Beautiful	Classy	Cuddly
Believable	Clean	Cunning

Cute	Flashy	Intelligent
Daring	Flexible	Jolly
Decisive	Fluent	Just
Dedicated	Focused	Kind
Demanding	Forward-looking	Knowledgeable
Desirable	Friendly	Leading
Detailed	Futuristic	Lifetime
Determined	Generous	Light hearted
Diligent	Gentle	Lively
Direct	Gigantic	Loner
Disciplined	Glamorous	Lovable
Discriminating	Global	Lovely
Dominant	Good	Loyal
Dynamic	Gorgeous	Macho
Eccentric	Graceful	Magnificent
Efficient	Great	Manly
Elegant	Gregarious	Masculine
Elite	Groovy	Mature
Entrepreneurial	Happy	Modern
Emotional	Hardworking	Modest
Emphatic	Healthy	Motherly
Endearing	High class	Motivated
Energetic	High performer	Nurturing
Enquiring	High tech	Objective
Enthusiastic	Honest	Obliging
Expert	Humble	Observant
Exploring	Humorous	Open
Extraordinary	Ideal	Optimistic
Extrovert	Imaginative	Orderly
Fair	Important	Patient
Fast	In control	Peaceful
Feminine	Independent	Perfectionist
Flamboyant	Intellectual	Persevering

Persistent	Reliable	Sure
Playful	Religious	Swanky
Pleasant	Resilient	Swift
Polished	Responsible	Tactful
Polite	Responsive	Talkative
Positive	Rich	Team-spirited
Posh	Romantic	Thoughtful
Practical	Rough	Thrifty
Pragmatic	Safe	Timid
Precise	Seductive	Tough
Proactive	Self-confident	Traditional
Productive	Selfish	Transparent
Professional	Sensational	True
Profitable	Serious	Trustworthy
Prolific	Sexy	Truthful
Proud	Sharing	Understanding
Punctual	Shy	Understating
Qualified	Simple	Vigorous
Quality	Sincere	Visionary
Quiet	Small	Warm
Racy	Smart	Well-mannered
Rational	Soft	Young
Raunchy	Solid	Youthful
Reasonable	Sophisticated	Winning
Rebellious	Special	Wise
Refined	Striking	World-class
Reflective	Superb	
Regal	Supportive	

Appendix C

Mini right/left brain questionnaire

Left brain			Right brain
I enjoy planning new things in detail	☐	☐	I enjoy doing new things on the spur of the moment
I am logical and rarely jump to conclusions	☐	☐	I can reach conclusions without following all the details of an argument
I rarely daydream or remember my night-time dreams	☐	☐	My dreams are very vivid and I often daydream
I try to find the reasons behind other people's behaviour	☐	☐	I can rarely see the motivation behind other people's behaviour
I prefer mathematical and scientific subjects to artistic subjects	☐	☐	I prefer artistic subjects to mathematical and scientific subjects
I am punctual and have a good sense of time	☐	☐	I am rarely punctual and have a poor sense of time

Left brain		**Right brain**
I am good at describing my feelings in words	☐ ☐	I find it difficult to put my feelings into words
I rely on the evidence when making a decision	☐ ☐	I rely on my feelings when making a decision
My files and reference materials are in perfect order	☐ ☐	I rarely bother to file things
I keep my hands still when I am talking	☐ ☐	I gesture a lot when I am talking
I rarely have hunches and prefer not to follow my intuition	☐ ☐	I rely on my instincts and follow my hunches
I rarely think in visual terms	☐ ☐	My impressions and thoughts often appear as pictures
I am good at explaining things	☐ ☐	I can understand what someone means without being able to explain it
I solve problems by keeping at them and trying different approaches until I find a solution	☐ ☐	I solve problems by putting them to the back of my mind and waiting for a solution to come up
I am very good at puzzles and word games	☐ ☐	I do not enjoy puzzles and word games
I have my feelings well under control	☐ ☐	I let my feelings show
I prefer reading non-fiction to romantic novels	☐ ☐	I prefer reading romantic novels to non-fiction
I analyse problems	☐ ☐	I deal with a problem as a whole
I am not particularly musical	☐ ☐	I am very fond of music

Index